Transition

UNDERSTANDING & MANAGING PERSONAL CHANGE

Transition

UNDERSTANDING & MANAGING PERSONAL CHANGE

John Adams, John Hayes, Barrie Hopson

Martin Robertson

First published in 1976 by Martin Robertson & Company, 17 Quick Street,
London N1 8HL

ISBN 0 85520 129 0

Typeset by Santype Ltd., Salisbury, and printed and bound in Britain at
The Pitman Press, Bath.

Contents

v

To our children whose major
transitions are still ahead of them

Samantha, Gillian
Sarah, Jonathan
Caitlin, Barnaby

*The important thing is this: To be able at any moment
to sacrifice what we are for what we could become,*

Charles Dubois

Introduction

There is increasing interest in and concern about the stresses generated by the rapid changes of modern living. People experience a number of transitions throughout their lives — from child to adult, school to work, single to married, job to job, married to divorced, geographical moves, and bereavement.

This book is a first survey of attempts that have been made to understand, and to help people in transition to understand, what is involved in giving up one mode of life and accepting another. It is a book that investigates the *processes* of individual movement from one relatively stable state to another. Evidence of two sorts is mounting and will be considered in the various chapters of this book. Firstly, changes in life patterns cause stress, and stress has physiological as well as psychological consequences. Put another way, one can get sick and tired of changing. Secondly, the personal reaction patterns to transition appear to occur in predictable, cyclical and describable stages. Take grief, for example. Parkes points out that

> Grief is not a set of symptoms which start after a loss and then gradually fade away. It involves a succession of clinical pictures which blend into and replace one another. ... we shall see how numbness, the first stage, gives place to pining, and pining to depression and it is only after the stage of depression that recovery occurs. Hence, at any particular time a person may show one of three quite different clinical pictures (1972, pp. 6—7).

We shall also see that the phases of various kinds of transitions hold a great many parallels with each other. We feel that through an understanding of the phases of transitions we can begin to move towards helping people cope with their transitions and thereby capitalise on the *opportunity value* we presume to be present in most, if not all, of them.

Jaques, in *As You Like It*, presents life as a transitional scenario within which the person progresses through seven life stages.

All the World's a stage,
And all the men and women merely players:
They have their exits and their entrances;
And one man in his time plays many parts,
His acts being seven ages. At first the infant,
Mewling and puking in the nurse's arms.
Then the whining school-boy, with his satchel
And shining morning face, creeping like snail
Unwillingly to school. And then the lover,
Sighing like a furnace, with a woeful ballad
Made to his mistress' eyebrow. Then a soldier,
Full of strange oaths, and bearded like the pard,
Jealous in honour, sudden and quick in quarrel,
Seeking the bubble reputation
Even in the cannon's mouth. And then the justice,
In fair round belly with good capon lined,
With eyes severe, and beard of formal cut,
Full of wise saws and moral instances,
And so he plays his part. The sixth age shifts
Into the lean and slippered pantaloon,
With spectacles on nose and pouch on side,
His youthful hose, well saved, a world too wide
For his shrunk shank; and his big manly voice,
Turning again toward childish treble, pipes
And whistles in his sound. Last scene of all,
That ends this strange eventful history,
Is second childishness and mere oblivion,
Sans teeth, sans eyes, sans taste, sans everything.

In this book we have deliberately ignored 'the whining school-boy' as well as 'the infant mewling and puking in the nurse's arms', and have focused attention on behaviour in adult life. In doing so we do not minimise the importance of transitional events in early life. Indeed much of our earlier work has concentrated on the transition points faced by 10—18 year olds in their vocational development (Hopson & Hayes, 1968; Hayes & Hopson, 1971). But recently we have become more concerned with adult transitions.

This book, perhaps more than most, reflects the histories of the authors, and our attempts to understand and cope with a variety of our own transitions.

The relationship between the three of us began in 1969 when John Adams arrived at Leeds University to spend two years working with John Hayes in the Organisation Development Unit of the Dept. of Management Studies. His first week in England coincided with running his first T-group in England in which Barrie Hopson was a participant. A close relationship developed, culminating in Barrie embarking on a three-month trip to the States on a Nato grant to study transitions with John Adams when he returned to National Training Laboratories (NTL) in Washington. Amongst all of us in the past few years we have experienced culture shock, geographical transitions, bereavement, redundancy, job change, marital separation, and major changes in life style. We became increasingly fascinated (when we were coping effectively, that is) by what was happening to us as we dealt with each of these transitional changes. The combination of scientific curiosity and total personal involvement proved irresistible, and we began to plan this book together.

Barrie Hopson and John Adams ran a workshop called 'Understanding and managing transitions' at Bethel for NTL in the summer of 1974. This convinced us more than ever of the value of trying to get this book together to further stimulate other people to become involved in transition dynamics. In the summer of 1975, John Adams attended a conference on life transitions sponsored by the Center for Designed Change at Sonoma, California. Here again a number of people met who discovered that they were not alone. Perhaps never in our history has self-management and control been such a vital ingredient in our survival and growth. It is exciting to be working in an area where intellectual fervour is beginning to bubble. We hope that some of you as a result of what you read here may be tempted to come in and join us.

OUTLINE OF THE BOOK

Chapter 1 describes how we see transitions as embodying the possibilities for both danger and opportunity. We want to look at what some of the dangers are, and describe some of the known paths to opportunity. It contains a great many definitions and concepts that underlie our thinking about transitions and their effects on people.

The remaining chapters in Part I spell out further what we mean by transitions and why we think the study of transition dynamics is important. They underscore the need for people to become more aware of their own and their friends' transitions. In chapter 2, Dale Lake and Geraldine Lake, in an essay prepared for this book, document and work towards defining changes people are making in their life styles. They suggest a large number of areas in which further research on life-style change is needed and discuss a number of existing theoretical frameworks for understanding the forces in the individual and his environment that are fostering new patterns of working and living.

Chapters 3 and 4 relate the experience of transitions to stress, and focus on the subtle and not so subtle dangers associated either directly or indirectly with transitions. Chapter 3 views the stress response as a biological/physiological chain of events and discusses both how major transitions trigger this chain of events and how chronic strain is now known to induce and/or maintain a widening variety of illnesses. Some ways of buffering the stresses associated with transitions are also introduced. Chapter 4, written by Douglas Duckworth for this book, looks at the way people define, analyse and cope with transition. When their coping is inadequate the outcome can range from simple dissatisfaction to severe debilitation. Suggestions are made for improved coping through learning to monitor the requirements a person establishes for him- or herself and the various components of his or her environment, and learning to alter the control strategies he or she uses.

Part II contains five chapters about various kinds of transition (intercultural experiences, career transitions, loss of employment, marriage, parenthood, divorce and death), the growth potentials contained within them and how they are experienced by individuals. These different kinds of transition will be experienced by most readers either directly or through their work with others. The material for these chapters comes from a variety of sources: research studies, literature reviews and the documented personal experiences of the authors.

Part III is related closely to Part II, but it is not precisely parallel in its chapters. Four chapters give accounts of various approaches and techniques that professionals are using today to assist people with their transitions.

Chapter 10 reviews methods for 'taking care of yourself' such as yoga and meditation, and chapter 11 describes a system of life and career planning that can facilitate transition experiences. Chapter 12, prepared for this book by Michael Mitchell, is a case study of a personnel transfer managed in such a way as to minimise the impact of this common organisational transition. Chapter 13, also specially prepared for this book by Douglas Duckworth, describes in detail a workshop on individual problem-solving.

Part IV consists of a single chapter that provides an overview of the present 'state of the art' as regards the study of transitions and points the way to needed further research and training programmes.

John Adams, John Hayes, Barrie Hopson
Leeds, England
June 1976

PART ONE

Towards an Understanding of Transition Dynamics

1. Towards an Understanding of Transition: Defining some Boundaries of Transition Dynamics

Barrie Hopson and John Adams

> In the ongoing flux of life, man undergoes many changes. Arriving, departing, growing, declining, achieving, failing – every change involves a loss and a gain. The old environment must be given up, the new accepted. People come and go; one job is lost, another begun; territory and possessions are acquired or sold; new skills are learned, old abandoned; expectations are fulfilled or hopes dashed – in all these situations the individual is faced with the need to give up one mode of life and accept another (Parkes, 1972).

Many writers discuss the future almost as if some 'gravitational force' were pulling us all towards 'Armageddon' at an accelerating rate. Whether Armageddon is nigh or not, it is clear that more of us are experiencing more surprises or disruptions in our lives, more frequently. Some are intentional, others not. In addition, as children and adults we move through a succession of life stages. Some of these are relatively stable periods, while others (e.g. the mid-life crisis and menopause) can be quite unsettling and cause us to re-evaluate our values and the goals we are pursuing in our lives. These transition points offer a great potential for personal growth and development, but for all too many people they trigger pain, both psychological and physiological.

We are concerned with mapping these transition points, and in so doing attempting to draw together ideas and concepts in a first tentative approach towards generating a model of transitional behaviour that will help predict human responses to these events. Such a model might also suggest ways in which people may be helped to survive and even gain from their transitional experiences.

3

TRANSITION DYNAMICS

The problems of understanding and coping with change in the world, while increasingly discussed, are seldom placed within a theoretical framework. One of the reasons for this is that it is the applied behavioural scientist rather than his theoretical counterpart who has shown the most interest in this area. He has adopted a practical orientation and has developed rough and ready models in order to help him and his clients understand the process of transition. These 'working models', while often invaluable as training and diagnostic tools, often fail to conform to the dictates of scientific theory, and these professionals, because of their nature and their trade, are unlikely to test out their assumptions, even if they were scientifically testable.

There have been a few systematic attempts to describe the human experience of transition. Fink (1967) and Parkes (1972) have described some of the stages that people pass through in coping with bereavement. Kübler-Ross (1969) has a systematic model to account for people dealing with the fact of their own approaching deaths, and the reactions of their relatives and friends to this. Adams (1969) discovered that applied behavioural science professionals in training pass through a number of identifiable stages. At the level of micro-transitions, Levinger and Snoek (1972) have outlined the ways in which interpersonal relationships change from superficiality to intimacy. At what could be called a midi-transitions level, vocational psychologists have plotted a person's career development (Super, 1957; Crites, 1969) and there has been some work done on the transition from school to work (Maizels, 1970; Kiel *et al.*, 1966) and mid-life career transitions (Sofer, 1970). In this book attempts are made to postulate predictable transition models to account for marriage, parenthood and divorce (chapter 8). Sociologists and anthropologists have done more work at the macro-level, examining the effects of technological change on traditional stable cultures (Mead, 1955), the functions of *rites de passage* in passing on cultural norms and cementing social networks (Van Gennep, 1960), or group responses to war and natural disaster (Fritz, 1957; Lifton, 1954; Archibald *et al.*, 1962).

What is still needed, however, is a model of transitional behaviour that allows testable hypotheses to be drawn from it, that gathers material from a number of different disciplines together in a comprehensible whole, and that provides a language that will set apart the study of transitional behaviour as an area of investigation in itself, instead of, as in the past, an aspect of research projects with an often quite different focus. This book was written as a first tentative attempt to link theory with practice, and this chapter will try to identify some of the key questions that theoreticians and practitioners might consider in the area of 'transition dynamics'.

We shall attempt to define what a transition is and the different forms of transition; we shall try to justify our belief that a study of transition dynamics warrants expenditure of energy and resources; we shall present terms that we find useful in discussing transitions; present a general model of transitions; summarise what is known about the effects that transitions have on people; examine the transition coping tasks and styles; and look at some typical problems that someone in transition has to cope with and how they may be helped firstly to cope with these problems, and secondly to benefit and grow from the transition, because our central thesis is that every transition contains within it 'opportunity value' for the individual to grow and develop.

What follows is not systematic enough to be called a model, and not ambitious enough to warrant the term theory. We hope that it might help to provide a framework for understanding and researching transitions. The framework is phenomenological in character.

What is a transition?

A transition is a discontinuity in a person's life space. Sometimes the discontinuity is defined by social consensus as to what constitutes a discontinuity within the culture. Van Gennep (1960) emphasises the importance of publicly recognised rites and rituals which demarcate the transition. He talks of a 'status passage' from separation through the transition to the incorporation of a new role. In chapter 6 we emphasise the importance of commonly accepted 'boundaries' in a career transition. Holmes and Rahe (1967) provide evidence to show the extent of cultural similarity in perceptions of what are important discontinuities. Most of them are represented in this book in Part II: death, marriage, birth, divorce, career change, geographical change, work change.

Another way of defining a discontinuity is not by general consensus but by the person's own perception. These two may not always coincide: for example, adolescence is considered to be an important time of transition in most Western cultures, whereas in other cultures (Samoa, for example; see Mead, 1928) it is not considered to be a time of stress, identity crisis, etc. Also, in the same culture some children will experience adolescence as a transition (i.e. as a discontinuity with all that implies), while others will not. Consequently it cannot be assumed that everyone experiences a transitional event, for example a change of job, in the same way.

For an experience to be classed as transitional there should be:

(i) *personal awareness* of a discontinuity in one's life space; and
(ii) *new behavioural responses* required because the situation is new, or the required behaviours are novel, or both.

A person can sometimes undergo a transitional experience without being aware of the extent of the discontinuity or that new behavioural responses are required. This at some point will probably cause the person or others adaptation problems. For example, following the death of her husband, the widow may not be experiencing strain, she might even be pleased that he is dead, but suddenly she becomes aware that no house repairs have been done, and a new dimension of loss becomes evident along with the awareness of new behavioural responses required.

What forms of transition are there?

They can range from macro-transitions like war, the effects of natural disasters, technological change, to micro-transitions at the individual level relating to a person's marriage, career, and relationships. A transitional event can be:

(i)   *Predictable-voluntary* e.g. marriage
(ii) *Predictable-involuntary* e.g. national service
(iii) *Unpredictable-voluntary* e.g. computer dating
(iv) *Unpredictable-involuntary* e.g. unexpected earthquake

Predictability is defined according to whether the transition can be anticipated or not.

Why is an understanding of transitional experience important?

We believe that for most people in the world there has been, or will be, a rapid acceleration in the number of transitions encountered in all aspects of their lives. Any transition will result in people being subjected to some degree of stress and strain. They will be more or less aware of this depending upon the novelty of the event and the demands it makes upon their behavioural repertoire. Thus, there will be a rise in the number of people experiencing an increased amount of stress and strain in the course of their daily lives. This justifies a more intensive exploration of transition dynamics.

What is the language of transition?

We found it necessary to define some terms very precisely. Below is a list of concepts we have found central to our work:

Transition	= a perceived discontinuity in a person's life space.
Event	= the stimulus that creates discontinuity.
Mover	= the person who is experiencing the transition.
Stress	= pressures of external factors on the person. This can be defined by the mover or by an external observer. This means that by any common consensus someone may be in a stressful situation, but he may not be experiencing any strain. Stress is defined here only as a stimulus variable.
Strain	= is a response variable. This is a person's experience of the stress variable, which is to some degree unpleasant, and the person would usually prefer not to be experiencing it. This is not to say that people will always do anything to avoid it. Some people only feel important, successful, or even alive when they are under strain. Their prognosis in health terms is likely to be poor (see chapter 3).
Biophysical strain	= a triggering off of the person's orientation response (OR) and adaptive reaction (AR). This happens whenever a stimulus pattern is changed, novelty is introduced, or a change is anticipated by the person. Excessive triggering

off has been shown to lead to illness (see chapter 3 and Sokolov, 1963).

Experienced = the degree to which a person is *aware* of the stress
strain factors, experiencing them as such, and his awareness of the biophysical strains they are generating within him.

(The distinction between biophysical and experienced strain is necessary as a person is not always aware of stresses which are actually affecting him.)

Identity = exists when an individual feels unable to implement his
strain self image in social roles he perceives to be important.

Proactive = a tendency to make things happen; to see the oppor-
orientation tunity value in a transitional event and move towards it, attempting to manage the event for oneself.

Reactive = a tendency to let things happen to one; even if the
orientation opportunity value of transition is seen, there is no attempt to manage the transition for oneself.

Decision = choosing one of two or more alternatives.
making

Decision = none of the alternatives is deliberately chosen.
avoidance

Coping = (i) managing feelings, i.e. utilising them and not being overwhelmed by them;

(ii) producing effective behaviours required by the new situation;

(iii) utilising the opportunity value contained in the new situation for personal growth.

Coping is more usually talked about in relation to the first two criteria. Coping in transition dynamics should always include the additional criterion of growing as a result of the transition.

Is there a general model of transitions?

We were heavily influenced in our thinking by Adams' (1969) model developed to describe and understand the professional development of postgraduate students in the Organizational Behaviour programme at

Case Western Reserve University, Cleveland, Ohio. Following extensive interviewing with thirty-three students, he developed a framework that described their passage, psychologically, through the programme, from being primarily self-oriented to involvement-oriented to instrumentality-oriented. Not everyone moved to the final phase, and they certainly did not move along each dimension at the same rate. He discovered that progression occurs first on the intrapersonal levels as described by level A (Fig. 1.1). Only when the person is clearly facing up to the reality of the situation for himself can he become deeply involved in meaningful ways in that situation (progression on level B). And then, only when he begins to understand clearly this involvement can he become instrumental in that situation.

Another way to view this is to consider the first two phases as reactive (dependence on the situation and reaction to the situation) and the second two phases as proactive (coordination of self and situation and integration of self in the situation). In this light, we can see that a person must become intrapersonally proactive before he can become deeply involved; and he must behave proactively in the situation before he can be consistently instrumental. This interpretation was borne out both by the definitions of the component parts of the profiles and by the variable 'overall focus', which gradually but consistently moved from level A (self-oriented) to level B (involvement-oriented) to level C (instrumentality-oriented) with progression through the profiles.

As we began to discover other work on different transitions, increasingly a general picture began to emerge. An understanding of the general framework at this point will facilitate the reader's grasp of the more specific models presented in this book.

The major point to be made in understanding transitions is that whether a change in one's daily routine is an intentional change, a sudden surprise that gets thrust upon one, or a growing awareness that one is moving into a life stage characterised by increasing or decreasing stability, it will trigger a *cycle* of reactions and feelings that is predictable. The cycle has seven phases in our current manner of describing them. The identification of these seven phases has come about through content analyses of reports from over 100 people who have attended transition workshops for the purpose of understanding and learning to cope more effectively with transitions they were experiencing and through extending the findings reported above.

(1) The first phase is a kind of *immobilisation* or a sense of being overwhelmed; of being unable to make plans, unable to reason, and

Fig. 1.1: Phases of personal and professional development

PHASE

		I Situation dependent	II Reaction to situation	III Coordination of self and situation	IV Integration of self in situation
A	Focus on self	Shock	Defensive retreat	Acknowledgement	Adaption and change
			Self as a result of the situation		
B	Focus on involvement	Inhibition	Action or opposition	Conceptualisation	Internalisation
			Self as a part of the situation		
C	Focus on instrumentality	Observation	Reflection or testing	Formulation	Implementation
			Self as instrumental in the situation		

LEVEL

unable to understand. In other words, the initial phase of a transition is experienced by many people as a feeling of being frozen up. It appears that the intensity with which people experience this first phase is a function of the *unfamiliarity* of the transition state and of the *negative expectations* one holds. If the transition is not high in novelty and if the person holds positive expectations, the immobilisation is felt less intensely or perhaps not at all. Marriage can be a good example of the latter.

(2) The way of getting out of this immobilisation, essentially, is by movement to the second phase of the cycle, which is characterised by *minimisation* of the change or disruption to trivialise it. Very often, one will deny that the change even exists. Often, too, the person projects a euphoric feeling. Those readers who recall seeing Alfred Hitchcock's film *Psycho* will remember that Tony Perkins spent a lot of time shrieking at his mother in the house on the hill. It is not until the end of the film that one learns the mother has been dead for some time, and it is her semi-mummified body with which he has been carrying on his 'dialogue'. That is an extreme example of denying or minimising the reality of a major change in one's life. It is important, however, not always to disapprove of denial. It is often a necessary *phase* in the process of adjustment. 'Denial is a normal and necessary human reaction to a crisis which is too immediately overwhelming to face head-on. Denial provides time for a temporary retreat from reality while our internal forces regroup and regain the strength to comprehend the new life our loss has forced upon us' (Krantzler, 1973). The importance of denial is discussed in chapter 9.

(3) Eventually, for most people — though not for Tony Perkins in *Psycho* — the realities of the change and of the resulting stresses begin to become apparent. As people become aware that they must make some changes in the way they are living, as they become aware of the realities involved, they begin to get *depressed* — the third phase of the transition cycle. They become depressed because they are just beginning to face up to the fact that there has been a change. Even if they have voluntarily created this change themselves, there is likely to be this dip in feelings. They become frustrated because it becomes difficult to know how best to cope with the new life requirements, the ways of being, the new relationships that have been established or whatever other changes may be necessary.

(4) As people move further into becoming aware of reality, they can move into the fourth phase, which is *accepting reality* for what it is.

Through the first three phases, there has been a kind of attachment, whether it has been conscious or not, to the past (pre-transition) situation. To move from phase three to phase four involves a process of unhooking from the past and of saying 'Okay, here I am now; here is what I have; here's what I want.' As this is accepted as the new reality, the person's feelings begin to rise once more, and optimism becomes possible. A clear 'letting go' is necessary.

(5) This provides a bridge to phase five, where the person becomes much more active and starts *testing* himself vis-à-vis the new situation: trying out new behaviours; new life styles; and new ways of coping with the transition. There is a tendency also at this point for people to stereotype, to have categories and classifications of the ways things and people should or should not be relative to the new situation. There is a lot of personal energy available during this phase and, as they begin to deal with the new reality, it is not unlikely that those in transition will easily become angry and irritable.

(6) Following this burst of activity and self-testing, there is a more gradual shifting towards becoming concerned with understanding and for *seeking meanings* for how things are different and why they are different. This sixth phase is a head level, or cognitive process in which people try to understand what all of the activity, anger, stereotyping and so on have meant. It is not until people can get out of the activity and withdraw from it a bit that they can begin to understand deeply the meaning of the change in their lives.

(7) This conceptualising, in turn, allows people to move to the final phase of *internalising* these meanings and incorporating them into their behaviour.

Overall, the seven transition phases represent a cycle of experiencing a disruption, gradually acknowledging its reality, testing oneself, understanding oneself, and incorporating changes in one's behaviour. The level of one's self-esteem varies across these phases and appears to follow a predictable path. Identifying the seven phases along such a self-esteem curve often gives one a better understanding of the nature of the transition cycle. This is done in Fig. 1.2.

Interestingly, the Menninger Foundation's research on Peace Corps volunteers' reactions to entering and experiencing training (a transition for each person) produced a very similar curve. More recently, Elisabeth Kübler-Ross and those who joined her death and dying seminars have also charted a very similar curve of the reaction cycle people go through upon learning they are terminally ill — the ultimate transition. This is presented in Fig. 1.3. (See also chapter 3 below.)

Fig. 1.2: Self-esteem changes during transitions

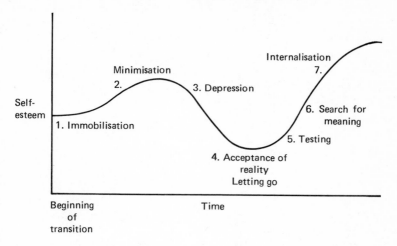

Before proceeding, we want to make it clear that seldom if ever does a person move neatly from phase to phase as it has been described and diagrammed above. It is rather more likely that these representations are of the general experience and that any given individual's progressions and regressions are unique to his or her unique circumstances. For example, one person may never get beyond denial or minimisation. Another may end it all during depression. Yet another might experience a major failure just as things begin to look up, and 'jump' back to a less active, more withdrawn posture.

What we wish to highlight is the *potential* for growth arising from any major disruption or calamity. One realises this potential and moves toward it when one lets go and fully accepts the situation for what it is, when one dies a 'little death' to become larger. Elisabeth Kübler-Ross underscores this idea excellently in her introductory remarks on the Imara essay from which Fig. 1.3 below is borrowed:

> . . . he explains that we must learn to die in order that we may learn to live, that growing to be who you truly are requires sometimes that you die to the life chosen for you by society, that each new step of growth involves a throwing off of more shackles restraining you . . . in order to grow, you must continuously die and be reborn, much as a caterpillar becomes a butterfly . . . although you receive your final opportunity for growth when you are at death's doorstep, your growth should not wait for this crisis in your life. By understanding

Fig. 1.3: Stages of personal grief

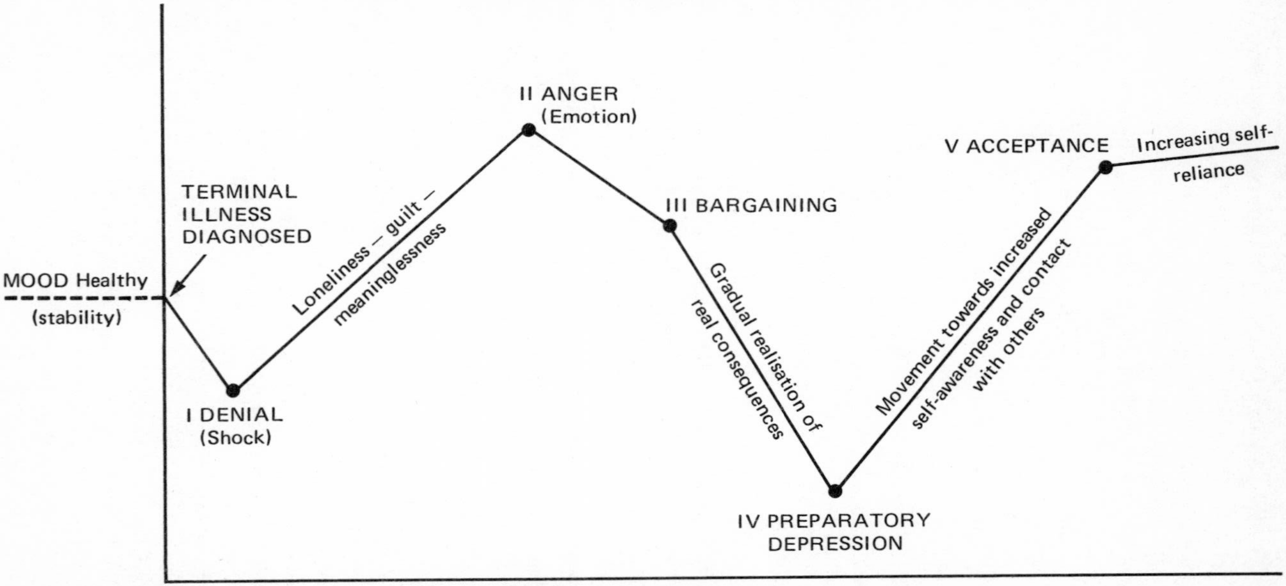

I DENIAL (Shock)

II ANGER (Emotion)

III BARGAINING

IV PREPARATORY DEPRESSION

V ACCEPTANCE

Increasing self-reliance

Movement towards increased self-awareness and contact with others

Gradual realisation of real consequences

Loneliness — guilt — meaninglessness

TERMINAL ILLNESS DIAGNOSED

MOOD Healthy (stability)

Source: Mwalimu Imara, 'Dying as the Last Stage of Growth' in E. Kübler-Ross, ed. (1975) p. 161.

the growth-producing properties of dying, you can learn to die and grow at any point you choose ... The qualities that predict your being able to deal comfortably and productively with death ... are the same qualities that distinguish a growing human being at any stage in his or her life (Kübler-Ross, 1975, p. 147).

What effects do transitions have on people?

It is important to note here that all transitions will involve some stress, including those considered by society to be positive changes, e.g. being left large sums of money, parenthood, marriage (Holmes and Rahe, 1967).

The severity of biophysical experienced strain is determined by a number of factors:

(a) The biophysical stress tolerance of the individual. This is not constant and varies according to the novelty of the situation and/or required behavioural responses, and as a result of the person's life history and general state of health. As with the concept of general ability there will be genetically determined limits of tolerance, even if these are impossible to measure.

(b) The number of stressful events operating at one time.

(c) The importance of the event to the individual.

(d) The intensity of the stress.

(e) The duration of the stress.

Stress cannot be avoided in life but the degree of strain can be partially controlled or managed. When the organism experiences strain the following occurs:

A lowering of adaptive responses: the perceptual field narrows and cognitive processes become more rigid. When people experience high levels of anxiety, they naturally tend to be rigid and inflexible in problem solving and other activities.

A reduction in resistance to other stresses: in building defences to cope with one stress, the person typically suffers a lowering of tolerance to other stresses.

Possible permanent damage to the biophysical system: Selye (1956) claims that experiments on animals and humans have shown that each exposure to a stressful event leaves an indelible scar, in that it uses up reserves of adaptability that cannot be replaced. However, this is a highly debatable point.

What are the coping tasks relevant to all transitional events?

We believe that there are common elements in any transition, which enables us to talk generally about transitional behaviour. We also assert that in dealing with any transitional event a person has two tasks to perform as he moves through the phases of the model:

(i) *Management of strain*: to manage the degree of strain generated by the stress in such a way that the individual can engage with the external problems caused by the transition.

(ii) *Cognitive task*: a transition will always necessitate adjustment. Any adjustment requires decisions to be made about the appropriateness of new and old behaviour patterns. The individual will be asking himself questions such as: How can I accept this situation? What behaviour is expected of me? What do I want from this situation?

How successfully he manages these two tasks will determine the speed with which he completes the transition.

Management of strain

Each individual will have a characteristic style of managing strain, which will incline towards being basically proactive or reactive. This could approximate to Rotter's (1966) distinction between being externally or internally controlled (see chapter 11, p. 178).

Examples of proactive strategies
Cognitive shielding — controlling the amount of stimulation in the environment by one or more of the following:

(a) Filtering — systematically disregarding certain stimuli in the environment according to some priority scheme.

(b) Queuing — delaying decisions during a heavy decision resolving period.

(c) Approximation — making decisions hastily and consequently less thoughtfully.

(d) Temporary drop-out — refusing to resolve decisions until after a recuperation period. This can appear initially as reactive; however, it is correctly termed proactive as the mover is deliberately opting out of the situation temporarily as part of a strategy to move in later but more effectively.

Personal stability zones — creating a stability zone in one's life space so that there is always someone, somewhere, or something to fall back on in time of stress. This often takes the form of ritualising activities.

Situational grouping — congregating with people who are about to experience or are experiencing similar discontinuities, e.g. ante-natal classes, induction courses, orientation programmes for first year students, women's and men's 'rap' groups, where the purpose of the grouping is to work on the problems and opportunities presented by the transition.

Crisis counselling — making use of professional and interpersonal resources.

Anticipatory socialisation — adjusting gradually to the discontinuity, e.g. half-way houses for alcoholics, ex-offenders and mental patients; if moving to a new firm, reading about it, meeting people who work there, etc. The main aim is to effect a gradual and managed change in one's life space. Chapter 12 gives an excellent example of how an organisation can ease the transition of a new manager into a department.

Support systems — this concept has been most clearly developed by Seashore (1974) who makes the use of appropriate support systems his key aid to coping with transitional stress. He points out to clients that the effective use of support systems can lead from social isolation to social integration; from vulnerability to assistance; from emotional isolation to intimacy; from feelings of powerlessness to feelings of self-worth; from stimulus isolation (in a rut) to broadened perspectives; and from environmental isolation to access to resources (see chapter 10).

Examples of reactive strategies
Withdrawal — opting out of the situation; trying to pretend it does not exist; suppression; repression.

Disengagement from the real problem — continuing with social role but withdrawing inwardly; claiming that one is powerless; displacement; projection. Chapter 9 shows how many people in approaching their own deaths spend some time reacting like this.

The cognitive task

When an individual behaves in a particular way he has made a decision to do so. Actions do not just happen. People make them happen or let them happen. In either case the individual is responsible for, even if not totally the cause of, what happens.

Decisions can be made, or avoided. One of the decisions an individual may make is to avoid making a decision, i.e. consciously to avoid choosing between one or more alternatives. Decision making is not necessarily a superior strategy to decision avoidance. Which of these approaches is most useful can only be judged ultimately by how far the individual's objectives are satisfied. There is sometimes conflict between short-term and long-term objectives. Successful decisions ideally should satisfy both. Decision resolution will usually bring with it a reduction of strain, and one way some people will choose to cope emotionally with the new situation is by resolving decisions quickly. This controls the degree of stress and consequently reduces the strain.

Each person, while using a variety of decision-resolving behaviours, will have a *general cognitive style* of coping with transitions which will incline them towards being proactive or reactive.

Cognitive decisions are resolved by individuals who use one or more of four main styles:

(i)   proactive decision making
(ii) proactive decision avoidance
(iii) reactive decision making
(iv) reactive decision avoidance.

Proactivity in itself is not always the most effective style for coping with transitions, although people who operate in this way are more likely to find they have control over their lives (Rotter, 1966), and people who experience themselves as having more control over their lives experience less alienation, dissatisfaction and depression (Seeman, 1971; Seligman, 1975). But proactivity in itself, without taking reality factors into account, can be dysfunctional. There may be a time when it will be less stressful simply to let others make a decision for one, especially if the outcome is not too important. One can rush into a situation without knowing all the facts, which might cause greater strain than simply not acting at all.

Each of the four styles has characteristic decision-making strategies, examples of which are as follows:

Proactive decision making
Shifting horizons — may lengthen or shorten his perspective on any given decision; so as to help choice he may consider the long-range and broad effects of an alternative, or he may prefer the narrow approach — 'crossing bridges when one comes to them'.

Altering requirements — creation of requirements in order to eliminate alternatives, e.g. 'for that job I think I need to enjoy meeting people — do I?'.

Elimination of alternatives — dropping the most unattractive alternatives until there is only one left.

Proactive decision avoidance
Sequential strategy — achieving all alternatives by accomplishing first one and then another.

Omnibus strategy — simultaneously accomplishing alternatives, e.g. using free time to pursue as a hobby what was an equally attractive vocational choice.

Changing the situation — avoiding choosing between a number of alternatives by creating a new situation where there are no alternatives, e.g. a girl who cannot choose which career to pursue gets pregnant. Although this in itself might give rise to all sorts of stress, the degree of strain experienced may be less for her than the dissonance created by the former situation.

Planned procrastination — e.g. avoiding a decision until more information is available, or more training or education has been acquired.

Reactive decision making
Unconsidered choice — a decision is made quickly, either because dissonance is too much to bear, or because the chooser is lowly motivated, e.g. to choose between alternatives by flipping a coin.

Reactive decision avoidance
Denial — refusal to believe that a decision has to be made.

Fatalism — assuming that something will happen to make his decision for him.

Fantasy — belief that some unlikely event will happen.

Procrastination — putting off making decisions.

If the individual is unable to manage the strain he will find the cognitive task exceedingly difficult if not impossible. Some individuals find that managing their strain comes easier than solving their problems.

For others the reverse is true. For some, by concentrating on cognitive tasks, strain will be managed, while for others strain must be managed before work on the cognitive task can begin.

Is it possible to generate a list of transitional coping styles?

In our early thinking about how people tended to react to new situations, we distinguished three tentative strategies:

Reactionary — refusing to accept the new situation, or when one does, rejecting it as having nothing new and valuable to offer compared to the previous situation where the person felt comfortable.

Going native — embracing everything in the new situation and rejecting the previous situation as having no value.

Both of these approaches deny the total self in the new situation, in the first instance rejecting the reality of the new situation and in the second, rejecting the self, which is largely an accumulation of past experience.

Self-confronting — the person asks himself what does this transition mean for him. Why am I in this situation? What is happening to me? How do I feel about it? Where am I now? What do I want from this situation? How will it help me to grow? Where might it help me to go? Every 'crisis' has 'opportunity value'.

Based on the theoretical statement that transition coping necessitates (a) managing strain and (b) solving cognitive tasks, it is possible to develop a more operational typology:

(i)   proactive decision making or avoidance and proactive strain managing strategy.
(ii) proactive decision making or avoidance and reactive strain managing strategy.
(iii) reactive decision making or avoidance and proactive strain managing strategy.
(iv) reactive decision making or avoidance and reactive strain managing strategy.

This is, of course, only a logical model. Empirical research is necessary to discover (a) the range of strategies that do exist and (b) whether they can be classified into these four major styles or whether a completely new typology is called for. We also need to know which styles are most effective for whom in different transitional situations.

What are some examples of typical problems faced by a mover during a transition?

She is vulnerable to pressure groups because she does not know what 'games' people are playing.

Her decision resolution capacity is impaired – she might resolve decisions quickly without much consideration or be unable to resolve decisions at all.

She will not know the cultural norms.

She will not know the right questions to ask, let alone have access to the answers.

She will discover that people, on the whole, find it difficult to empathise with the newcomer to their social system.

She will experience a narrowed temporal frame of reference, being primarily aware of a sense of immediacy, e.g. one new day at the end of her first week constitutes approximately 20 per cent of the time that she has been there, compared to someone who has been there for 5 years when one new day represents less than 0.4 per cent of the time she has been there. Consequently, the latter's feelings about that day will be quite different from the mover's feelings about the same day.

How can the mover be helped to adapt and even profit from the transition?

There is certain information that he needs about himself:

(i)   Knowledge of his own needs and re-evaluation (see chapters 11 and 13).

(ii) The relationship climate he likes to be in.

(iii) The kinds of role he prefers to occupy.

(iv) What personal anchor points help him to cope with discontinuities.

(v)   How he typically tends to respond to new situations. Is he satisfied with the results? If not, what can he do to change this response pattern?

There is certain information that he needs to know about the new situation:

(i)   *The task expectations* others hold for his role.
(ii)   *Social expectations*, appropriate mode of address and dress, what is acceptable and unacceptable social intercourse.
(iii) *Data* relevant to the situation, e.g. who is that man and what does he do? What social resources are there for widows?
(iv)   Any *jargon* that is used, e.g. an 'M and F file'; three 'blocks' away; the SSRC.
(v)   How he can attain *support and information* in the new situation, e.g. by seeking out key people to discover the above information; capitalising on one's newness and differentness; discovering a friend/colleague whom he can trust, gripe with, and with whom he can test out feelings and thoughts. Developing a variety of support groups is a highly effective way of managing transitions.

There are certain skills he will need to develop:

(i)   How to move into a new situation with as little immobilisation, minimisation and depression as possible.
(ii)   How to exit from the old situation, i.e. letting go.
(iii) How to manage the anxiety generated.
(iv)   How to behave in the new situation so as to maximise his chances of fulfilling his objectives.

Is the mover the only person responsible for a successful transitional experience?

We believe he is not. A transition is dependent upon:

(i)   *Pre-transitional body*, organisation, group, culture, etc.
(ii)   *Post-transitional body*, organisation, group, culture, etc.
(iii) *Mover*

Successful transitions demand work on all three fronts. Unfortunately, it is often more difficult to influence (i) and (ii), and it is easier for helping agents to concentrate on the mover.

Is it possible to train people to cope more effectively with transitions?

This has to be empirically tested. Our general hypothesis is that people experiencing transitions will have similar tasks to cope with, namely, managing strain and dealing with cognitive tasks presented by the transition. We are assuming that to a considerable extent people's reactions to being in transition are learned as opposed to being inherited. To the extent that individuals' reactions are learned, we should be able to develop preventive, educative and re-educative strategies to help them more effectively manage their affairs and relationships at lower psychological costs, and derive greater benefits from the opportunity values imbedded in every major transition.

This means that a training programme could be generated to help develop more effective coping styles (i) for a number of people either experiencing different transitional events, or who are anticipating transitional events, or (ii) as general training for any presently unknown future transitions.

Debate and experimentation are necessary to ascertain whether these groups can be mixed or whether they should be separated when it comes to a training workshop. Criteria of a successful training programme should include:

(i)   A clearer perception of the person's overall life needs;
(ii) A clearer perception of the person's present needs;
(iii) An understanding of her approaches to managing strain and resolving decision situations;
(iv) A collection of data on her typical response pattern(s) to a new situation;
(v)   Her demonstration of new skills acquired deemed to be appropriate to more effective coping, according to her own objectives.

Do we now have a clearer understanding of transitional behaviour?

This chapter has attempted to move towards a conceptual framework for understanding transitions and for predicting behavioural outcomes from transitions. We have concentrated on the mover. It has been hypothesised:

(1) That a transition is a discontinuity in a person's life space of which he is aware and which requires new behavioural responses.

(2) Transitions may be macro, micro, predictable or unpredictable, entered into voluntarily or involuntarily.

(3) They also follow a predictable course. Progress through the phases can be accelerated, and some phases will be less important than others depending on the meaning of the transition to the person.

(4) All transitions involve stress which can produce biophysical strain, whether experienced or not.

(5) The amount of stress and degree of strain can be partially controlled or managed.

(6) All transitional events require —
   (i) management of strain generated by the event
   (ii) cognitive tasks to be resolved.

(7) Each person will have a characteristic style of managing anxiety and resolving cognitive tasks. These are termed proactive and reactive orientations. Four types of coping styles are outlined:
   proactive or reactive decision making or avoidance; and
   proactive or reactive strain management strategy.

(8) The mover can be helped to adapt and profit from a transition; it is hypothesised that it is possible to train people to develop more effective coping styles, and in particular to develop their proactive orientation, thereby increasing their satisfactions and furthering their growth.

(9) Every transition has opportunity value for the person but he does not often take advantage of the opportunity.

The final question is always 'why'? Why spend the energy, use the time, deplete the resources, all of which could be directed to something else? We know of no better answer than a statement of John Wood at the Sonoma, California conference on life transitions in the summer of 1975:

We come out of nothing, and we are going back to nothing when we die. When something in our life changes, we are confronted with nothing again. We are trying, all the time, to become familiar with that nothing. I have a lifespace filled with ideas, feelings, people. In life changes, that lifespace breaks up, and then it comes back together again in a new form. What we are trying to do is break that completely and be all one, be in that nothingness again, but *know* it. Whether we focus on something outside or inside, we're moving toward that barrier . . . to break it.

2. Life Styles: Their Diagnosis and Change

Dale G. Lake and Geraldine S. Lake

When reality becomes illusion
change is imminent
When illusion becomes reality
change is manifest

LIFE STYLE IN THE POPULAR MEDIA

A few hours drive south of Denver on 160 acres of rolling plain there is a modest barn-like structure which serves as the focus of a lovely pastoral setting. A few horses are visible and a simple structure, used for a home. Inside the barn one does not find the usual paraphernalia of stalls, farm tools and hay, but rather, an immaculate shop in which a single man is at work on a 1940 vintage airplane.

A conversation with this man reveals that not too many years ago he was a well-known engineer for NASA, living in a major north-eastern city. In the last two years he and his wife (who had always wanted to raise horses) had dismantled their pattern of life in the urban north-east in favour of a more rural setting in which he buys old planes, fixes them and resells them to farmers, while she raises horses.

Changes at the top

The interest in dramatic breaks in career lines has been growing for some years. At the height of general public interest the *Wall Street Journal* in 1971 ran a series of front page articles on 'life styles'. Witness the excerpts below

By Eric Morgenthaler
Staff Reporter of *The Wall Street Journal*

Two years ago, Willard H. Sahloff was at the height of a successful career in the appliance industry.

The 61-year old Mr. Sahloff had been since 1953 vice president of the housewares division of General Electric. He commanded an army of 10,000 workers, who under him manufactured and marketed 300 houseware models. He was listed in 'Who's Who' and known throughout the business as 'Mr. Housewares'. In all respects, he fit the image of a satisfied and successful executive.

But then Mr. Sahloff made a move that isn't part of the image: He announced he was retiring early to take up other business interests, giving up the career he had doggedly pursued for 40 years. And further, he revealed he had been planning the move for 10 years.

'I was very happy with General Electric, and I left with the greatest of reluctance,' recalls Mr. Sahloff, who now is involved in several lesser business ventures but who still gets 1,500 Christmas cards each year from former associates. 'But I decided I just didn't want to keep waking up at 3 o'clock in the morning and making notes to myself. You have a hell of a lot different life than I do now when you're running a big company and are responsible to its shareholders.'

Contradicting an Axiom

Mr. Sahloff's bailing out seems to contradict a cherished axiom of success: that the rewards at the top of the ladder are so great that men will stay there as long as they can. That seemed to be true for a long time, but indications are that there is a major switch taking place in executive attitudes towards security and success.

The result is that more executives, like Mr. Sahloff, are doing what 15 years ago would have been nearly unthinkable — leaving the executive suite and taking off in new directions within the 'System'.

Alternative life styles

1971 saw a peak in the popular interest in life-style change. This is not surprising, since Toffler's *Future Shock* had just been published in the previous year and was still a best seller. So intense was the interest that dozens of 'trade-type' magazines flourished and even today a Baltimore paper has an entire section entitled Life Style. At first, much of the popular interest was in 'alternative' life styles, that is, life styles that depart significantly from those considered 'acceptable' in mass culture. A spokesman for the alternative life style was the *Black Bart Brigade*, a paper that began publishing in November of 1971. In its first issue it declared the following.

> We're not quite sure where this notion got started, but those who defend it often talk about the impossibility of teaching an old dog new tricks. That may very well be if we are talking about dogs and very, very old ones. The fact is that many men and women, not only in their 30's and 40's, but well into the 50's and beyond, have discovered that they were on a treadmill to a rather hollow old age security, and realizing nothing of their vigorous middle years in the process. In many cases these folks form the mature backbone of a goodly number of agencies for social change, and in many others they simply find their own quiet way into a life that is more rewarding, more living than any they could obtain as a cog upon a wheel in a giant machine whose purpose no one really understands any longer.
>
> The *Black Bart Brigade* is all about this phenomenon. We think that some agency has got to counteract the widespread tendency to relegate alternative life styles to the young in years. We believe that when life begins to seem pointless and devoid of real meaning, that it is not because the prime years are hopelessly behind, but rather that a whole new life should be opening ahead of us; that we are no longer to be constricted by the narrow vision of the past. We feel that the desire for change and freedom is the sign of a healthy and alive person at any age.

A concept for study

Even as the media were stressing the bizarre aspects of changed life styles, and as advertising began to recognise the dollar appeal by pushing such slogans as, 'Buy the car that fits your life style', a few popular writers began to see the knowledge-building implications of the life-style concept. Foremost among these was Alvin Toffler. In his book, *Future Shock*, he captured the many divergent forms of personal revolution occurring in our culture and dubbed these changes — 'life style changes'.

How we choose a life style, and what it means to us, looms as one of the central issues of the psychology of tomorrow. For the selection of a life style, whether consciously done or not, powerfully shapes the individual's future. It does this by imposing order, a set of principles or criteria on the choices he makes in daily life . . . . To be 'between styles' . . . is a life crisis (Toffler, 1970, p. 306).

With the recognition of life style as an important concept for building knowledge, we turn now to look at formal research into this complex phenomenon.

CONCEPTUAL FOUNDATIONS FOR LIFE STYLE

A casual reading of mass media's treatment of life-style change might lead one to believe that it is a one-time, unique event. In contrast, there are formal theoretical orientations which view the human being as a maturing social organism in which change is natural, continuous, even necessary. For instance, Erikson's (1963, p. 270) formulations:

(1) that the human personality in principle develops according to steps predetermined in the growing person's readiness to be driven toward, to be aware of, and to interface with, a widening social radius; and

(2) that society, in principle, tends to be so construed as to meet and invite this succession of potentialities for interaction and attempts to safeguard and to encourage the proper rate and proper sequence of their unfoldings.

These are in turn translated into eight 'ages of Man', the last four, intimacy, generativity, acceptance and integrity all likely to have considerable impact on the way an individual behaves in the settings of family, work and recreation. Indeed, Erikson himself hints at a relationship between the stages of development and life style:

Although aware of the relativity of all the various life styles which have given meaning to human striving, the possessor of integrity is ready to defend the dignity of his own life style against all physical and economic threats (Erikson, 1950, p. 268).

And in so stating, he is indicating that when the final stage is reached, life style also becomes stable.

In a similar, but more focused vein, Kohlberg (1969) has described a theory of development with a primary focus on moral behaviour. The importance of cognitive-developmental theorists is their advocacy of a distinction between discrete behavioural changes or learning and *changes in mental structure*. Structure refers to the general characteristics of shape, pattern or organisation of response rather than to the rate or intensity of response or its pairing with particular stimuli. Cognitive structure refers to rules for processing information or for connecting experienced events.

The cognitive-developmental theories of Erikson and Kohlberg assume that mental structure is the result of an interaction between certain organismic structuring tendencies and the structure of the outside world. This assumption sets the theoretical stage for a view of life-style change that is connected to the natural cognitive development of the organism. Thus, the theoretical precedent has been established, although the task of formulating a cognitive-developmental theory of life-style change remains.

Life-style research

Work on such theories is under way. Gould has been studying phases of adult life with a sample of 524 men and women, and has teamed with Sheehy (1974) to develop a theory of seven stages of adult development and has specifically tried to analyse separately man's development, woman's development and, uniquely, developmental stages of couples.

In still a third viewpoint, Levinson (1972) has distinguished the following gross chronological areas of adult male development: (a) early adulthood from roughly age 20 to 35; (b) the mid-life decade age 35—45; (c) middle age, from 45 to 65; and (d) several elderly periods, as yet unidentified. An interesting aspect of this work is the suggestion that crises are the stuff of which transitions are made. Crises are good. They keep us from slipping into a rut. A person can expect periods when his particular life structure is forming, hurdles when it is breaking up and reforming, and periods when it is relatively stable. Many changes can take place within each period. But a person moves from one to the next only when he starts working at new developmental tasks and builds a new structure for his life.

Levinson introduces the 'dream' as a core element in the development of young adults. This is the vision of self-in-the-world, the imagined possibility that generates excitement, aliveness, energy, and hope. The major task of the twenties is to build a life structure around that vision. However, it must be pointed out that Levinson is studying a sample of 40 men. The woman's role must be to share the dream of the man. As the man realises the dream he will often choose a second woman to be his 'testimonial' of what he has become. Levinson assumes that there must be parallel life phases for women but little or no research has been done on women's life styles.

Levinson is not alone in recognising the role of the self in the development of life style. Super (1957), in a continuing series of studies conducted on a longitudinal sample of subjects over the last twenty years, has shown the many ways that self-concept manifests itself in vocational preference as a translation of self-concepts differentiated along such lines as self-esteem, abstraction, certainty and stability.

The relationship between work, as it is carried on in organisations, and life style has been studied by Bier (1967) and Friedlander (1970). They have been developing the view that there is a relationship between the structure and functioning of organisations and styles of living. Further, once organisation structure and processes are crystallised, they tend to foster the style of life and form of man from which they were originally derived. Such conceptualisation has led these theorists to propose three basic life styles that interact with various kinds of organisation to result in task accomplishment and human fulfilment. The life styles are:

Formalistic, which takes direction from authorities, guidance from precedent and policy, has faith in rules, laws, policies and order, and strives for advancement and prestige in order to achieve security and comfort.

Sociocentric, which takes direction from discussion and agreement with others who are close, guidance from close relationships with others, has faith in group norms, and strives for intimacy and acceptance, in order to achieve intimate relationships and shared values.

Personalistic, which takes direction from within the individual, guidance from self-knowledge of what one wants to do, has faith in one's own sense of justice, and strives for experimentation and self-discovery.

In order to study these life styles and how they interact with various kinds of organisation structure such as bureaucratic, collaborative and coordinative, Friedlander has developed a paper and pencil factor analytic measure of the three life-style orientations. He has stimulated an exciting array of studies on life-style issues such as exploration of role and life style, leadership and life style, interactions between people with similar and different life styles, the repercussions of people with different life styles operating in incongruous organisation structures, and he is studying methods of adapting life styles. Friedlander is also developing concepts of progression through life styles in the cognitive-developmental tradition.

One other cognitive-developmental theory merits review in the context of life style. It is unique because its focus is related primarily to the learning style of the individual adult. It is relevant because all of the above theorists would agree that the period between life styles is a crisis period. In stressful crisis periods we are likely to fall back upon our most rudimentary skills for learning. Therefore, the theory and research of Kolb (1974), which has at its core a model for adult learning, contributes an important potential link for understanding *how* one actually moves to a new life style. Kolb's theory proposes a descriptive model of adult learning as a process for translating experience into concepts that in turn are used as guides for choosing new experiences. The learner, if he is to be effective, needs four different kinds of abilities: concrete experience abilities, reflective observation abilities, abstract conceptualisation abilities, and active experimentation abilities. The dominance of one or more of these abilities does much to determine the style the individual develops for choosing new experiences in life. We think Kolb's theory has high potential for uncovering and explaining the ways that individuals develop and change such aspects of total life style as family patterns, work settings and recreational settings.

Practice of life-style change

The pervasiveness of life-style changes has not escaped the attention of practitioners who work in organisational development, encounter groups and therapy. Perhaps the most notable example is a workshop invented by Art Shedlin and Herb Shepard entitled The Life Planning Workshop. In this workshop various exercises are orchestrated to help participants review their life goals, identify change targets and develop plans for achieving new goals. More recently, Adams and Hopson have developed an experimental workshop to assist individuals in managing life transitions, whether such transitions are from one culture to another or from one life style to another (see chapter 11).

In still another area of application Dr Frieda Porat (1974), who founded the Center for Creativity and Growth, has described case studies of life-style change in her book, *Changing Your Life Style*. Various other centres and institutes throughout the U.S.A. and England now purport to offer life-style changing experiences.

Review

So far we have described recent interest and research in the area of life-style change. We have viewed life change as a topic for the media, as a focus for theory and research and as an area for application. Having conducted such a review, we agree with Toffler that 'how we choose a life style and what it means to us looms as one of the central issues of the psychology of tomorrow.' In what follows we wish to portray, in broad vignettes, one view of that future.

FUTURE RESEARCH ON LIFE-STYLE CHANGE

Obvious foci for studies of life style are family, work and health; family and work because so much of life is enacted in these areas and health because it is so dependent on the *way* we manage the stresses of work and family. Most researchers in the areas of family, work and health will readily admit that the areas are related conceptually and experimentally. However, each area has tended to develop its own characteristic research formats; e.g. survey methods on worker satisfaction, family case studies, and clinical and animal studies in health. We were unable to uncover a single approach in any of these separate areas or even on life style itself that was sufficiently comprehensive to help us understand how a life style develops and changes. (Even the excellent works of Levinson and Friedlander must be included in this generalisation because Levinson has limited his studies to a longitudinal study of 40 men and Friedlander has woven his research into the fabric of organisations.)

Several traditional professions — especially in the fields of medicine, law and sociology — compile records of lives and draw inferences from them. Consider hospital dossiers. They are usually heaps of badly organised facts about- the patient's previous illnesses, symptoms, remedial measures taken, and notes on his ward behaviour. The medical record often seems meaningless and arbitrary to the hospital staff, who thus need reminders to 'write up' the patient.

Legal records resemble medical dossiers in that they exhibit at times a rather stilted and arbitrary character, even though the legal model stresses evidence. The ideal legal case calls for careful documentation and testimony. Courts of law follow rules of evidence for establishing credibility. It is interesting, however, that due process depends on the same sort of ideographic analysis that an adequate description of life pattern will need.

From sociology there is an ideographic tradition referred to as the *course of life* (Leonard Cain, 1964). The core idea is that at different ages one is expected to behave in different ways and receive certain treatment from others based on that behaviour. Perhaps the most carefully structured sociological subdivisions of time are those by Goffman (1959) in his work on careers.

Jean Piaget and Barbel Inhelder (1958) have made the most substantial contributions in psychology to holistic methodology – particularly in the specification of age norms. What is missing, however, is a more ambitious life-stage system research on theory such as Erikson's. The real problem with this research and our interest in life styles is that studies tend to be conducted with the very young and the very old. A few important exceptions have been published by Buhler (1968) and Kelly (1955).

A researcher who has been concerned with holistic or organismic concepts of life is Dailey (1971). He describes his own research as an attempt to do life assessment. In his words,

> A subjective life history is one in which the investigator using methods more holistic than objective, attempts to learn not only what happens but also what it means to the person (p. 36).

Dailey's own work culminates in recommendations for retraining researchers to do holistic research. His life assessment instrument, which requires a 3–4 hour interview, illustrates the magnitude of research instrumentation needed for studies of life style.

To conduct studies of life style and its change, all of the following methods will be needed to produce integrated knowledge:

(1) Survey methods in order to determine what the rate and incidence of life-style change is;

(2) personality measurement methods capable of weighing value orientations toward objects, persons, places and self;

(3) historical life pattern assessments (such as Dailey's) for determining sources of motivation;

(4) assessments of physiological stress; and

(5) learning style measurement methods.

The orchestration of all these methods into the single focus of life-style change should provide substantial gains in knowledge.

Needed research

Work

First there is the need to weave separate studies of work and family into emerging views of life style. Some research has already hinted at this need. For instance, one of the most ambitious studies of the meaning of work in today's culture was commissioned under Elliot Richardson while he was Secretary of Health and published in a volume entitled *Work in America.* The commission was quick to point out that work is not an isolated aspect of life,

> it is central for most adults, it makes a major contribution to identity and self-esteem, it brings order and meaning to life. Work offers economic self-sufficiency, status, family stability, and an opportunity to interact with others in one of the most basic activities of society.

Therefore, the commission concludes,

> If the opportunity to work is absent or if the nature of work is dissatisfying (or worse), severe repercussions are likely to be experienced in other parts of the social system (p. 186).

— and we would add 'other parts of the person's total life pattern'.

That the centrality of work in one's life space is being reduced can be inferred, says the commission, from the growth of communes, adolescents panhandling in Georgetown, North Beach, etc., shifts to the four-day week, welfare loads increasing and retirements at earlier ages. It is difficult to know what the implications of this reduction are without life-style studies to help understand what such a reduction will mean in family life, recreational life, and to the basic physical and psychological health of individuals. Indeed, the commission itself, after analysing sources of dissatisfaction in work, trends, alternatives to the present situation, ways to improve work, etc., found

> that work, health, family stability, education, and other matters of major concern do not reside in discrete compartments, but rather that we live in a closed system — 'spaceship earth' to use Kenneth Boulding's phrase. These spheres of action are mutually influential (p. 23).

The commission concludes:

> Because work is central to the lives of so many Americans, either the absence of work or employment in meaningless work is creating an increasing intolerable situation. The human costs of this state of affairs are manifested in worker alienation, alcoholism, drug addiction, and other symptoms of poor mental and physical health (p. 186).

Notice that the manifestations are likely to appear elsewhere than on the job.

Family

Turning the focus of this section to the family does not mean that work is to be left behind. The two are interdependent. The cases of Terkel's (1974) blue collar workers give many instances in which frustrated workers will displace job-generated aggression on family, neighbours, and strangers.

A common experience of human relations trainers is described by Art Shedlin (1974, unpublished):

> One October day a well-dressed, obviously successful, robust man of about 45 came in to talk with me. (I didn't realize it at the time, but he was the first of many who were to come — all saying about the same thing.) He seemed placid, confused, and angry all at the same time, with the anger a subtle overtone. The lyrics of the theme song went something like this 'Here I am at 44, successful, respected, productive, a competent executive making $40,000 a year — but there is "the taste of ashes" in my mouth. My kids are growing up but I've lost touch with them — when I'm home I'm only half there, daydreaming and worrying about myself instead of being with them. All the traveling I've had to do has somewhat estranged me from my wife, causing a kind of flatness in our life together. Sometimes I feel like chucking the whole thing — then I think of all the ways I'm

locked in to the security of where I am — the pension plan, the stock options, the insurance, and so forth. All that is good for the family. But in a way, I'm not "in" the family. I don't know what I want to do — at times I don't even know what I *want*.'

The O'Neills (1974) provide us with the reciprocal woman's view:

Betty has been married for seventeen years, has three children ranging in age from fifteen to five, and lives in the suburbs of a large city. Her husband, Sam, drives to work in the city. Betty has not held a job since her marriage and defines herself in terms of being a wife and mother. She believes herself to be successful in both these capacities and has long been content with her role in life.

But then gradually, over a period of several months, Betty begins to feel restless. Her youngest child is now in first grade, and for the first time in years Betty has a certain amount of genuine leisure during the day. She is surprised to discover that these hours of privacy seem somehow empty. She has always said that she wished she had more time to herself, but now that she has it she isn't quite sure what to do with it. Sitting alone in her kitchen in the late morning, drinking her fourth cup of coffee, she wonders what it will be like when the children are older and still less dependent upon her. A feeling of incipient uselessness creeps over her at times — and she isn't even forty yet (p. 30).

Not to be overlooked is the child in the family. Philippe Aries (1962) has presented an analysis of the changing role of the child from the Renaissance to the present day. Aries informs us that the concept of childhood as a separate period of life with special characteristics is relatively modern. Today, the combined wishes of the family and the effect of school has been to remove the child from participation in society much beyond the previous cultural patterns.

A study of life styles should help us to understand the dilemmas of individual life stress in the above by forcing us to view the family holistically as a system in which intergenerational conflicts of life style are occurring, each pressed upon the family by the restructuring going on in the individual. Indeed, we may find that the movement of any one individual in the family into a new phase of life style will precipitate subsequent life-style changes in the others. It is not too hard to imagine that as the boy moves into adolescence and his physical and sexual prowess increases, his new found behaviour could intensify his father's concern over a loss of meaningfulness and youthfulness associated with an impending life-style change in the thirties.

Health

The question of health illustrates the interdependence of work and family even further. Chapters 3 and 9 show clearly that major health changes are precipitated by stress, whether created in the family, at work or in the culture.

Holmes and Rahe (1967) devised a simple objective procedure for recording significant recent life history events in work, family and recreation. Their questionnaire lists typical, change-inducing events (for example, marriage) and tabulates an annual life-change unit score for the person being studied (see Fig. 9.1, p. 145). Studies using the Holmes and Rahe life-change scale show: that major illnesses are most likely to follow major life changes (for 3000 naval recruits; Rahe *et al.,* 1968); that coronary heart disease was higher among 39 Swedish subjects who increased their scores on the life-change scale six months prior to its manifestation (Rahe *et al.,* 1971); that sickness at sea could be predicted by changes occurring prior to sailing (Rubin *et al.,* 1969; N-2556); that when compared to controls 54 Swedish males suffering myocardial infarction had higher life-change scores in the two years prior to onset (Theorell *et al.,* 1971); and only one contrary finding, in which it was reported that students with mononucleosis reported fewer life changes than did a heterogeneous group of students (Wilder *et al.,* 1971; N-283). Even in this study the authors suggested that mononucleosis patients were defensive about the imaginary nature of their disease and thus under-reported stressful events.

The second example comes from Friedman and Rosenman (1974), who have taken a large sample of clinical patients and, by examining eating habits, use of time, emotional stress, competitive behaviour, etc., have derived what they call the 'type A pattern'. This pattern is, in their words, 'an action-emotion complex that can be observed in any person who is aggressively involved in a chronic, incessant struggle to achieve more and more in less and less time . . .' In addition to observing their subjects they also give them a simple task of reading instructions that requires aggressive verbal behaviour, and then they measure the voice patterns electronically and can separate type A's from type B's. They claim that there is a much higher incidence of various forms of heart disease in type A's.

Friedman and Rosenman's *Type A Behavior and Your Heart* (1974) is a dramatic testimony to the effects of a life pattern on health. It is dramatic (a) because these are medical doctors who have uncovered a psychological pattern, (b) because they have physiological measures to identify a psychological type, and (c) because they claim it is related to a particular pathology. Friedman and Rosenman are quite convinced and quite convincing that the individual who creates a life pattern that is a losing race against time is inviting heart disease at an early age. In addition, there are some other elements — the authors claim — that can be added to the life pattern which even *increase* the likelihood of heart failure. They are, in order of danger, smoking, a diet high in cholesterol, and 'violent' exercise such as jogging against a stop watch or handball. The authors' arguments are, for the most part, supported by research (with the exception of 'violent' exercise) and while one wonders why alcohol is hardly mentioned, it does seem safe to conclude that their work leaves little room for doubt that total life pattern can be identified as a predictor of heart disease.

Even Friedman and Rosenman's prescription for changing type A life patterns is a testimony to the holistic nature of work and family. They prescribe, among other things, that the type A seriously consider joining a religious group 'in order to find a source of peacefulness'. They also recommend changing eating patterns, including taking time for breakfast, and spending more time with children and spouse.

Again, we conclude that the above separate studies have illustrated the need for new holistic studies and we think life style can provide a vehicle for conducting such studies.

The rate of life pattern change

Another research task that needs to be conducted through polling techniques of Harris or NORC, is to determine just how prevalent major life pattern changes are in our culture. Toffler (1970), of course, says change in relation to objects, people and places will continue to accelerate.

> Whether upward, downward or sideways, the future holds more, not less, turnover in jobs . . . (p. 113).

> Not infrequently the new job involves not merely a new employer, a new location, and a new set of work associates, but a whole new way of life. Thus the 'serial career' pattern is evidenced by the growing number of people who, once assured of reasonable comfort by the affluent economy, decide to make a full 180 degree turn in their

career line at a time of life when others merely look forward to retirement (p. 14).

The primary difficulty in this research effort will be to sort out factors that are obviously related but are still distinct from a life pattern change (such as job turnover). Above, Toffler makes the claim that it may very well lead to life-style change. However, there must also be job changes that leave the basic life pattern untouched and life pattern changes that are not related to job turnover. The woman who has been a housewife for the last twenty years and goes to work outside the house after the children leave would probably have to develop new life patterns due to the combination of place of work change and the reduction in child responsibilities. Early retirement from the military might also involve a change in life pattern that would not show up as a turnover statistic.

Many more studies could be derived from a basic commitment to study the consequences for work, family and health of life-style changes. To list a few possibilities:

examinations of alternative life styles in such settings as communes and religious sects;
rigorous experimental studies of the comparative effects of different training laboratories on life-style transitions;
targeted studies of special groups such as women, pre-retirement, newly retired and minorities;
mobility patterns of families and their life styles, etc.

In addition to such studies, a new, more operational definition of life style would have to emerge. Skinner has rightfully pointed out the danger of using popular terms in undertaking scientific studies:

The important objection to the vernacular in the description of behavior is that many of its terms imply conceptual schemes. I do not mean that a science of behavior is to dispense with a conceptual scheme but that it must not take over without careful consideration the schemes which underlie popular speech. The vernacular is clumsy and obese; its terms overlap each other, draw unnecessary or unreal distinctions, and are far from being the most convenient in dealing with data (Skinner, 1938, p. 7).

Thus, one goal of life-style studies must be to redefine and increase our understanding of it by identifying and defining some of the underlying patterns of combination and alteration that characterise life patterns. Carnap (1953, p. 438) has referred to this task of redefining concepts as the problem of *explication*: he points out that making more exact a concept that is used 'in a more or less vague way either in every-day language or in an earlier stage of scientific language' is often important in the development of science and mathematics.

Implications for action

If we only increased our knowledge about how to research life-style change and its impact on salient aspects of life such as work and family, our efforts would be incomplete without applying this knowledge. What follows is more suggestive than exhaustive. It identifies areas for action without describing strategies for implementation.

The work of Shedlin, Shepard, Adams, and Hopson mentioned above provides a point of beginning. Similarly, Kolb's work on learning styles is a good place to begin; by increasing the awareness of those experiencing the strain of life-style change, his theories could be used to teach individuals how they might use their own learning style to facilitate change.

In-house company or organisation efforts to retrain workers, transfer professionals, or increase the percentage of women and minority workers will all involve elements of life-style change for those individuals, and these efforts might be improved by understanding the larger consequences of organisational training efforts.

Many governmental agencies provide pre-retirement seminars for employees. These seminars might be strengthened if, in addition to the typical topics dealing with housing and security, the larger life-style issues of the impending loss of power and the simultaneous need to take increased control and initiative over one's total life activities were added.

The instrumentation which must be developed for better research on life style could contribute to the individual's ability to diagnose his/her own need to change. Or conversely, it could help to identify periods of stability. A family armed with sensitive diagnostic tools might find more satisfying ways of understanding and coping with intergenerational conflicts stimulated by one or more life-style changes in the family.

Finally, better knowledge of life style, how it develops or stagnates, how it is enacted in work and family, could provide the basis for a national institute for the improvement of the quality of life with which the individual or group might contract for as long as a two-year period for such periodic services as *diagnosis; workshops* on initiative taking, risk taking, family health, sexual adequacy, religious experiences and role changes; and inclusion in a *network* of persons experiencing similar kinds of stresses. Over time, such an institute could create widely disseminable self-contained multi-media packages.

SUMMARY

This has been an attempt to show that the concept of life style, popular with the mass media, is also an exciting new arena for research and action. It implies a comprehensiveness, a holism, a purposefulness, much needed in the fragmented research current in studies of family and work. It is vital to the further development of our understanding of human transitions.

3. Stress and the Risk of Illness

John Adams

Transitions, regardless of what sort they are, represent a disruption in one's routines. Hence, they cause a disruption of equilibrium. Even positive, carefully planned transitions lead into new areas for the individual and to the disruption of that person's routines to some extent. The stress response ('strain') is a major factor to consider in the study of transitions because transitions are always, to a greater or lesser degree, strain inducing.

Modern living is stressful. Society is changing rapidly causing changes in values, life styles, career patterns, family expectations and so on. Over the past few years, popular and professional books, magazines and journals have focused increasingly on stress and its impact on people. On any newsstand one can find books on stress and how to escape from it. Likewise, professional publications in the behavioural sciences are dealing with the same issue. While 'strain' may be defined somewhat differently from one publication to the next, the clear trend is towards defining it as a non-specific physiological response to disruption, and towards relating the chronic experience of this response to the risk of various illnesses and other health changes (e.g. accidents). To a growing number of doctors and behavioural scientists, strain is becoming the basic bridge between psychology and medical pathology.

Strain is the body's physical, mental and chemical reaction to disruptions, which prepares one to handle the unfamiliar or the frightening. It is both good and bad. Strain is needed for alertness and the performance of high quality work. In emergencies, it is needed as a source of increased energy and strength. On the other hand, chronic or prolonged strain can cause or heighten the effects of a vast array of diseases. For example, in *Stress* (McQuade & Aikman, 1974) the table of contents reads, in part:

PART TWO: What Stress Can Do To You

    Chapter 1: The Cardiovascular System:
                 Heart Attack, Hypertension, Angina, Arrhythmia, Migraine

Chapter 2: The Digestive System:
Ulcers, Colitis, Constipation, Diarrhea, Diabetes

Chapter 3: Stress and the Immunity Screen:
Infections, Allergies, Auto-immunity, Cancer

Chapter 4: The Skeletal-Muscular System:
Backache, Tension headache, Arthritis, the Accident-prone

In each case, the authors make a detailed accounting of case examples and population studies which suggest strongly that prolonged exposure to stress can cause or heighten each of these conditions. The authors describe the differing personality characteristics of persons prone to different diseases and show how stress eventually leads to bodily breakdown.

An improved understanding of one's own transitions or the intention to help others manage their transitions more effectively must be accompanied by an understanding of stress and of how chronic strain increases the risks of illness. The next section of this chapter describes the non-specific stress response in greater detail. Following that, some historical and current perspectives relating stress to illness are developed. A third section reviews the relationship between organisational variables (as stressors) and illness and begins to indicate ways of alleviating or buffering the impact of stress.

THE STRESS RESPONSE

If one's body is invaded by a certain kind of virus, one's lymphatic system will send out a tailor-made kind of cell, called an antibody, which will attack that particular virus, almost like fitting a key to a lock. Following the success of the antibody in overcoming the virus, the antibody remains in the system and the person remains, at least for a time, immune to further attacks by the same virus (e.g. measles). Since the 'common cold' is made up of a great many combinations of viruses, it is one illness we don't seem to become immune to. In any event, this is an example of our body's making a specific response to a specific invasion. The stress response is always the same, regardless of the invasion.

The stress response triggers the autonomic nervous system, which ordinarily serves to keep our bodies in equilibrium through controlling our metabolism and growth rates. It does this through acting on our thyroid and pituitary glands, telling them when to release hormones into our bodies. It is called the autonomic nervous system because it is autonomous. That is, it normally is beyond our conscious abilities to control it. The autonomic nervous system also is set off frequently by disruptions from outside, and this is the beginning of the stress response. In other words, it is other people and events out in the environment we must relate to that set off the stress response. With this in mind, we can view stress not as a bad thing to be avoided but as a fact of our lives.

Doctors and psychologists are becoming concerned, however, because of the number of times events disrupt our sense of continuity and set off the stress response. Surprises set it off most often — things like getting fired, having an accident, or being asked for a divorce. But changes we decide to make — like looking for a new job or adopting a new career — also cause disruptions that set off the stress response. And now we are learning that normal life developments like menopause or turning thirty create their own turbulence and therefore set off the stress response too!

The chemical reactions occurring during the stress response are meant to equip the body to fight or take flight, by increasing blood pressure and metabolism rate, increasing the production of cholesterol, and producing adrenalin. Society has made it less necessary for us to fight or flee with any great frequency, but our bodies have not evolved as fast as has society, and the disruptions of everyday living still set off the stress response cycle once needed for survival. Over a period of time, if we set the stress response off regularly, there is a cost to be paid. The list of diseases, as we saw above, looks somewhat like the table of contents from a basic pathology text. The eventual wear and tear of chronic stress responses lowers resistance to these maladies and also seems to intensify their impact.

There is a tremendous difference between people both physically and in terms of their personalities. While much is yet to be learned, it is fairly clear that these differences greatly affect our eventual reactions to chronic stress.

Different people are either born with or develop different equipment than their neighbours. Some of us have inherited weaknesses like poor eyesight or weak livers because those things run in our families. Others of us acquire weaknesses through accidents, illnesses, or personal neglect or abuse. All of us have some weak links, physically, which are susceptible to the gradual wear and tear of chronic stress.

People also develop different personalities. Psychiatrists tell us that we learn very early in life whether or not it is 'permissible' to experience and express feelings. For example, if we are raised in an environment where it is not alright to cry or not alright to be angry, we learn very quickly to hold our breath when we have such feelings, and therefore develop shallow breathing habits. This can make one's respiratory system susceptible to breakdowns.

We also learn very early in life what sorts of relationships to have with people. For example, boys are taught that men are self-reliant and do not have intimate relationships with other men or with very many women. Society tends to say we should develop one intimate relationship and does not encourage us to develop a network of support systems which, we shall see later, probably can help alleviate strain (see pp. 52—3 and chapter 10).

What all of this adds up to is that many of the stress-related diseases listed above tend to have clusters of behavioural characteristics that differentiate them from the others. For example, coronary prone people typically tend to be highly competitive and driven; they fall easily into conflict with authority figures; and they are determined to out-do their parents. Very active and energetic people tend to be coronary risks (see, for example, Friedman & Rosenman, 1974).

Ulcer patients typically also are go-getters, but under the surface they are holding down a strong need to be nurtured. They tend to have a lot of hostility in their systems which is blocked from expression by their need to be loved. Ulcer patients also tend to get into marital troubles quite readily (see, for example, Wolf, 1965).

Cancer patients are different. They have often had a life of loneliness and exhibit deep-seated melancholy, despair, disappointment and hopelessness. The onset of cancer often follows shortly after a severe disruption to or termination of a crucial relationship (see, for example, LeShan, 1966).

Arthritic patients tend to be more domineering people and yet are often socially shy at the same time. They express their feelings in aggressive actions. Many athletes fit this category. As they get older and have less energy, they are less able to utilise these outlets and tend to develop arthritis in one or more of their joints (see, for example, Brooke, 1960).

It is thus indicated that people who tend to 'come down with' these different diseases have different physical make-ups and different personalities. To reiterate, we all have our weak links.

When these diseases are induced or maintained by stress, they are not easily cured. As an example, thirty people in a recent study had surgery done on their ulcers. During the next year, seventeen developed new ulcers, seventeen developed physical signs of anxiety like tics and phobias, five became asthmatic, four developed high blood pressure and one contracted tuberculosis (Silverman, 1968). There is no complete medical cure for diseases where a major stress factor is involved.

HISTORICAL AND CURRENT PERSPECTIVES ON RELATING STRESS AND ILLNESS

Claude Bernard, the famous nineteenth-century biologist, thought that the 'seeds' of disease were all around and inside us all of the time. The diseases, or dis-eases, did not have an effect on one's body unless one's body was in a state to 'receive' one of them. Most frequently, according to Bernard, our bodies maintain an equilibrium that resists disease and the seeds therefore cannot grow.

During the same period, however, microbiologists like Louis Pasteur were receiving more attention from the medical world as they identified and learned to destroy pathogenic microbes, like those causing diphtheria. Over the years, conquered diseases have disappeared or become rare, but others have always replaced them. We are still building and expanding hospitals. We still do not know for sure why people get sick.

The pendulum, however, seems to be swinging from 'Pasteur' back towards 'Bernard'. Pasteur, when near death, reputedly said that 'Bernard was right. The microbe is nothing, the terrain [state of the body] is everything.' However, Pasteur's achievements outlived his dying words and have strongly influenced the practice of medicine.

Bernard's work was revived in the 1930s by Walter Cannon, a Harvard physiologist who described a 'wisdom' of the body that sets off adjustments to change and disruption. Cannon noted that the same adaptive responses were triggered by a wide variety of intrusions.

Even earlier, around the turn of the century, Johns Hopkins psychiatrist Adolf Meyer recognised that the human organism's adaptive system can become overloaded and break down. He kept life-charts or biographies of his patients which showed that people became ill shortly after clusters of major changes in their lives much more frequently than chance would predict. Harold G. Wolff, a psychiatrist at Cornell, studied these phenomena and began to relate life settings and emotional states to specific diseases.

Thomas H. Holmes, formerly a co-worker of Wolff's at Cornell and now at the University of Washington, took the work of Meyer and Wolff even further in developing a scale for predicting one's susceptibility to stress diseases. By 1965, Holmes and his colleagues had evolved their Social Readjustment Rating Scale to its present widely known form (see Holmes & Rahe, 1967). After being discussed by Alvin Toffler in *Future Shock*, this scale has appeared in the *New York Times, Reader's Digest* and nearly every popular and professional book concerned with relating stress to illness susceptibility. It is also described briefly in this book in chapters 2 and 9.

This scale consists of 43 life-change events. Each event has been assigned a number of points (through an extensive research process), which represent the average relative amount of readjustment required to restore one's equilibrium after experiencing that event. A great many studies have been conducted and are now being conducted using the Social Readjustment Rating Scale. While the results vary from one study to the next (due to different populations and differing research designs) one thing remains constant across these studies — the more readjustment points one amasses during a period, the greater one's likelihood of becoming ill in the not too distant future. And, according to Holmes, the higher the total points, the more severe that illness is likely to be!

This section is concluded with a few brief mentions of a variety of specific studies that have related stress and illness.

Jay M. Weiss (1972) of the Rockefeller University in New York subjected two rats in each experiment simultaneously to the same physical stressors (electric shock) while varying the psychological stress (predictability of the shock). While an audible signal told one rat when to expect the shocks, the second rat heard the signal randomly. A third rat was confined in the same manner as the other two but received no shocks or signals. The control rat (no shocks or signals) developed very few ulcers. The rat that heard the audible signals randomly developed ulcers five times larger than the rat that heard warning signals! In these experiments, *unpredictability* emerged as the key factor. That is, the less expected the disruption, the greater the impact of the stress response.

Seligman's (1975) work on the phenomenon of 'learned helplessness' demonstrates clearly in animals and humans that distress and depression are generated when a subject does not have control over his environment. If responses are rewarded randomly instead of being contingent upon certain behaviour, then 'learned helplessness' appears and continues to affect the subject even in future tasks where in actuality he now has control.

John C. Cassel of the University of North Carolina has been studying the experiences of first time mothers. For those experiencing a high degree of stressful readjustment during their pregnancies, 30 per cent of those who received a great deal of love and support during the readjustment period prior to delivery experienced complications in childbirth; while 90 per cent of those who received little warmth and support experienced childbirth complications (from Lamott, 1975, p. 10).

Cassel has also found changed hormonal levels in people deprived of warmth and support. In a related study, he found that divorced men have a death rate three to five times as high as married men of the same age (ibid.).

Lawrence E. Hinkle and William N. Christensen looked for 'Asian flu' among twenty-four women by examining samples of their blood for the presence of the influenza virus. The women had varying concentrations of the virus, but the amount of virus was uncorrelated with the onset of influenza. In nearly every case, the women who succumbed were those who had recently gone through a bad emotional experience (ibid., p. 13).

In 1949, Franz Alexander noted that while hypertension was virtually unknown among African blacks, it was an exceedingly widespread disease among American blacks. Black psychiatrists William H. Grier and Price M. Cobb attribute the high incidence of hypertension among black ghetto dwellers to 'being black, and perpetually angry, and unable to express it or do anything about it.' Similarly, Ernest Harburg, of the University of Michigan, tested the blood pressures of blacks in high and low stress areas in Detroit. He found that, all other things being equal, 32 per cent of the people tested in the high stress area had hypertension while 19 per cent of the people in the low stress area had hypertension (ibid., pp. 31–2).

S. L. Syme, of the University of California, has investigated the relationships between social changes (transitions) and heart disease. The data he has collected have led him to three conclusions:

(1) Men whose adult life setting is different from that in which they grew up (typically rural to urban) are three times as likely to have a coronary as those whose life setting remains the same.
(2) The more often a person changes a job, the more likely he or she is to have a coronary.
(3) As rural areas become urbanised, the incidence of heart disease increases (ibid., p. 36).

These are but a few of an almost endless list of studies which have been conducted linking stress and physical illness. Readers interested in further such examples are referred to W. McQuade and A. Aikman (1974) and K. Lamott (1975). Both of these books are easily read and themselves contain further references for investigating the relationships between stress and illness. As a means of summarising the studies cited above, the following conclusions can be drawn:

(1) The incidence of illness is positively correlated with the amount of life change or transition one undergoes.
(2) Unpredictable disruptions cause more severe stress-related diseases than predictable disruptions.
(3) Lack of feedback on the success of attempts to cope with strain-inducing events causes more severe stress-related diseases than when relevant feedback is present.
(4) Interpersonal warmth and support during stressful periods seems to reduce the impact of the stress response.
(5) Viruses alone do not cause all illnesses. The incidence of bad emotional experiences seems to upset the body and allow the viruses to take over.
(6) Hypertension occurs much more often in environments characterised by high stress and few ways to respond to that stress.
(7) The more major life changes (jobs, location, etc.) the higher the risk of coronary heart disease.

ORGANISATIONAL STRESS AND ILLNESS

John R. P. French, Jr., and his colleagues in the Institute for Social Research at the University of Michigan have for several years been involved in a series of research efforts investigating the consequences of various organisational factors on the health and emotional well-being of the members of organisations. Their findings not only corroborate the relationships between stress and illness mentioned above, but also begin to point the way towards comprehensive ways of buffering oneself from the impact of strain-inducing events.

One of their major studies was conducted at the Goddard Space Flight Center of NASA (French & Caplan, 1972). The theory they tested in this study is that occupational stressors, as modified by individual differences, induce psychological and physiological strains which, in turn, induce coronary heart disease. This is represented in Fig. 3.1. Their findings indicate the extent of the impact of modern working life on organisational members. The findings are reviewed here by looking briefly at physiological and psychological strains related to each of the proposed organisational stressors. Each of the strains in their study has been shown in previous studies to be a risk factor in coronary heart disease.

Role ambiguity: lack of clarity in one's work resulted in dissatisfaction, threat, under-utilisation and a sense of futility.

Role conflict: conflicting demands or apparently overlapping responsibilities resulted in dissatisfaction, tension, threat, and increased heart rate.

Fig. 3.1

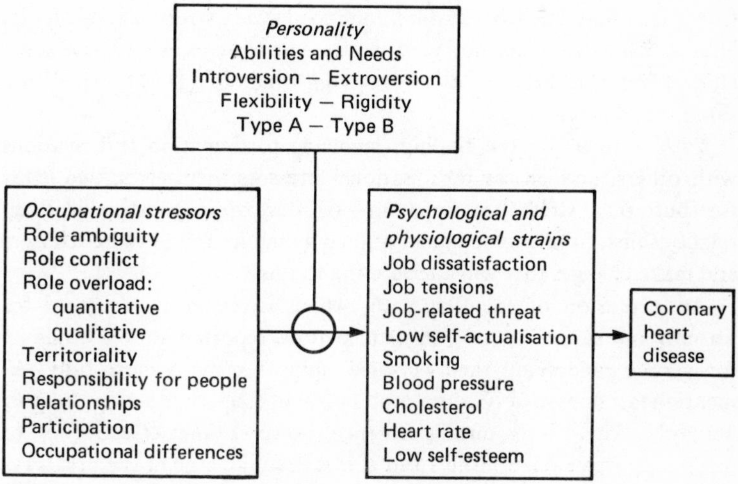

Quantitative and qualitative role overload: when one had too much to do or work that was beyond one's capabilities, the result was dissatisfaction, lowered self-esteem, threat, raised cholesterol levels, and increased smoking and heart rate. Interestingly, subsequent studies have shown the opposite conditions (too little to do and unchallenging work) to have similar outcomes.

Territoriality: when one had to cross organisational boundaries regularly, such as being an administrator in a scientific setting, one experienced quantitative and/or qualitative overload and the attendant strains.

Responsibility for people: more or less responsibility for others than was desired led to increased smoking, blood pressure and cholesterol levels.

Relationships: poor relationships were a prime cause of role ambiguity and role conflict.

Participation: high authentic participation resulted in low psychological strain, positive attitudes towards work and high productivity.

Occupational differences: administrators in the scientific community (NASA) were found to have the highest incidence of quantitative role overload and the most occasions to cross organisational boundaries. They also experienced coronaries at three times the rate of scientists in the same research centre.

Alleviating the impact of stress

One might now ask what can be done to alleviate stress or to buffer its effects. While there are not yet any clear-cut answers, we do have some clues from the French, *et al.* research findings (1972), which are summarised here.

With a focus on the findings involving participation and relations with others, and on the organisational stressors themselves, two paths for buffering stress are apparent: (i) develop supportive working relationships; (ii) examine organisational dynamics found to be stressors and make changes that will alleviate the strains.

An extension of the first path, which is related to the need for warmth and support during stressful periods reported above, would be for people to develop their personal support systems more fully. As mentioned, our society does not encourage us to develop support networks. There is mounting evidence, however, that effective use of one's supportive relationships can alleviate strain. One of the best ways to get through a stressful period is to talk it out. In depth. With feeling. Yet how many people do this with a friend. a clergyman, or a doctor? Most people have very few friends they feel close enough to, to turn to for counselling. Often one's few close friends are so much like one that they cannot offer a different perspective in any event. We all need others to help us focus; help us test reality; help us find intimacy, self-worth and perspective; help us take responsibility for ourselves.

The second path is organisational change. The norms or ways of doing things in organisations induce a lot of strain in people. As was described above, unclear responsibilities or mixed messages from one's superior can set off one's stress response. So, too, can too much work or too little work. Even having to work with people trained in a different area can be strain-inducing! People in organisations can examine their ways of working and make changes to reduce ambiguities, to balance work loads and to develop good working relations. For some time, organisational psychologists have pointed out that such changes can improve productivity and satisfaction. Now doctors and psychiatrists are beginning to say these changes may help us live longer or in better health.

A third pathway should be mentioned in closing, that of taking care of one's self. As was pointed out, some of us do not take very good care of ourselves, and all of us have developed characteristics of which we are at best only partly aware. Research indicates that good nutrition, exercise and relaxation habits help alleviate the impact of stress. We can also manage our strain more effectively if we are aware of our preferences, needs and peculiarities. For example, if a person has high needs to work in a cohesive group, he or she will find assembly line work stressful; whereas someone who would just prefer to 'do his thing' and not worry about a group may not find the same assembly line job to be stressful.

This third path of self-awareness and self-management is the central theme of chapter 10, which delves more deeply into aspects of the self and examines the effectiveness of some of the currently popular techniques for helping individuals become more self-aware and self-responsible.

4. Human Coping Processes

Douglas Duckworth

When a person undergoes a transition, a variety of coping tasks are generated for him. These can range from the management of his own affective responses to the novel situation, through to the modification of the situation in the direction of his personal preferences. Understanding the nature of coping processes, therefore, and the way in which they can be made more effective, is an important prerequisite for an adequate theory of transitions. This chapter, and the closely related chapter 13, address these issues.

A useful starting point for understanding coping processes is the recognition that a person requires certain things of himself, and of the various components of his environment. At one extreme, items such as food and water are involved, and at the other, patterns and standards of behaviour. These things are not automatically forthcoming: under normal circumstances a person's requirements are only adequately catered for to the extent that he actively arranges that this is so. The term 'coping' is commonly used to describe the processes that occur as a person tries to satisfy his requirements in the face of obstacles, difficulties and the requirements of other people. Many of the most significant and meaningful experiences in a person's life will be associated with his coping activities: experiences of power and helplessness, of success and failure, of routine and novelty, of joy and sorrow, of stress and tranquillity, and so on. The ways in which he exercises and develops his coping skills will also have implications extending beyond the immediate situations in which he deploys them. His level of physical well-being may even be affected.

For the purposes of this chapter, coping will be regarded as a series of *control* activities where a person is attempting to exert influence in such a manner that his various requirements are catered for. These control processes will be explored a little further, together with some of their ramifications, and then attention will be focused on one particular route by which a person might be helped to manage his control activities more effectively.

CONTROL PROCESSES

From an early age, a child seems to make efforts to control his actions with a view to exerting some influence and control on his environment (White, 1959). Seligman (1975, p. 141) has described the origins of these attempts in this way:

> To his grief each infant learns that mother is not a part of self, but part of the world: the synchrony between motor commands and the sight of mother moving around is much less than a perfect correlation — although it is not zero except in the most impoverished environments. I suggest that those 'objects' become self that exhibit near-perfect correlation between motor command and visual and kinesthetic feedback; while those 'objects' that do not, become the world. Then, of course, begins the lifelong struggle to raise the correlation of the world's changes with motor commands — the struggle for control.

At first, the experience generated by such activity may be an end in itself. Indeed it may always be so to some extent. But an infant's apparently innate tendency to explore and control develops into something that has very functional consequences for him. For if an individual is to survive as a biological system, then unless he remains attached to a life-support system he will have to exert some control on his environment simply because it will not automatically provide him with all the things he needs for survival.

In addition to having physiological requirements, as a person grows up within his various social groups he will acquire a range of beliefs about what behaviours and attributes are desirable or obligatory for himself and others, and what end-states of existence are desirable for himself and others. Rokeach (1973) has termed the first category of beliefs 'instrumental values', and the second category 'terminal values'. A person may consider, for example, that among other things it is desirable to be competent, courageous and logical, and that such states as happiness, inner harmony, self-respect and social recognition are worth striving for. Once more, these required behaviours, attributes and experiences will not automatically arise, but will tend only to exist to the extent that they are created by the person, as he exercises his control skills.

A person's development will usually be characterised by the acquisition and exercise of increasingly sophisticated control skills. For example, when an infant is playing with his toy bricks he is in a situation where the *physical* consequences of his actions are of central importance for achieving his goals. He will seek to control the movements and positions of the bricks by means of movements of his hands and arms. But as he grows older, he will learn that actions can have social meaning. In many of the situations he encounters he will find that it is the *psychological* consequences of his socially meaningful actions that are of central importance for achieving his goals. Exercising control in such settings will call for skills that are of quite a different order of sophistication.

An analytic unit for describing the various levels of control processes involved in human functioning has been developed by Miller, Galanter and Pribram (1960). They call it the TOTE unit. TOTE is an acronym for Test-Operate-Test-Exit. The *Test* or monitoring phase of the control process consists of establishing whether there is congruity or incongruity between a representation of a current state of affairs and a desired state of affairs. If there is congruity, *Exit* takes place and attention or control moves elsewhere. But if there is incongruity then some activity follows, the *Operation*, which is directed at changing the current state of affairs so that it becomes congruent with the desired state of affairs. A vital supporting system here is an internal representation of the controller and his environment that can guide the generation and implementation of an effective plan. Miller *et al.* call this the *Image*. A further *Test* is carried out, and once more, depending upon the outcome, there is either an *Exit* from the loop, or further *Operations* are performed. One of the main concerns of Miller *et al.* was to illustrate the usefulness of the TOTE unit for explaining how a person manages to integrate all the hierarchical complexities of a behavioural plan into a smooth sequence of actions. For the purposes of this chapter, however, the major usefulness of the unit lies in the fact that it provides an outline description of the processes that occur as a person seeks to exercise control in specific situations. This property will be examined more fully in connection with training strategies (pp. 59–61).

When considering human control processes, one further complexity must be taken into account: the fact that a person has the capacity to monitor and intervene in his first-order control activities. Harré and Secord (1972) have presented an extensive philosophical analysis of the nature of a person, partly based upon the work of Strawson (1959) and Hampshire (1965). They conclude that this capacity represents a major difference between men and other organisms, and suggest that it underlies the most characteristic form of human behaviour: the conscious following of rules, and the intentional carrying out of plans. Coupled with language powers, it permits a person to talk about his actions in anticipation, while they are going on, and in retrospect.

DEFICITS IN CONTROL SKILLS

Most social groups seem to operate criteria for evaluating a person's control activities both in specific instances, and at a more general level. Fairly common criteria are such things as whether a person exhibits appropriate types and intensities of emotional arousal, whether he can establish and maintain social relationships, and whether he can earn his living by approved methods. Through applying the criteria judgements are made about how well a person is coping or managing. It is interesting to note that although people are expected to cope satisfactorily in the various sectors of their lives, in the extensive formal education that they receive many kinds of control activities receive little or no attention. For example, people may be taught the specific technical skills for their jobs, but not taught how to exercise social control in their work places, or how to moderate the attempts of others to control them. Most people are taught that death terminates a life, but not taught how to manage the potentially complex process of responding to the death of a close friend. When a person discovers that his subject of research or study has lost its meaning and fascination, or that he cannot relax and enjoy his holiday as much as he would like, then even if it occurs to him to try and formulate corrective strategies, generally he will have little but folklore to draw from.

When a person does not have the knowledge or skill to exercise control in some specific situation, or series of situations, there can be various kinds of outcome for him, ranging from simple dissatisfaction to severe debilitation. Sometimes a fairly straightforward deficit in a control skill can have serious cumulative consequences for a person's life style. At a later stage this might lead to a therapist or counsellor being faced with a complex person-situation problem to resolve. Some of the disorders discussed by Harré and Secord (1972) are of this kind. They postulate that abnormal forms of social behaviour could appear for two distinct kinds of reasons. The *ethogenic* form of some recognised kind of abnormal behaviour would represent the consequences of a failure by a normally organised person to understand and employ the rules of social life correctly. In contrast, the *pathological* but complementary form of abnormal behaviour would represent the consequences of the malfunctioning of the organism as a neurological system. Thus there could be ethogenic and pathological schizophrenia, paranoia, autism, neurosis, and so on. Intermediate cases are also a possibility; for example, a disturbance that was originally the product of ethogenic failure could eventually lead to malfunctioning of the neurological system.

Seligman (1975), in developing his theory of learned helplessness, has reviewed the experimental evidence relating to the state of affairs where a person perceives that his attempts to control a situation are being ineffective. It appears that the person *learns* that the outcome he desires is independent of his responses. Various kinds of changes are associated with this learning. Firstly, the person tends to stop trying to exercise control. Secondly, he comes to believe that his attempts are ineffective, and he finds difficulty in learning that he could be effective. Finally, if the situation is a traumatic one, the person tends to experience heightened anxiety, followed by depression.

Within the general field of psychosomatic medicine an extensive series of investigations has been going on for a number of years into the possible relationships between life events and illness (e.g., Rahe *et al.*, 1964; Holmes & Masuda, 1970). The life events that have been studied have one common feature: their advent either is indicative of, or requires, a significant change in the ongoing life pattern of a person. Also important is the fact that only some of these life events are negative or stressful in the traditional sense: many of them are socially desirable, for example marriage. In general, the findings have been positive. Among other things they have shown that magnitude of life change is very significantly related to the time of disease onset and to the seriousness of the chronic illness experienced. In the light of these studies, various questions can be raised, such as: To what extent are life changes uncontrollably linked with disease processes? Can a person learn to manage his covert responses so that life changes have a reduced physiological impact? Can a person manage his functioning so that some state of psychosomatic health moderates the impact of life changes? These and other questions suggest fascinating and maybe useful lines of research, and highlight the importance of control processes as a subject for further investigation.

HELPING A PERSON TO MANAGE HIS CONTROL ACTIVITIES

In a society where professional help is available, an adult person will probably seek it on one of two main grounds. He may seek it because he thinks he cannot function or cope adequately in terms of socially accepted indicators of normality. Alternatively, he may seek it because he wishes to enhance some of his control skills in order to operate more effectively and so realise more of his desirable end-states of existence. The helping process in the first case is commonly termed 'therapy', and in the second case 'training'. When a client has a specific control problem, and would experience difficulty both in devising and in implementing any strategy for gaining control, it is probably appropriate for the helper to devise a strategy and guide the client through all the intermediate steps that are intended to culminate in effective control. Thus a person with a particular kind of phobia may be helped systematically to desensitise himself, with the result that he gains control over his fear responses (Wolpe & Lazarus, 1969; Lang, 1969). For control problems where the client could implement a strategy for gaining control, but cannot himself devise an appropriate strategy, then once more the level of help that is appropriate is fairly clear. But what if a person explicitly wants to increase the *general* effectiveness of his control activities: that is, his effectiveness across a variety of situations, including, as in transitions, *novel* situations? I am proposing an approach that has two main parts to it. The first part involves the client learning to monitor the requirements he sets up for himself and the various components of his environment. The second part involves him learning how to alter the basic approach or strategy he uses in control situations, so that his control tends to become more effective in those situations.

The first part of this approach is important because there are occasions when a person can eliminate (or at least moderate) a control problem, and thus pre-empt (or simplify) the usual process of resolution. This is based upon the fact that although a person may find that he has learned an array of specific requirements and therefore is faced with a parallel array of control problems, he has the capacity as a human to become aware of these requirements. He also has the capacity to modify at least some of them should he so choose. When a requirement is changed, the nature of the control problem is changed accordingly. In the simplest case, for example, a person may decide after all *not* to require something, and in so doing he eliminates his control problem. In order to implement this part of the approach in a training programme, a person would have to be taught how, in any control problem he faced, to evaluate the requirement that he had set up.

A significant feature of the second part of the approach is that a person is learning about control processes at a level that transcends any specific control problems, but that nevertheless can be applied to them. In considering how to implement this second part of the approach in a training programme, the model of control developed by Miller *et al.* is useful. Their model is in a sense a description of 'ideal' control: it specifies the processes that must occur if a system is going to be effective in achieving the things it requires. If a person is trained so that his control processes conform more closely to the form prescribed by this model, then the actual effectiveness of his control activities may increase. Some major prescriptions implicit in this model of control are listed below, together with the extra prescription derived from the first part of the approach. Possible training strategies are also outlined.

(1) *The controller must possess an adequate internal representation of himself and his world.* A person can be trained (a) diligently to observe and consider the consequences of his own and others' control activities so that gradually he accumulates more useful internal representations, and (b) to use such information sources as books and human experts.

(2) *An incongruity must be recognised.* In non-obvious cases a person can be trained to perceive the range of cues, from feelings of mild dissatisfaction to definite emotional states, that can be indicative of incongruities.

(3) *Constructive activity must follow the recognition of an incongruity.* A person can be trained so that he tends to respond constructively to an incongruity, as opposed to remaining passive. He can be persuaded that he is capable of exercising control in many situations; he can learn that the exercise of control is rewarding; he can learn to attenuate any emotional reactions that are associated with incongruities, which sometimes lead to avoidance behaviour or disruption of responses; and, he can learn to formulate his required states of affairs so that the responsibility for action rests upon himself and not elsewhere.

(4) *An incongruity must be articulated.* A person can be trained (a) to infer and articulate both the state of affairs that he requires, and the state of affairs that exists (or, that may exist), so that the difference

between them is evident, (b) to articulate this incongruity at several levels of generality so that later he can choose the level that is most useful to work at, (c) to specify those consequences (actual or potential) of the state of affairs that exists (or, that may exist) that give it significance, and (d) to infer the assumptions and reasoning that lie behind his requiring a particular state of affairs.

(5) *The validity and personal utility of a requirement must be evaluated.* A person can be trained (a) to examine the possibility of resolving the incongruity by altering his specific requirement, (b) to check that the pursuit of his requirement is not self-defeating in the sense that it frustrates other important requirements, and (c) to check that the requirement is not a product of what Ellis (e.g. 1973a) has called an irrational belief: the belief that something *should, ought,* or *must* be different from the way it is. As Ellis has shown, such beliefs tend to have self-defeating consequences of various kinds.

(6) *An incongruity must be resolved by an operation that changes the state of affairs that exists (or, that may exist).* A person can be trained to generate a range of possible operations, and then to select and implement an operation that is within his response capabilities and that will resolve an incongruity (D'Zurilla & Goldfried, 1971).

(7) *The success of the operation must be assessed, and if judged unsatisfactory, another operation performed.* A person can be trained (a) to assess the success of his attempts to resolve an incongruity, and (b) to create and implement another operation if that is necessary, utilising the extra information generated by the 'failure'.

An account of a training programme I designed to implement this approach, together with some preliminary results from an analysis of the evaluation data, is given in chapter 13. The experience with the programme showed that it is quite feasible to translate the broad training strategies into a specific programme for a particular sample of participants, and the results from the evaluation indicate that this approach can be a powerful way of intervening in the control activities of clients.

PART TWO

The Experience of Transition

5. The Potential for Personal Growth Arising from Intercultural Experiences[1]

John Adams

It is currently stylish to publish papers making predictions about the future. Often included among the predictions is that the 'size' of the world will continue to 'shrink' via improved communications and transportation, and that nationalism will also become a less important social factor. This shrinkage is due to increased mobility, multinational corporations and television, which can bring any event, anywhere in the world, into our living rooms instantly. Thus, it is becoming increasingly important to understand cultures other than our own.

As life speeds up and becomes more complex, more people will be confronted more frequently with unfamiliar new situations. That is, an increasing proportion of us will have to learn to enter into and emerge from time-bounded situations that are in varying degrees strange and ambiguous. One example of this is the American businessman who is asked by his firm to spend three months helping to set up a new office in Greece. In addition to knowing business principles, he will also have to be able to adapt quickly to the Greek language and way of life if he is to be successful.

One way to look at personality is that it is at least in part a pattern of responses to one's environment (e.g. Fink, 1967; Adams, 1969; Harvey, Hunt & Schroder, 1961; Rosoff, 1970). As one becomes familiar with one's environment and adapts to it, one's personality emerges in the form of reasonably stable patterns of behaviour. In this sense, one learns to become rooted in one's environment. Deprivation experiments demonstrate that the removal of the environmental stimuli brings on hallucinatory and psychotic behaviour quite rapidly.

By any index, the environment in which we live today is changing at an accelerated rate. Consider, for example, some of the things that have been added to our way of life during the past twenty-five years: commercial jet travel, missiles and space flight, nuclear power (for good or evil?), computers, super highways, super institutions, super agriculture, pesticides, environmental pollution and television. One half of U.S. population is 25 or under, and these additions are not 'new' to them, but are readily taken for granted. Taken together, these conjure up associations of speed, movement, change, opportunity, danger. . . . They suggest that the idea of rootedness in the environment is changing; from being rooted in a reasonably stable environment to being multi-rooted in a series of different and more fluid environments (see Bennis & Slater, 1968).

The purpose of this chapter is to describe the reaction processes one goes through from the time one enters a new situation to the time one is able to be a fully functioning and contributing part of that situation. In this chapter we capture some of our own experiences, and those of others, and identify the common threads of these experiences in the form of a learning model that describes the potential for personal growth arising from intercultural experiences. Many writers have described 'culture shock' as an adaptive process, but few, if any, have suggested that intercultural experiences lead potentially to increased adaptive capabilities.

Personal growth, as we use the term here, means the development of increased adaptability and a stronger sense of self. If a person learns to feel that the centre of gravity of his own universe is rooted in his self, he will be better able to be meaningfully involved in a variety of changing situations with a strong base of continuity from which he can extend himself both for learning and for applying his past experiences. Lacking this, in his various involvements in varied situations he may well become like a 'yo-yo' as he moves from place to place and never changes.

Nina Rosoff spent three months as a staff consultant in behavioural science for a large industrial organisation in Denmark. John Adams spent two years in teaching and organisation development consulting in England. Both of us took the time and opportunity to travel extensively in Europe. Our method of developing a learning model was quite simple. We each kept detailed personal journals of our day-to-day work activities, feelings and experiences. We brought these together, along with the ideas suggested by several others who had had similar intercultural experiences, and looked for common themes. Out of this, and out of the theoretical thinking we have each done, we tried to capture the essence of our separate experiences in a learning model.

This is not a research paper, but we hope that it will lead to specific ideas for research and to training schemes that will facilitate personal learning from intercultural experiences.

SHARED EXPERIENCES

We should point out that though the lengths of our respective sojourns were quite different (three months and two years), our separate experiences in adjusting contained many parallels. This leads us to believe that the experience of time in a relatively strange time-bounded situation is quite elastic. The longer stay resulted in somewhat longer phases that were also of greater 'intensity'. Both of us, however, completed much the same cycle of reactions to our adopted cultures. There is certainly a variety of personality factors that also affect the length and intensity of reaction phases, which we shall not attempt to discuss here.

While each of us intended to enter our new cultures with ebullience and the attitude that we would be able to get along very well, we were quickly frustrated as those expectations turned out to be based in a false security and on stereotypes. At the very first, we found ourselves to be tired much of the time, and either we didn't *want* to go out or do much to get acquainted with our new environments, or we felt more secure staying *at home.*

> At first, I just felt like staying home in the evenings after work. (N.R.)

This seemed to be more due to *anxiety* in the face of dealing with all the new stimuli, than from an actual confrontation with the new culture.

> I was afraid of all the newness and just wanted to come home and stay. (J.A.)

We felt very alone during the early weeks and spent an inordinate amount of time writing letters to friends 'at home'.

> I'd buy food, eat, work, and write many letters to the people in the States that I care about and miss a great deal. (N.R.)

At the same time, we were quick to grasp at the invitations of new friends, and we soon found ourselves to be getting out quite a lot. There was a curious mixture of wanting to meet new people and of being quite content to sit at home or alone in the office if others didn't initiate the interaction.

What one might call *survival and maintenance* were of primary importance. Getting to the store, finding out where the public transportation was and how to use it, getting food by speaking a new language or dialect, and using unfamiliar money, all turned out to be 'major projects' the first few times.

> Today was a frustrating day when everything seemed to go wrong or long. Went to Bursar's office and found I needed to go downtown to get a national insurance card so I went to the bus stop and then returned because I didn't have passport and work permit (didn't need them) — went back to my office and Ted Stephens popped in to inform me of two additional courses I need to teach. (J.A.)

> Came home around 1.30 and picked up my passport and work permit and drove downtown — only to get lost and soaking wet looking for the Social Security office. Returned home about 3.00 and at 4.00 went to meet Maria. Downtown again to register with Police. Hurry, Hurry and find out stores don't stay open on Thursday night after all. So—o, got part of uniform and came home. We all got thoroughly drenched and mad at each other. Ycchh! (J.A.)

During these initial weeks, activities like these often took a long time to accomplish because of our reluctance to ask for help or because when we did ask, we could not understand the reply. We felt that we wanted to prove to ourselves that we could manage on our self-reliance, and that, as foreigners, we did not want to appear to be ignorant or helpless.

> I often find myself lumbering through stores, curious about what I see, and rarely asking anyone for help. And when I do have the courage to ask, I find it's difficult to understand what's been said to me, and so I clam up again. (N.R.)

We were not able to plan ahead effectively because our thinking was forced onto the 'here and now' issues. How can one plan ahead when it takes a whole day just to go to the police station to register as an alien? As a result, our *orientation to time* during the early weeks was such that time passed, or seemed to pass, very slowly. We each learned that the experience of the passage of time is a very elastic phenomenon, in that after a few months time seemed to be passing by incredibly rapidly. A day at the end of the first week is about 15 per cent of the time in the new setting (and this probably largely spent dealing with the details of getting settled), whereas a day after three months represents only a bit more than one per cent of the time spent in the situation.

A major portion of our attention was focused on the *obvious and gross differences* that confronted us, like language (or dialect), money, and transportation. We became, for a time, preoccupied with the details of understanding these with the mistaken idea that once we understood we would have accomplished the major part of our assimilation.

As these major differences faded as sources of trouble, providing for home and family and becoming *relevant and productive* on the job became more important; but here we were unclear about what was expected of us. Again, we were reluctant to ask; but we assumed that the work system, at least, would operate pretty much as it had in the States. Being somewhat anxious about all of this caused us to keep to ourselves most of the time and to be concerned with the *quantity of work* we were doing. We thought we were working hard during these early weeks and months and it was only later, in retrospect, that it became clear to us that we weren't really getting anywhere and that a vague sense of insecurity remained.

It has taken me about six weeks to realize I've been inundated with busy work that is essentially irrelevant to why I came to the organization. (N.R.)

When we did mingle with co-workers, we found ourselves professing such *ideologies* as collaborative efforts and better team work for the staffs we had joined. We have been trained in these and found these qualities to be strangely lacking. We became more certain later that these efforts had most likely been an outgrowth of our needs to feel included, rather than having necessarily been the most appropriate suggestions for the organisational settings in which we found ourselves.

Nevertheless, we quickly found ways to be 'busy' and we were each soon overloaded with commitments that were later to become burdens. This preoccupation with being involved, active and mobile (we began travelling a lot very early) provided us with the illusion that the work we were engaged in was both relevant and important. But after a short time, we began to see more honestly that we were doing mediocre jobs on a series of 'one night stands' that were far from pushing our abilities.

It really brought home to me the fact that everything I've done to date has been hand to mouth and one-shot stuff. I really need some continuity to stimulate me. (N.R.)

As consultants and teachers, we were not doing a good job, we were getting *depressed*, and we were not having the impact we thought we were having. We were working busily on a lot of minor, but familiar, activities.

> I don't need to do all of this worrying! I need to start to develop a more productive attitude. I think half of my depressive feelings have to do with my lack of professional productivity. (J.A.)

This eventually led to a great deal of self-questioning about how we could learn to fit in and make our contribution; and how to handle continued frustration and depression. We soon became homesick and we wanted to be with close friends and familiar ways of living. The *subtle cultural differences* now began to emerge into our awareness; the mannerisms, characteristics of relationships, life styles and so on.

Though we experienced this in different ways, the *pain of being different* was felt acutely, along with the *pain of not knowing* if one could, should, or would ever be able to adapt. We again began to look for the familiar and to pull inward.

> I went for a walk downtown with Jim and really felt like withdrawing after a while. He is really wrapped up in anti-American scapegoating things and his comments really made me want to get the hell out of things — to go home, or something. Anyway, I realized that I'll never be fully a part of things here. (J.A.)

At this point, we were also easily irritated and easily became cynical about the ways of our new neighbours.

> As all of this has been happening, I've begun to notice more things I don't like here. I feel I've been slow to notice some of it, but the main thing is the depersonalized nature of things ('one' needs —, etc.) and the tremendous prejudices . . . (J.A.)

A high point for each of us were the visits of American colleagues and friends, when we could discover that we were still deeply valued and loved. These encounters were not all pleasant, but they were awakening, for we discovered quickly that we were not thinking, acting or influencing to the degree to which we had before we left the States. We had allowed ourselves to become *narrow, uncreative and intellectually lazy*. Each of these visits, however, seemed to provide stimulus for us to move ahead, and to do so in more effective and more satisfying ways. We began to feel like 'ourselves' again.

As I began to contribute in an intellectually creative and productive way to my colleagues, they began to respond. I felt less threatened by the newnesses and differences. Being capable of managing the differences made me feel like myself. (N.R.)

Another factor that helped us was our continued *positive moving* towards the environment and the people. It was important to us to be able to speak their language and to understand their mannerisms. We were the foreigners, not them; we were the minority, not them; we had the 'accents', not them. A new experience for most Americans! We wanted to become more like them and less foreign.

Gradually, we each came to feel we were deceiving ourselves as well as the people we were trying to relate to. We experienced a growing sense of inauthenticity in our attempts to become 'natives'.

As for the cultural 'differences', I'm still learning a lot about the English way of life and beginning to be concerned about my style — of speaking, of being, of working — I've been using bloke, bloody, bob, quid, etc., a lot and also pronouncing more and more words in 'English'. These have been conscious attempts to gain acceptability. (J.A.)

As a result, we did not continue to use our newly acquired local slang vocabularies or pronunciations for very long and became more satisfied with our American accents, vocabulary and mannerisms while continuing to meet people both socially and at work. As Arning (1965) points out:

.... When an executive goes native, as men sometimes do when assigned to one region for an extended period of time, he may become less alert to the possibilities of applying logically his knowledge ....

We began to feel much more satisfied with our lives abroad, as we increasingly felt accepted for ourselves and our behaviour. At this point, we felt we were being *realistic* for the first time about how much we were able to accept the systems we were working in and about how much they were accepting us. It was during this 'midway period' also that we began to gain a better understanding of what we had experienced initially.

I feel like I'm right at the edge of a 'golden era' in our stay here and I can't seem to get into it. (N.R.)

We had both been struck by the number of times we had found ourselves daydreaming and recalling incidents we had 'forgotten' that occurred in our childhood and adolescence.

> George and I talked a lot about culture shock and consulting. One thing both of us have found is that we're doing more looking back into our childhood days and remembering things more clearly more often. Perhaps it is part of the developmental nature of possibilities attached to culture shock. (N.R.)

More of these memories were of old events that had to do with acceptance, rejection and self-confidence. We were *growing up again* and reliving these events in our new cultures. It is known that these kinds of recollections commonly happen when anxiety unconsciously reaches proportions that are not manageable by means of one's normal coping repertoire. In severe neurotic cases, this kind of 'regression' signals the impending failure of the repressive mechanism (see, for example, Aldrich, 1966). This is not to say that we were about to 'blow up', though that might be a possibility in some cases. These memories did, however, provide us with new perspectives on just how anxious we had been without really having known it.

We now feel confident that those people who do not learn much from their intercultural experience, those who return home bitter or depressed or disenchanted, are usually those who do not continue, or perhaps never start, the process of what we call *positive moving*. Those people who withdraw from the new culture and avoid meeting it directly are not likely to learn much from their experience; it is more likely that their growth process will stagnate or even regress until they can finally return 'home'. Meanwhile, their experience of the new culture becomes increasingly insular and biased by fantasy, anxiety and self-fulfilling ideas about failure.

It is natural to expect the people in any country to be curious about life in another country and, with growing familiarity, to become more candid with their stereotypes and feelings. As our new friends aired their views of American behavioural science, American men, American women, American education, American money, and America in general, it was not surprising that we adapted to their culture by using their language and by dressing in their clothes in order not to be too different. It is also not surprising that we had recollections of earlier, usually adolescent, incidents involving self-acceptance and self-confidence.

> The feeling I have of trying to adapt to this place has a purity about it. I relate this to feeling like I did as a kid when I was trying to prove myself by being best at everything I did . . . a kind of testing my own power, strength, intelligence, etc. (N.R.)

In essence, because of the variety of new stimuli, our 'survival' was to some degree threatened. We each chose to cope, and saw other foreigners coping, by doing whatever seemed necessary to be seen as a part of our new friends and their way of life.

The fact that we perceived the focus of many of these new stimuli to be upon our roles is important. In America, roles are often taken as identities. Being questioned about our Americanness, maleness, femaleness, professionalism, and so on, on some level forced each of us to become defensive of ourselves and of the roles we 'are'. Having to define who we were, what we were, and why, allowed us to gain *greater clarity about ourselves*. Our colleagues who have been through similar experiences think, as we do, that talking out who we were and what we were doing allowed us to become more aware of the degree to which we had learned to characterise people, places and things.

We were able gradually to develop *longer term involvements* in activities that were useful to our clients and satisfying to us. We began to see meaningful paths available to us and we became more selective about what we would become involved in.

> Saying no to Morgens was difficult because I knew he needed help. But involvement on one-shot projects now feels like a real drain on me. I feel unrooted if my energy is not going into work which will be maintained and become stabilized after I leave here. (N.R.)

As our satisfaction with life in our new homes continued its upswing, we noted that we were more like we had been before our arrival — back to being ourselves and doing things in comfortable ways. It seemed that the more able we were to *reassert ourselves* (to ourselves) and the less we worked at 'going native' for the sake of acceptance, the better off we were. There still existed, about two-thirds of the way through our visits, a fear of relaxing and letting go, a lingering fear of rejection.

> I think generally that I'm depressed about all of this because I'm not really comfortable here yet. I feel like I'm not a stranger anymore, but I'm also not yet an accepted part of the system. It's a lonely and powerless feeling. (J.A.)

We continued to become more satisfied with ourselves and our new lives, becoming more confident of ourselves in our new settings and developing more optimistic biases towards events and toward ourselves. *Success experiences* in the new cultures were valuable keystones to each of us. These seemed to provide the impetus which continued to push us along and which shifted our attitudes from having a strange, new world *imposed* upon us, toward a sense of the *opportunity*, adventure, risk and challenge of our new worlds.

> It is a strange feeling to realize that the different foods, dress, sounds, sights and people, which once were so foreign, have become a part of my everyday life. I feel excited, alive, and challenged. I'm so glad I came here. (J.A.)

We became aware that we were in cultures where we could try out new behaviours and attitudes. This is what we had each intended originally, but we only discovered it in reality during the latter portions of our stays.

> My hope is that by trying to write and speak the language more, and by new behaviors, I will gain more self-confidence. After all, I'm in a place where I have no historical past or relationships with which to contend. All I have is now. The mere idea is both frightening and freeing. (N.R.)

In essence, we used an increasing amount of time to define ourselves to ourselves; to recreate, to establish new parts, to drop old patterns that we no longer wanted to maintain. We each began to feel that we were developing as persons and in our perspectives on people and life. It was very much like shedding old lives, contexts and perspectives, and putting on *new lives, contexts and perspectives*. With this different view, we began to feel more certain about ourselves, and more powerful and influential in guiding our own lives.

We were reminded of the fable in which the wind and the sun argued which was the more powerful. During the course of their debate, a man passed along wearing a cape. The wind offered to demonstrate his power by blowing the man's cape away, but the harder he tried, the more tightly the man clutched at his cape. Then came the sun's turn, and he peacefully smiled on the man, who soon took off his cape better to enjoy the sunshine.

Leaving our 'new' homes, friends and countries proved to be at least as difficult as arriving.

The trip to the States will happen last among these, but it's the most salient in my mind right now. I need to get myself prepared for this trip as I never have done before. I need to really put in a good performance at the conference and I need to be very much in charge of myself when I go home. (J.A.)

The sense of freedom and expansiveness that we had acquired abroad lost its intensity.

I didn't realize how much I would hate leaving. I feel like a part of me is being torn away. I wonder how permanent my own development will be when I leave here? I wonder if who I am is just a reflection of my environment? Have I really changed? Once again, only TIME will tell. (N.R.)

It felt very much like coming home from a vacation to return to work. Many questions arose in our minds and it was difficult to decide to return at all. We were aware of the time and how little of it we had left.

The thing that is really hitting me yesterday and today is the dilation of time. It is almost as if it has in reality slowed down. Perhaps this is due to the fact that I have left psychologically and am waiting impatiently to leave physically. I don't have the answer, but it is certainly quite a powerful and central experience. (J.A.)

Perhaps the biggest issue in transitory living is that it becomes difficult to do any immediate here and now living. Things in the present situation are let slide while things in the future situation are postponed. It's a weird sort of limbo of deferred living. (N.R.)

While problems of transportation, geography, money and language did not cause us many problems upon returning, other issues and questions began to ruffle our feelings. These were things like: If I am different now, how will I be seen? Who will my friends be? Will I be as successful? Will I find an equally stimulating job and equally fulfilling avenues for continued growth? How will it feel to be without my new friends here?

I spend a lot of time thinking about renewing old relationships in the States, and about the new ones I'll have to form. I am guessing that I won't be so close to old friends there and I do want to do a great deal of early relationship-building with new people. (J.A.)

As Americans returning to America, we were not treated as unique as we had been when we first went abroad. Though we described this earlier as having been a rather uncomfortable experience, it had provided us with entrees and opportunities. We wondered if we would still be 'part of *our* crowd'. We had each spent a considerable portion of our time abroad building relationships and establishing 'places' for ourselves. We wondered how difficult re-establishing these would be.

We also had many questions concerning the permanency of any changes we had undergone and the likely longevity of any resolutions we had made about being different when we returned. How many of the changes we thought we had undergone would turn out to be delusions? (see Pagés, 1971). Would we be able to maintain the changes in the absence of the friends and cultural surroundings from which they emerged?

As it turned out, we found our separation to be quite difficult. We were now embarked upon another intercultural experience which, in new and old ways, in exciting and depressing ways, in real and unreal ways, offered new opportunities. When we left America, we had taken her for granted and gone to another culture to learn for ourselves. Again, we would be doing the same thing.

I know things will be very different and much faster-paced than here — and I am reluctant to start investing energy there in thinking these differences out. (J.A.)

DOES THIS MAKE SENSE?

As we reviewed the preceding section, a pattern emerged which we can discuss. This pattern, as presented in Fig. 5.1 below, is descriptive of the natural processes of adaptation and growth that we each experienced. These experiences are arranged in a framework that outlines more or less chronologically: (1) primary feelings and reactions; (2) overriding concerns; (3) ways we adapted to these feelings and concerns; (4) the outcomes of these efforts; and (5) those attitudes, activities, and so on, that provided energy throughout our sojourns. These are each divided into four phases of 'development', A–D, which are discussed below.[2] One should realise that there is certain to be overlapping among these phases, which are separated here for the purposes of discussion.

Fig. 5.1

PASSING OF TIME

	1. Feelings and Reactions	2. Primary Concerns	3. Coping Activities	4. Immediate Outcomes	5. Continuing Energy Sources
A	Anxiety – what will it be like? Slow passage of time Frustration Imposition of culture	Survival Maintenance Self-Reliance Obvious cultural differences Being productive	Getting settled Stay at home – but go out whenever asked Maintain links with old friends Keep very busy with trivia	Confusion Fatigue	1. Risk taking 2. Openness to new ideas 3. Desire to learn about self; about new culture
B	Depression Pain of being different Regression Stagnation – narrow, uncreative, intellectually lazy	Subtle cultural differences Need to feel acceptable, included	High quantity of work Hit and miss activity Professional ideology Going native Increasingly cynical of local way of life	Over committed Lack of influence Inauthenticity	4. Positive moving toward the culture 5. Supportive relationships
C	Opportunity value of culture Rapid passage of time Excitement	Need to understand, influence, grow, contribute Quality of Work	Colleague relationships Self-reassertion Self-testing Choice & continuity of involvements	Growing up again Realistic perspectives Increasing influence, satisfaction, self-clarity	6. Patience 7. Success experiences
D	Sadness at leaving Happiness at going 'home' Anxiety – what will it be like? Slow passage of time	Where is my home? Do I have a new identity? Will I be accepted now that I am different?	Resolutions about what I will be like when I get home Withdrawal of energy	New lives, contexts, perspectives, confidence	

A. Getting settled can be an unsettling experience

Initially we had a mixture of expectations, which might be stated as follows. We initially held stereotypes, impressions, and so on, about our new cultures that led us to believe they would be different from what we were used to. At the same time, we did not expect that *we* would have to change. As we found this latter expectation to be wrong, we became anxious and frustrated (1). We felt a strange way of life had been 'imposed' upon us. The focus of our concern and attention (2) was on the survival of our 'selves' as we knew our 'selves', upon proving that we were self-reliant, upon overcoming the obvious differences (and thus 'accomplishing' assimilation) and upon becoming quickly productive and useful.

While we were getting settled (3) we were also keeping in touch with the familiar environment of our friends at home. At the same time, we were eager to meet new people when they came to us. Wherever possible, we found that we tended to gravitate, at this point, towards others who were in similar states of cultural uncertainty.

We generally felt busy doing things that we soon found to be trivial activities (filing papers, getting parking permits, and so on). The result (4) of this early activity and of the mixed expectations about the new culture and about ourselves in the new culture, led not too surprisingly to our being very tired and generally confused much of the time.

B. Will I ever really be a part of all this?

With growing frustration over not being 'assimilated' as rapidly as we expected, we became depressed (1). We continued to feel that we would be able to adapt without going through any changes in our own attitudes, but we also felt increasing pains at being different. We found we were thinking in narrow, uncreative, lazy, stagnant ways. It was at this point that we became aware of emergent recollections of childhood rejection incidents. The concern (2) that became central to us was with overcoming the subtle differences between the two cultures we were straddling (e.g. mannerisms, values, and so on). We tried to be acceptable and included.

We tried to accomplish this through a variety of superficial activities (still resisting self-change) (3), and we became involved, in a hit or miss fashion, in a variety of short-term activities. We relied on our professional backgrounds to guide us into areas of acceptability and inclusion. We tried to look, act and talk like the locals. As this failed to lead to satisfaction, we found ourselves reversing this and becoming cynical about the new culture.

The outcomes (4) were that we found ourselves over-committed in activities we did not want. We found that we were not influencing our situations, and we felt unreal and inauthentic.[3]

C. *This is more like it!*

As these feelings of lack of influence (we have been trained as professional 'influencers') and of inauthenticity (authenticity is a value we hold very dear) reached uncomfortable levels, we realised we were at a choice point: either to turn inward and probably continue to cycle between phases A and B, or to open ourselves to the culture and learn from it. With this realisation we began to see 'opportunity value' inherent in the differentness of the new culture (1), we became more excited and the passage of time seemed to hasten.

Our primary concerns (2) were no longer with being accepted — we found we were more acceptable when we did not try so hard — but with our needs to understand, influence, grow and contribute. Our activities (3) became more meaningful to us (and to our clients) as we exercised more choice over our involvements. We began to reassert and test ourselves for learning purposes rather than to 'prove a point'. We began to work collaboratively with our colleagues, and we became interested in the quality of our work rather than the quantity.

The outcomes (4) of this seemed to be that we were growing up again. We were developing realistic and broadened perspectives. We now felt more satisfied and influential. We were clearer about who we were and what we could expect to achieve. Hall and Whyte (1963) also indicate that such trips abroad generally cause the person to become more aware of his modes of behaviour which were previously unconscious to him in the native culture he grew up in and learned to take for granted.

D. *Go home? But I am home! Or am I?*

As the time for returning to America approached, time seemed to slow down again and we were faced with mixed feelings (1). On the one hand, we were now going to return home and see our friends and involve ourselves in activities there. And this made us very happy. On the other hand, we had learned how to be both useful and happy in a new culture. Leaving this was painful, for we now had close friends and important involvements in both places.

Our major concerns (2) during the last few days, aside from packing and flying issues, were wrestling with the issue of where home really is for each of us. We finally reached the conclusion that home is wherever we are, and that the move now facing us was not likely to be our last. For the first time, we experienced ourselves as being at the centre of our own universes. We began making resolutions (3) about how and what we were going to be when we got back to the States.

We did not know that we were about to go through phases A—D all over again (though in different ways). The final outcomes (4) of our stay were mostly that we had developed new lives, new contexts, new perspectives and new self-confidence.[4] Along with this came the feeling that life-long friends are becoming a thing of the past and that we still have a lot to learn about the formation and break-up of reasonably intense short-term relationships.

These are things that always seemed to help

Throughout our visits we found sources of energy and courage. These are important in that they were present throughout the phases we have described. We feel these factors provide much of the potential for realising personal growth opportunities and therefore for the design of training programmes for intercultural learning.

(1) *Risk taking.* Regardless of how our experiences looked to us in retrospect, we each found that we were continually putting ourselves at risk personally, interpersonally and professionally as a means to learning and growth. This does not mean we were trying to make fools of ourselves (though this sometimes happened), but that we were searching for new ways to stretch and challenge ourselves.

(2) *Openness to new ideas.* We worked hard at this and found rewards from viewing ourselves as learners. We know many unhappy people who have decided they have nothing new to learn about the way they live. There is at least a correlation here, if not a direct cause and effect relationship. Lundstedt (1963) states that adjustment in overseas sojourns is enhanced by universalistic tendencies, rational attitudes, openness and flexibility.

(3) *Desire to learn.* This is related to openness. We left the U.S.A. with the intention of using our experience in new cultures as a means of learning about ourselves and others. Many Americans, when abroad, seem more interested in 'teaching' than in 'learning'.

(4) *Positive moving toward the culture.* We sometimes felt like re-establishing a familiar cultural island on which to live, but we always learned something useful about ourselves and our new friends when we resisted this temptation and continued to immerse ourselves in the newness of the culture. Both Morris (1960) and Sewell and Davidson (1961) found that the *amount* and *depth* of social interaction engaged in by individuals in their new cultures were positive influences on their adjustment.

(5) *Supportive relationships.* We each found that the most meaningful parts of our experience were the relationships we formed, and that people *would* encourage us to experiment. It was not necessary to worry about failure or success so much as learning from the outcome of our experiments, because these people were able to communicate that we were acceptable to them as people. One insight here is that people willing to form this kind of relationship are not so rare as one might think, once one is content to be oneself, rather than trying to be 'just like' the natives. M. B. Smith (1955) supported this conclusion in his finding that maintaining self-esteem, gaining acceptance and *making friends* were among key variables influencing the ease or difficulty of adjustment of foreign students studying in the United States.

(6) *Patience.* Without a continual effort at quietly creating an inner sense of calm from which patience is drawn, fear and the reality of a hurried pace of newness can easily create physical illness and emotional despair in living in different cultures. Though it was sometimes difficult, we generally felt better when we forced ourselves to assimilate new concepts and differences one step at a time, rather than expecting to be able to grasp the 'whole picture' immediately.

(7) *Success experiences.* Perhaps the greatest source of energy came from being successful at something in the new culture. Such experiences ranged from learning that in England one passes one's cigarettes around when having one oneself and in Denmark one cannot drink without 'skoaling' everyone, to the design and execution of successful consulting interventions. Though one needs to create these for oneself, they are likely to occur more frequently when the preceding six variables are in good working order.

INDICATIONS

What has been described here indicates there is a push toward personal growth arising from intercultural experiences. Many colleges and universities have known this, intuitively at least, for some time and have responded with 'junior year abroad' programmes. What we have found is that the fact of studying or working or even sightseeing abroad does not in itself lead to personal growth. Rather, there are indications from our experiences that this process is stimulated by being immersed in the 'differentness' of the place and by struggling with the task of finding one's way, by making the unfamiliar familiar, by risking to lead a choiceful rather than a choiceless life. When this is approached as an active learning task, rather than as a natural by-product, the rewards are at least commensurate with the effort.

The experiences described herein as a result of such efforts, suggest that frustration and depression result from trying to join the new culture by means of rote adoption of the culture, or by trying to prove one's worth to the culture. When these attempts fail, at least three choices become obvious: complete withdrawal (go home), isolation, or authentic involvement. If one chooses the latter, and if at the same time one sheds the idea that the differentness of the culture is imposed upon one, and replaces this with the view that the differentness means opportunity for growth, then the frustration and depression can quickly turn to excitement and satisfaction. We see this shift from 'imposition' to 'opportunity' as being key to the learning process.

NOTES

1. The original version of this chapter was a working paper written by John Adams and Nina Rosoff.
2. Other writers have identified similar stages to those advanced here. Oberg (1960) identified stages of: 1. Incubation, 2. Crisis, 3. Recovery, 4. Acceptance, and 5. Return. Smalley (1963) identified stages of: 1. Fascination, 2. Hostility, 3. Adjustment, and 4. Biculturism. Neither, however, discusses in any detail the personal growth opportunities inherent in their 'adapted' stages of Acceptance (Oberg) and Adjustment (Smalley).
3. At this point, we were each acutely aware that the American culture was changing rapidly and that we really were not yet a part of our new cultures.

Feelings of being 'homeless' or culturally rootless were nearly immobilising at times. In retrospect, one concern we have is that we see a growing number of people shuffling back and forth among cultures without ever getting beyond this phase of intercultural reactions. Though these people seem to be joining an 'international elite', they also often appear to be losing their cultural links — a 'dangerous' process for those whose job it is to represent one culture to another.

4. Where most writers have described the cross-cultural adjustment of 'slump and recovery' as a U curve, Gullahorn and Gullahorn (1963) have more correctly described the process as a W curve wherein the individual faces at least as severe an adjustment test when he returns to his native culture.

6. Career Transitions as a Source of Identity Strain

John Hayes and Patricia Hough

This chapter presents a descriptive model of an individual's relationship with organisations and explores career transitions in terms of how boundaries are encountered. In an attempt to move away from the narrow view of the organisational career as a hierarchical progression, Schein (1971) has described the dynamics of the career in terms of a sequence of boundary passages in which the individual moves up (across hierarchical boundaries), around (across functional boundaries), or more centrally into the organisation (across inclusion boundaries). We define a boundary as that which lies between two conditions that are seen to be different by the organisation, the individual, or both. In our view the organisational career is a dynamic relationship between the individual and an organisation (or organisations), and while an important event in such a relationship may be the crossing of an organisational boundary, an equally important event, both for the individual and the organisation, may be the individual's decision not to cross a boundary, or the organisation's decision not to permit an individual to cross a given boundary.

Using this concept of boundary we intend to explore certain aspects of the relationship between the individual and the organisation. In particular we shall consider the individual's and the organisation's orientations to boundary crossing, the consequences, both short and long term, of crossing or not crossing boundaries both for the individual and the organisation, and the ways in which they cope with these consequences. In this context boundaries are only important when they are perceived to exist by at least one of the parties to the relationship.

There are, within most organisations, generally accepted views about the 'normal sequence' of career movements, in which individuals pursue certain routes at certain rates through the organisation. These views give rise to expectations about the 'normal' transitions an individual should experience. As Becker and Strauss (1956) point out, they usually relate to age; in other words there is a temporal pattern associated with a spatial pattern. Thus a person entering an organisation at position A may expect to cross certain boundaries and be in position B by time t. This gives rise to what Roth (1963) describes as career timetabling; the development of expectations about transitions. Roth argues that these norms for movement arise from the precedent of what has happened to others in the past, and a kind of bargaining between the individual and the organisation for what is appropriate to him in the present and the future. In this way the individual and the organisation attempt to impose some structure on an uncertain situation (the future). However, career paths frequently deviate from the 'normal' in a variety of ways. The individual may not expect to move while the organisation does not share this expectation or vice versa. How and why does the individual come to define himself as ready to separate himself from his current status and cross a boundary to an alternative status? What happens when the organisation is unwilling or unable to support and facilitate this boundary passage? What happens when the organisation attempts to separate an individual from a status he is reluctant to lose? This chapter attempts to explore these and related issues.

The dynamics of boundary crossing can be examined within the context of the model presented in Fig. 6.1. Phase I of this model is concerned with the general orientation to boundary crossing that both the individual and the organisation bring to any boundary situation. Within this we shall explore some of the factors that contribute to the development of these orientations.

Phase II of the model is concerned with what happens when an individual is confronted with a particular organisational boundary. He may desire transition and satisfy his desire by moving across the boundary. On the other hand his desire may be frustrated and he may fail to cross the boundary. Similarly he may prefer no transition and actually experience either transition or no transition. Thus an individual's attitudes and feelings with regard to transition and the actual transition he experiences are congruent in A and D and incongruent in B and C.

Phase III of the model explores the possible consequences of this process. Crossing or not crossing an organisational boundary at a particular point in time could lead to changes in the way a person is viewed by others, to changes in the way he sees himself and to changes in his behaviour. Thus, for example, in situations B and C the individual

Fig. 6.1: Model of career transitions

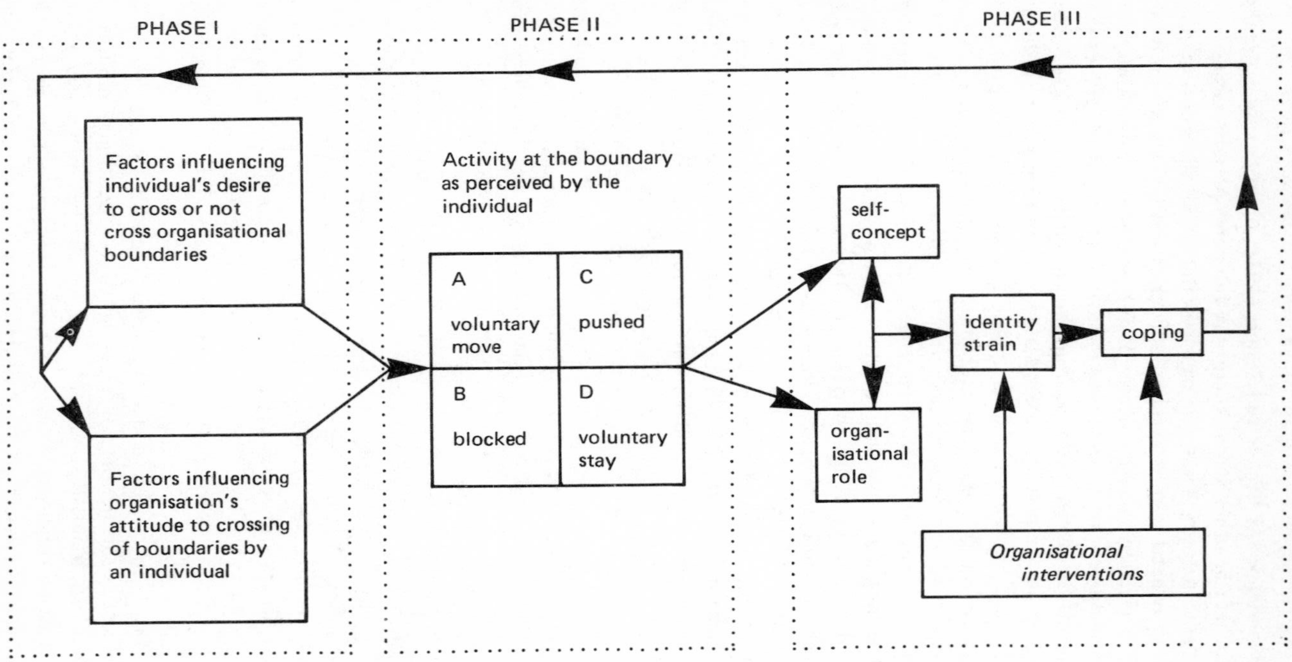

PHASE I

Factors influencing individual's desire to cross or not cross organisational boundaries

Factors influencing organisation's attitude to crossing of boundaries by an individual

PHASE II

Activity at the boundary as perceived by the individual

| A voluntary move | C pushed |
| B blocked | D voluntary stay |

PHASE III

self-concept

organisational role

identity strain

coping

Organisational interventions

is either prevented from moving (blocked) or forced to move (pushed) by forces outside his control. Individuals who experience such frustrations may react in a number of ways. In their attempt to tolerate or reduce the anxiety aroused individuals will adopt coping behaviour that could be either functional or disfunctional for themselves or for the organisation. Phase III will also have implications both for how the individual approaches subsequent boundaries and for the organisation's attitude towards future boundary passage by that individual and by others.

PHASE I

The organisation's attitude towards boundary crossing

People are an important and expensive resource for most organisations. In a changing environment a flexible labour force is essential if this resource is to be used effectively. It is, therefore, in their own interest for organisations to encourage the kind of boundary crossing that will facilitate the optimum use of manpower resources. Management development, training programmes and the many attempts to influence and mould the individual's behaviour, attitudes and values are clear examples of the organisation's commitment to the encouragement of certain kinds of boundary crossing.

The need any organisation has for existing and new kinds of labour will fluctuate. Labour may be redeployed in such a way that people may be required to adopt new roles or to continue in similar roles in a different part of the organisation. The organisation may also recruit from and release people onto the labour market as the need arises.

Industrial growth and the need to fill existing positions as they fall vacant have confronted organisations with the need to consider deliberate and conscious strategies for the development of talent. They have had to prepare individuals to cross hierarchical boundaries and assume more responsibility. In describing what he calls the agricultural approach to the enlargement of competence, Gellerman (1968) captures the essence of management development.

Competence can be encouraged to grow in the same sense that a tree can be encouraged to grow. This is not done by leaving it to develop as best it can in competition with others (the jungle approach) and not solely by giving it an occasional dose of fertilizer (the education approach), rather competence grows when it is systematically nourished, pruned of its errors and transplanted, as it grows larger, to new ground on which it has ample room to flourish.

Industrial training and re-training are concerned with matching the available labour supply with organisation needs. Ideally, one product of training programmes is people equipped with the necessary skills to perform new roles. While this is a necessary condition for them to cross functional or hierarchical boundaries, often it is not sufficient to ensure smooth boundary passage. Industrial disputes are often rooted in the many concerns, not related to proficiences, that are associated with such movement: will it result in loss of status? Will encumbents of the new role enjoy the same level of remuneration? Is the organisation prepared to offer some compensation for the inconvenience incurred in crossing the boundary? etc.

The crossing of inclusion boundaries involves learning the values, norms and required behaviour of an organisation, department or work group. For example the novice may be on the pay-roll but he is not automatically a full member of the organisation. If he has anticipated the norms of the organisation or work group he is joining then the process of organisational socialisation will merely involve a reaffirmation of these norms through various communication channels. If, however, he comes to the organisation or work group with values and behaviour patterns that are considerably different from those expected by the new group then adjustment may involve difficulties. The organisation will attempt to socialise the individual, separate him from his old values and behaviour patterns and encourage him to seek a new status that is compatible with the environment he has entered. Organisations have an interest in promoting the crossing of certain inclusion boundaries because it provides a means of building commitment and loyalty as well as facilitating the smooth functioning of the organisation.

Organisations differ in their boundary characteristics. Schein (1971) argues that organisations vary in the number and degree of permeability of the boundaries they embrace and in the nature of the filtering properties associated with boundaries. For example, a military organisation may possess numerous functional boundaries separating the different line and staff activities, but in order to ensure manpower flexibility in combat situations it may maintain highly permeable boundaries and pursue a policy of rotating personnel. In a university, on the other hand, functional boundaries are likely to be considerably less permeable in the sense that a professor of folklore would probably find it very difficult to move to the chair of high energy physics.

Many variations in boundary characteristics will stem from the nature of the organisation's task and the nature of the organisation structure that has evolved to accomplish that task. However, not all variations will have such 'functional' roots. For example, the filtering systems associated with boundaries may be functional and vary with the nature of the task and responsibilities involved, or they may be non-functional and include such properties as social and ethnic factors: Which school did he go to? What does his father do? What is his religion, skin colour? etc.

Discouragement of boundary crossing

There are occasions when the organisation will actively discourage boundary crossing. Usually these relate to situations in which the organisation believes that a person will make a more effective contribution to the organisation's success in his current rather than in some other role. An extreme example might relate to the organisation's attitude to people crossing the external inclusion boundary. Training is an investment in human capital. Unlike investment in plant and machinery, investments in human capital are not owned by the organisation. The worker is free to leave the organisation and when he does the investment in human capital leaves with him.

Clearly a wide range of factors contribute to the organisation's attitude towards boundary crossing and, as we have seen, not all of these are related to the functional needs of the organisation. Further, while we have drawn attention to various factors that will influence an organisation's attitude to boundary crossing in general, we have largely ignored those factors that will influence its attitude to boundary crossing by a particular individual. In this respect the organisation will be influenced by the quality of the data it has about that person and will depend upon the nature and success of its appraisal systems.

The individual's desire to cross boundaries

People voluntarily seek to cross organisational boundaries for a number of reasons. Foremost amongst these may be the desire to change their environment in some way. Change may be sought either to provide the individual with new stimuli or to give him a sense of mastery over his environment. Many studies exemplify this wish. Hendrick (1943b) postulates a work principle which suggests that pleasure in work is a consequence of the gratification of the instinct to master (or alter) the environment. He suggests that work is primarily motivated 'by the need for efficient use of the muscular and intellectual tools, regardless of what secondary needs – self-preservation, aggressive or sexual – a work performance may also satisfy.' He calls this thesis the *work principle*, 'the principle that primary pleasure is sought by efficient use of the central nervous system for the performance of well-integrated ego functions which enable the individual to control or alter his environment' (Hendrick 1943a).

Neff (1968) suggests that some people try to satisfy through work the need to be creative. At one level creativity may be synonymous with novelty; the re-arrangement of traditional components into a new or unique pattern. 'Creativity generally strikes us as a form of human activity that is quite idiosyncratic, expressive of the unique qualities of a particular person.' Only very few jobs, scientific research, painting, or business enterprise and the like, can satisfy the need for this kind of creativity. At another level, however, creativity might be defined as the creation of an additional unit of something that is quite familiar; thus the typical industrial worker can be engaged in creative activity. 'Only when the process of automation proceeds so far that his connections with production become entirely attenuated, does the worker feel utterly useless.' However, long before this stage is reached the individual may find that familiarity with a work situation affects the level of stimulation and the opportunities for creative experience. Thus he may be induced to engage in some exploratory behaviour which eventually leads him across an organisational boundary.

Boundary crossing may also be sought as a means of attaining higher remuneration, greater security, more congenial social relationships, a new identity (within the organisation and possibly within society at large), or as a means of escape from some disagreeable aspect of organisational life. Encouragement to cross boundaries may also be welcomed as a signal of recognition by the organisation.

The individual's general orientation towards boundary passage may have already been influenced by the host of social factors that affect his vocational development long before he enters the world of work (see Hayes & Hopson, 1971, chapter 3). Whatever the precise reason, many individuals will have a positive orientation towards boundary crossing because they evaluate many transitional opportunities in terms of gain, as a means of closing the gap between their ideal world and the world as it is. Others, however, may be reluctant to see the personal growth opportunities from transition and be predisposed to see boundary passage in terms of potential loss.

PHASE II: ACTIVITY AT THE BOUNDARY

Fig. 6.2 illustrates what the individual may experience when confronted with an organisational boundary. His orientation may be either to seek or to avoid boundary passages, although what actually happens may ultimately be determined by the organisation.

Fig. 6.2: Activity at the boundary

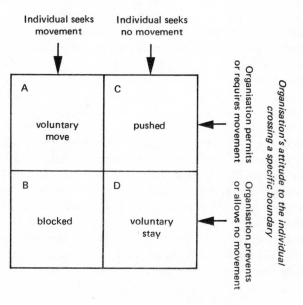

Individual seeks movement

The individual may wish to cross an organisational boundary in order to move *towards* some attractive position or *away* from an unattractive one. Thus the individual may seek to move across boundaries in search of success, challenge, self-esteem, power, influence, money, the opportunity to develop his special skills and potential, etc. Alternatively, he may wish to cross boundaries in order to remove himself from a dissatisfying situation within or external to the organisation. He may want to get away from undemanding, over-programmed or boring work, a depressing environment, and the like.

Voluntary move

When an individual wants to cross a boundary the organisation may be happy to allow this to happen or powerless to prevent it. In these circumstances the individual's preference for boundary passage will be realised.

Blocked

In some circumstances the organisation or even factors external to the organisation may block the individual's desired transition.

    External factors. Conditions in the labour market are an important external factor that could hinder transition. Opportunities at both national and local level, on an industrial or occupational basis, significantly affect the individual's chances of securing alternative employment. When unemployment is high an individual may be unable to realise the movement he seeks across either internal or external organisational boundaries.

    Discriminatory policies of potential employers in other organisations can block movement. Thus, for example, some organisations may be disinclined to recruit new entrants over a certain age, since they feel such employees will cost more, may be less receptive to new learning, and will have a shorter pay-off after training. Similarly, locking out policies of those organisations that promote from within may act as 'barriers' to prospective employees from other companies.

    Internal factors. Some organisations aim to prevent a loss of human capital by acting in such a way as to restrict individual movement. The organisation may consider the individual to be worth more where he is, want to avoid the cost of recruitment and selection, prevent the loss of knowledge and technical experience and the acquisition of trade secrets by competitors. The organisation may also want to prevent an individual moving internally because he is judged to be lacking in competence or unready for a move.

In such circumstances the organisation can deliberately prevent movement in a number of ways. For example, hierarchical movement may be blocked simply by refusing promotion, inclusion movement by excluding the individual from important decision areas, and functional movement by the pursuit of policies of narrow specialisation. In more general terms the organisation may deliberately make the individual's situation seem more attractive than alternatives by offering higher salaries, very congenial working conditions, appeals to his ego or sense of loyalty, etc.

Not all blocks to movement are deliberately engineered by the organisation. Movement may be restricted simply because there is nowhere to move (waiting for dead men's shoes), or through paternalistic employment policies that offer high wages, pension schemes, security of tenure, and the like which may unintentionally inhibit movement by raising the cost of boundary passage for the individual.

Individual seeks no movement

In contrast to those individuals who seek to cross organisational boundaries, there are those who for various reasons become locked in their current role. For personal reasons they prefer not to cross organisational boundaries.

As already mentioned in Phase I, some people are quite satisfied with their present situation. They may be interested in and committed to the job, enjoy its prestige, or have a strong loyalty to the organisation or work group. Even for those who are not altogether happy with their present position, the risks involved in transition may be too great to bear, especially so when they have acquired their present position on the basis of experience rather than paper qualifications, or where they have built up special skills that would be difficult to transfer. The fear of making a poor move, of going from bad to worse, may be heightened in those situations where the individual's chances of regaining his old job are low.

Extra-organisational factors may also influence the individual's attitude towards transition. These may include children's education, the care of sick or aged relatives, geographical ties, the complexities of a dual-career family and such economic factors as the cost of housing in alternative areas.

Pushed

In this case the individual's desire for no transition may be frustrated because of external forces that push him across an organisational boundary. The individual may be subjected to such forces because, for example (i) his current position disappears, (ii) he is seen by the organisation to be 'in the way', or (iii) the organisation wants to make better use of him elsewhere.

(i) For various reasons an organisation, or part thereof, may go out of business. Bankruptcy, technological change or restructuring of the organisation could lead to the disappearance of work roles and the need for people to cross functional or (if they have to leave the organisation) external inclusion boundaries.

(ii) An organisation may judge an individual to be incompetent, or at least relatively so in comparison to younger, better trained or more effective workers. Technological change may render existing skills obsolete and create the need to remove some workers to make way for new. People can also be pushed across inclusion boundaries if, for example, a sponsor leaves the organisation and his successor does not want to retain his predecessor's protégés within 'the inner circle'.

(iii) The organisation may push an individual across boundaries to exploit his skills more effectively elsewhere. This could occur, for example, when a plant is opened at some new location which requires the transfer of key personnel familiar with the organisation. Expansion or natural attrition may also demand the promotion of existing employees who might be quite content to remain where they are. Management development could also involve frequent functional moves to give reluctant employees a breadth of experience.

Voluntary stay

In this category the individual's desire for no transition is fulfilled. After evaluating the potential costs the individual prefers not to cross a particular boundary and the organisation is content to accept this situation or is unable to change it. For example, the opportunity to cross a hierarchical boundary may be rejected because of the costs this would incur in disaffiliating from an immediate work group (i.e. the cost of crossing, simultaneously, an inclusion boundary).

A factor sometimes ignored by an individual when examining the various costs and benefits of crossing a particular boundary at a given point in time is that in many organisations there exist recognised career phases within which certain kinds of transition are facilitated, even encouraged. Thus the rejection of an opportunity today may affect both the possibility of similar boundaries being open in the future and his chances of crossing them.

PHASE III

Identity strain

Identity strain exists when an individual feels unable to implement his self-concept at work. People develop a set of expectations about various roles. After they have crossed or not crossed particular organisational boundaries they assess their role and attempt to integrate it with the way they view themselves as a worker. Where the individual is unable to implement his occupational self-concept in his perceived role he may be motivated either to modify his self-concept, or to change in some way his perceived role, or in extreme circumstances to withdraw from the situation. In those situations where the individual's desire for, and experience of, boundary passage are congruent it seems likely that he will experience relatively little identity strain compared with those situations where his desire for, and experience of, boundary passage are incongruent. There may even be circumstances where no identity strain is experienced.

Voluntary move

Boundary passage is voluntary. The individual wants movement and achieves it. When he has correctly anticipated the nature of the role to which he is moving, he is likely to experience little difficulty in adjusting his self-concept and behaviour to the new situation. In those cases where anticipatory socialisation has been less adequate adjustment might involve greater strain; the individual may be confronted with unexpected experiences and signals from others. Nonetheless he is likely to be motivated to arrive at a satisfactory adjustment to this new situation as soon as possible and is unlikely to revert back to old definitions and assumptions when confronted with the unanticipated.

Voluntary stay

Again the individual achieves what he wants, that is he remains where he is. It is likely that this situation will present fewest problems and least strain. An exception may be where the individual receives signals from others that indicate that he has deviated from accepted career patterns and timetables. In some circumstances the individual may respond to these signals, re-evaluate his predicament, and modify his orientation to transitions. He may even receive signals that indicate that any future attempts to cross boundaries will be blocked and these may produce similar reactions to those which will be dealt with below.

In contrast there are those situations where the individual's desire for and experience of boundary passage are incongruent. It is in those situations that we would expect the most difficulty with coping.

Blocked

In this case the individual is thwarted in his desire to cross a boundary. He feels he should be crossing a particular boundary, but various external factors prevent this. There is a clash between his and the organisation's timetable and the individual fails to become what he expected he would be. His self-esteem is damaged and he may suffer humiliation in the eyes of others. Humiliation and therefore identity strain might be less when, for example, an economic recession reduces opportunities throughout the organisation. In these circumstances an individual may find it easier to cope with no promotion because this is an experience common to other people and does not reflect on his own competence. Coping could be considerably more difficult if he were the only person to be passed over for promotion.

Pushed

Boundary passage is involuntary. The individual's desire for and experience of movement are incongruent. Most strain and the greatest difficulties in coping may be experienced when boundary passage creates an unanticipated change in the way the individual defines himself, and where this change reflects on his competence and status. Thus a 64-year-old worker anticipating retirement may find it easier to adjust to redundancy or early retirement than a 54-year-old employee, particularly when the younger man feels the circumstances of his redundancy reflect unfavourably on his competence.

Difficulties might also arise when an individual experiences a boundary passage that others define as a success (i.e. it reflects favourably on his status and competence) but that he himself did not desire.

The personal experience of identity strain

We have seen that there are certain circumstances in which organisational pressures are likely to cause an individual to experience identity strain. This type of strain would be expected to occur most frequently where the individual feels either blocked or pushed in relation to a particular organisational boundary. The *degree* to which strain is felt by an individual will be a product of the situation *and* of his own disposition.

Identity strain will arise when the individual's organisationally related needs and wants are not satisfied. This might occur, for example, when an individual is divested of power, influence or belongingness. A person who has a high need for achievement or power might experience more inner strain if he felt his advancement was blocked than one whose high affiliative need made it attractive for him to stay with the same work group. Career blockages exist only where needs or ambitions create the desire to press onward across a boundary. For those people whose identity is not heavily invested in the progression across organisational boundaries the strain felt when their careers are blocked may be far less significant. Also those for whom deprivation is consistent with their self-concept may not necessarily experience identity strain.

People with similar needs may still have very different personalities and consequently deal with frustrated needs in a variety of ways. Looking at personality in one way, for example along Rotter's (1966) internal-external control dimension, we might expect an externally controlled individual to shift the focus of blame for loss of role onto other people, the organisation, or forces beyond his control. He might by-pass the humiliation and identity strain of an involuntary loss of role by making organisational policy, his superior or an external situation the scapegoat and may reduce the incongruence between his experience and his awareness of the situation and be better equipped to cope with his new status. What is more, he may be able to avoid the personal stigma that might otherwise attach to him. In contrast the internally controlled person may take upon himself the burden of humiliation, and assume that the timetable clash he is experiencing is a reflection upon his own adequacy.

Coping behaviour

People cope with identity strain in different ways. Some feel they can only remain passive in the face of the organisation as Sofer's 'giant straddling the major career corridors', while others will expend a great deal of energy trying to get their way and by-pass the blocks.

Any one person may adopt a number of coping strategies, over time, in the attempt to reduce the strain he feels. These strategies may or may not be rewarding (or functional) to the individual and to the organisation. We have found it useful to look at the behavioural expressions of the coping strategies in addition to the personal orientations they reflect, as a way of exploring how functional each coping style might be for the individual *and* for the organisation.

When a person experiences identity strain as a result of a thwarted or undesired move he may, initially, find it difficult to understand what is happening. He may be overwhelmed. Alternatively he may respond by 'blowing his top' (Goffman, 1952). Whatever form the immediate reaction may take this will often be followed by some form of denial, an attempt by the person to minimize the issues he has to cope with. As the incongruities associated with identity strain persist he may begin to recognise their existence and seek some way of coping with the situation.

Merton (1957) provides a useful framework of adaptations in his paradigm for deviant behaviour, which Levenson (1961) has applied to career blockages. These consist of ritualism, rebellion, innovation and withdrawal. We can add to these what might be considered the normal adaptation of acceptance and apply them to ways of coping with identity strain in organisations.

Acceptance. Attempts to modify an unsatisfactory situation may involve risks that the individual feels weigh the balance in favour of accepting the present state of affairs. This may involve feelings of humiliation, lack of competence, being the subject of 'status asynchron-isation' when younger men have gone further, etc. In the short term these feelings may be reconciled through rationalisation, projection or denial. In the longer term the individual may eliminate identity strain by adjusting to a new self-identity in which he accepts a changed set of assumptions about himself. This transitional process may be very similar to those described in chapter 9.

Ritualism. When an individual feels unable to accept the situation in which he finds himself he may go so far as to reject the norms of the organisation, give up his desires for boundary passage of particular kinds, and continue only with the form of his role, the organisational ritual. He loses interest in his work and settles down to minimum performance in order to preserve outward appearances. Thus he maintains his position in the organisation, but detaches himself from it inwardly. His detachment may, of course, be merely a front to preserve his social persona while he continues to harbour his original desires. He may tell the world he does not care about his organisational position, and almost convince himself, but still look for new opportunities. After some time the person who adopts this coping strategy may find it unrewarding and change tactics. He has tried to remove the identity strain by shedding the part of himself that was involved in the organisational career, but may experience more strain in doing without that sub-identity.

Rebellion. This type of coping with identity strain can be described as direct action since the individual adopts behaviours that are intended to change the situation rather than himself. He rebels against the way in which the organisation deals with boundary passage, may equate 'normal' behaviour with failure and act in opposite ways. These may well be aggressive, and range from personal ruthlessness to direct sabotage. The individual may find his action goes unrewarded since he is operating outside the framework of organisational norms. Although he might achieve a certain kick out of lousing up the system, in the long run he may satisfy neither his own ends nor those of the organisation.

Innovation. This coping strategy is another form of direct action but one in which the individual tries to attract attention to himself and his desire for boundary passage by innovatory behaviour within the organisational frame. He may mount a kind of public relations campaign in his attempts to advance in order to be noticed by the powers that be. Within such a campaign he may be trying to say two things: (a) the organisation sees me as having limited potential, but it is incorrect in its perceptions and does not appreciate my strengths, or (b) the organisation correctly perceives me as being limited in my current role, so I need to initiate some change (possibly changing role) in order to realise my potential. If the pressures he exerts are seen as legitimate he may be successful and be able to influence the direction of his career. In this case the organisation might recognise the value of his innovation as contributing to its own development too.

Withdrawal. In the extreme case of feeling totally unable to accept the norms of the organisation the individual decides to leave and to seek alternative employment. He is effectively refusing to change himself, feels that he cannot change the situation and therefore opts out. In the long run this could be rewarding if he finds a more satisfying position for himself. His withdrawal may also please the organisation.

Ways the organisation can help cope with identity strain

Camouflage. If an individual has failed to cross boundaries he wanted to cross, or if he is pushed across boundaries he would have preferred not to cross (e.g. demoted), the organisation may be able to camouflage this situation so that, while it may still be painfully apparent to the person concerned, it is disguised for others in the organisation. Thus, for example, the individual may be given less power and responsibility, in effect be demoted, but allowed to retain his title and salary, he may even be given an increase in salary or kicked upstairs to a harmless job. He is, in other words, allowed to save face in much the same way as the executive who is asked to resign and allowed to leave the organisation gracefully, rather than being dismissed under a cloud.

Similar strategies may be used to help the individual come to terms with his own potential within the organisation. Rather than abruptly halting the progress of an individual when he has exhausted his potential for further advancement there may, over a period of years, be a variety of lateral moves 'for experience' that provide the individual with the opportunity to come to terms with a less ambitious timetable and, eventually, an appropriate career ceiling.

Compensation. The experience of identity strain may be eased if the individual is offered some compensation. Thus the manager who is given an undesirable promotion to an isolated area may be compensated in terms of salary, housing, domestic assistance or other fringe benefits, or with the belief that this is a necessary step towards some more desirable identity. The manager who is relieved of his duties may find it easier to maintain his self-respect if he is compensated with some form of golden handshake or early retirement plan. Similarly, the manager short-listed to succeed his boss may find it easier to accept the appointment of an outsider if he is compensated with the headship of a fairly autonomous sub-department, in other words, if he is offered some alternative identity.

Counselling. Any person within the organisation (peer, boss or some kind of specialist resource) may help the individual cope with his identity strain through a formal or informal process of counselling.

Counselling can serve an *adjustive* function and assist the individual develop a more appropriate balance between his self-concept and his career. Leona Tyler (1961), discussing the problems of adjusting aspirations downwards, argues the need to develop counselling situations that facilitate attitude change, and suggests that by working in situations 'rich in acceptance and understanding, so that defensiveness is minimised and the person is able to grasp and accept his own limitations, realism and clear thinking may gradually win over inflated expectations'. Adjusting aspirations upwards as well as downwards may be considerably aided by appropriate counselling.

Counselling can also serve a *motivational* function to arouse and stimulate new ways of thinking about careers. Thus, the ambitious man who finds himself blocked might be encouraged to explore possible alternatives, the kinds of boundary they would present and their permeability.

Finally, counselling can serve an *evaluative* function and help the individual assess for himself his needs and explore how these might best be satisfied. In this way counselling can help the individual evaluate different opportunities and decide which, if any, to pursue.

Minimising the occurrence of identity strain

The more unrealistic the individual's expectations about his progress through the organisation, the greater will be the likelihood that he will experience identity strain. It is possible for the organisation to help prevent, rather than cure, identity strain through doing all in its power to enable and persuade the individual to assess, realistically, his own potential and the opportunities within the organisation for exploiting that potential. Chapter 9 explores the doctor's role in coordinating different parties' perceptions of the subject's transitional status. Within the organisation honest recruitment information, induction procedures and feedback on performance and training needs help the individual maintain a balanced view between his personal growth potential and job opportunities within the organisation. Failure and identity strain may also be avoided if the individual can be encouraged not to commit himself to positions or statuses he is unlikely to attain.

Where supervisors and managers are aware of the personal needs of their subordinates they are better able to design jobs and organisational life that will promote growth and improved functioning. Without this knowledge, identity strain may be an unnecessary by-product of day-to-day management. Similarly, an awareness of the career implications of organisational decisions can help minimise unnecessary problems.

Finally, the organisation can help minimise identity strain by ignoring failure or sub-optimal contributions to organisational goals and allowing certain people to proceed along 'normal' career paths or to maintain their current position when 'rational analysis' indicates the need for some change.

SUMMARY

This chapter has explored career transitions in terms of how boundaries are encountered. Such encounters are likely to promote identity strain when they lead to circumstances in which people feel unable to implement their self-concept. It has been argued that the organisation can intervene in order to help the individual to cope more effectively with this strain or even eliminate many circumstances that lead to the initial generation of identity strain. Such 'career concern' on the part of organisations can make a major contribution to the personal growth of organisational members and, at the same time, be the key-stone in the design of policies to make the most effective use of human resources.

7. Loss of Employment

John Hayes

Loss of employment is rarely viewed by those bereft of the opportunity to work as simply loss of an income source, a problem that could be resolved by generous unemployment benefits and special pension schemes. We live in a work-oriented society in which occupational achievement, rather than inherited wealth, ownership of land, or distinguished family name, has become the primary basis for prestige and reputation. In such a setting it is not surprising that loss of employment has many varied and complex implications for the individual.

If Economic Man were an adequate description of the average worker, then it would be reasonable to assume that a person would cease working once his material needs were satisfied. Testing this hypothesis Morse and Weiss (1955) asked over 400 men whether they would continue working if by some chance they inherited enough money to live comfortably without working. They found that 80 per cent of the total population, and over 90 per cent of all those between the ages 21 and 34 replied that they *would* continue working. Brown (1954) investigated what actually happened to those who were the recipients of large, unexpected, sums of money. He considered three London factory workers who won on the football pools sums of money which, suitably invested, would have provided sufficient income for them to live on for the rest of their lives. He found that after only a short period of leisure they all returned to work, two of them to highly repetitive jobs and one to a job as a fitter.

These findings suggest that work is more than a means to purely monetary ends. Morse and Weiss asked those who stated that they would continue working their reasons for feeling this way. They received a wide variety of answers. Approximately two-thirds of all respondents gave answers that they classified as 'positive reasons'. These were: working keeps me occupied and gives me an interest (32%); working keeps me healthy and is good for me (10%); the work is enjoyable (9%); it justifies my existence (5%); gives me a feeling of self respect (5%); provides the opportunity to be associated with people (1%); other (1%). These positive reasons accounted for 63 per cent of the total sample. Slightly more than one third of the sample gave negative reasons for continuing to work. They said that without work they would 'feel lost' (14%); wouldn't know what to do with their time (10%); feel bored (4%); feel useless (2%). Some said they would continue working from habit, inertia (6%), and some said they would continue working to keep out of trouble (1%). It would appear, therefore, that quite apart from being a source of income, work is a central and important element in the lives of many people in society today.

Loss of employment: A psycho-social transition

Changes in that part of the world with which an individual interacts are important or unimportant depending upon the influence such changes have on the assumptions the individual makes about the world. Parkes (1971) argues that this assumptive world is the only world we are aware of; it includes everything we know or think we know. It includes our interpretation of the past and our expectations of the future, our plans and our prejudices. Any or all of these may need to change as a result of changes in one's 'life space', whether or not these changes are perceived as gains or losses.

When major changes in life space are lasting in their effects, take place over a relatively short period of time and affect large areas of the assumptive world they are identified by Parkes (1971) as psycho-social transitions. Loss of employment, whether through redundancy or retirement, is, for most people, an example of such a transition. Parkes illustrates this point by suggesting that loss of a job deprives a person of a place of work, the company of workmates and a source of income. Morse and Weiss would probably add to this list a source of activity and interest, a source of identity and self-esteem and a sense of purpose. Thus loss of employment can produce many changes in an individual's life space and corresponding changes can be expected in his assumptive world. For example, assumptions about the way in which each day must be spent will change, and assumptions about the sources of money and security will change as will the individual's faith in his own capacity to work effectively and to earn a living. Parkes also suggests that his view of the world as a safe, secure place will change, his expectations of his future and that of his family will change and he is likely to have to replan his mode of life, sell possessions and maybe even move to a place where his prospects are better. Parkes argues that the individual's altered assumptive world will cause him to introduce further changes in his life space, to set up a cycle of internal and external changes aimed at improving the fit between himself and his environment.

Even the loss of a job one has never had can be difficult to cope with because one's assumptive world contains models of the world as it is and as it might be. The man who might be promoted to works manager rehearses in his mind the world he hopes to create. He engages in a kind of anticipatory socialisation aided by the rich imagery of his new comfortable office, efficient secretary, challenging assignments and respectful subordinates. It may be almost as hard to give up such expectations and fantasies as it is to give up objects that actually exist. Thus the man who is not promoted actually loses something very important. The change he has to cope with is a change in his own assumptive world.

This chapter focuses attention on loss of employment through retirement and redundancy since most people will experience at least one of these psycho-social transitions at some time in their lives. Both retirement and redundancy have a number of similarities. Firstly, as already indicated, they affect a large part of the individual's assumptive world. Secondly, they take place over a relatively short period of time. This is true even for retirement, which the individual can anticipate. Yesterday he was a worker, today he is not. He moves from a familiar status to one with which he is unfamiliar. Thirdly, they are not controlled by the individual but by external sources. The economic situation, technical change or management whim can determine that certain people are to be made redundant. Organisation policy, the availability of state pensions and convention can determine when people will retire. Those who do not want to be retired from their job at a particular age may be powerless to do anything about it. Fourthly, these are transitions that generally lead to a reduction in the range of possible roles and status, whereas most other widely experienced major life transitions (e.g. employment, marriage, parenthood) increase the range of roles and status for the individual. Finally, they are both recent phenomena: rapid development and accelerating change have been associated with changes in the industrial structure and occupational changes within particular industries. In addition, geographical changes in employment opportunities have meant that the demand for certain types of labour in given areas has fluctuated. Inevitably, these fluctuations have resulted in redundancies. The number of retired workers is also growing as a proportion of the population. The developed nations, with their vast productive capacity, have created surpluses which can be used to support a non-working, retired segment of the population. This ability to support non-productive people coincided with a demographic revolution and the emergence of an ageing population. It is not surprising therefore that in most developed countries minimum state pensions and maximum retirement ages have been institutionalised. Against this backdrop organisations have been adopting these (or even earlier retirement ages) to support their reward systems, which rely heavily on a throughput of people to ensure promotion opportunities and to maintain a flexible labour force.

REDUNDANCY

The way people view themselves and the way they are viewed by others is strongly influenced by the work they do. It is not surprising therefore that many of the studies of unemployment in the 1930s in Europe and in the U.S.A. reported by Eisenberg and Lazarsfeld (1938) indicate that redundancy not only threatens a man's sense of economic security but also shatters his sense of proportion, destroys his prestige in his own eyes and, he imagines, in the eyes of his fellow men, leads to the development of a sense of inferiority and a loss of self-confidence. In short, redundancy has been found to have numerous depressing effects and is often associated with a decline into apathy. Bakke (1960) also drew attention to how a straightforward event in a family's relation with the outside, economic world, i.e. loss of job for the father and source of income for the family, initiates a process of change that has ramifications for all the functional sub-systems of the family. Loss of employment, therefore, produces changes not only in the life space of the redundant worker, but also in the life space of his family system, requiring all to make adaptive personal changes.

An examination of the research reported by Bakke (1960) and Beales and Lambert (1934) in England, of Zawadski and Lazarsfeld (1935) in Poland and Gatti (1937) in Italy and the work described by Eisenberg and Lazarsfeld (1938) in America suggests that the process of adjusting to redundancy can be divided into a number of stages.

1. Shock

The initial reaction to redundancy seems to be one of surprise, shock, fear and a feeling of injury. The extent of shock appears to be greater (a) when work is an important ingredient in the person's definition of himself, (b) when the expectancy of re-employment by his old employer is low and (c) when redundancy is a novel experience. Wedderburn's study (1965) of redundancy amongst railwaymen included men who had worked on the railways all their lives, as had their fathers before them. To these men redundancy came as an enormous emotional shock. Statements such as 'the whole world has changed, you have a feeling of abandonment, loneliness, and you feel isolated' clearly indicated that unemployment rudely challenged their assumptive world. However, in industries where redundancy is a recurrent phenomenon people tend to integrate unemployment into their life style. The trauma of redundancy is modified by the heightened expectancy of subsequent re-employment.

2. Search and maintenance

Studies frequently point to a period of renewed hope, optimism, active job hunt and the maintenance of social activity. It would appear therefore that many newly unemployed invest themselves in active coping behaviours. Wedderburn (1964) noted, for example, that the most commonly expressed reaction to redundancy by white-collar workers after the cancellation of a Government defence contract in 1962 was to 'get cracking' in looking for another job. However, the extent of this investment has been found to vary. For example, Sheppard and Belitsky (1966) found that achievement motivation was related to the job seeking behaviour of the unemployed. They found that the degree of achievement motivation was related to such behaviour as (1) the time the worker waits, after being laid off, before starting his job search; (2) the number of different companies he considers during his first month of unemployment; (3) whether or not he approaches out of town employers; (4) whether he restricts himself to contacting only those companies he has heard beforehand are hiring new people; (5) the range of occupations he considers; and (6) the total number of job seeking techniques used. They further found a clear relationship between achievement motivation and job finding success among workers over the age of 22.

The job hunt may serve functions other than the location of new employment. Some redundant workers embark on the search for work in order to maintain the routine of working life and provide a reason for continuing to rise early and engage in activity outside the home. Time spent at home, once the garden has been dug and house repairs completed, tends to be purposeless activity. The job hunt provides purposeful activity that is seen as being legitimate and deserving of support within the family. It is a form of mitigation. While there is hope of re-employment the redundant worker can deny the need to seek a new status and establish a new pattern of relationship within his life space.

During this period the usual rhythm of family life is maintained. The father continues to spend time outside the home seeking work, social activities, wherever possible, seem to be maintained and, according to Bakke, the division of labour in the home is altered very little. Also changes in relationships are usually for the better. The father sees more of young children and the bonds between them are often strengthened. The wife usually accepts her husband's plight and supports him both within the home and outside.

As the period of unemployment extends the situation as experienced by the redundant worker and his family slowly begins to change. Savings are eroded, financial problems present themselves and the necessity for increasingly severe adjustments becomes obvious.

3. Threat to identity: depression and withdrawal

The belief that 'things will turn out alright in the end' is shaken and it becomes obvious that life cannot continue as if nothing had changed. The unemployed worker may intensify his job search but, as Zawadski and Lazarsfeld's analysis of fifty-seven autobiographies of the unemployed in Warsaw suggests, his mood increasingly reflects fading hopes and the belief that his efforts will be futile. Repeated failures to secure employment are depressing and, for many, the ritual of collecting unemployment pay and social security benefit begins to symbolise the fact that their fellow men and society at large recognise they are no longer able to support themselves and their family. Their sense of identity in the outside world is under pressure.

The redundant worker's identity is also threatened within the family. The wife may begin to provide an alternative source of income by seeking outside work for the first time, or by increasing the amount of time she devotes to paid employment. This results in a redivision of labour within the home. The wife delegates domestic chores to the children and begins to assume duties previously reserved for the husband. Bakke reports that she begins to assume a greater degree of responsibility for management and for distributing the available income. He also notes that the husband, considerably discouraged and tired out by his search for work, often takes this excuse to withdraw from his parental responsibilities in other respects, so that decisions as to the activities of the several members of the family descend upon the mother. Consequently the husband's status in the eyes of both wife and children tends to decline. This is sometimes accompanied by older children, who contribute to the family's income, demanding more freedom in view of their increased importance as family providers.

Crises become more frequent as opportunities for conflict between husband and wife and father and children increase. Family life becomes less satisfying for all and little energy is devoted to forward planning. Nonetheless, Bakke reports that to the outside world the family, and particularly the wife, attempt to provide a united and loyal front.

4. Disorganisation and crisis

If the period of unemployment is prolonged there is a possibility that the redundant worker and his family will be plunged into a period of crisis and disorganisation. Various studies note a period of active distress, of hopelessness, and of frequent attacks of fear, for example of being homeless, and the feeling that life and society has forgotten them.

The wife may become bitter. Bakke reports that she frequently questions the sincerity of her husband's search for work and expresses the suspicion that he is loafing. She stops defending the father from the criticisms of the children and she even criticises him outside the home. Eisenberg and Lazarsfeld summarise a number of studies that indicate that the children are often robbed of any sense of security and leadership, fall into bad ways, endure poor health, suffer emotional disturbance and do less well at school.

Severe depression, divorce, even suicide are all possible outcomes of this phase. However the evidence from the great depression, as reported by Bakke and Eisenberg and Lazarsfeld, suggests that many people are surprisingly resilient. Nevertheless, the period of disorganisation and failure is a testing time. If the family remains disorganised for long there is a very real possibility that it will break up. The husband may decide that all is lost, give up seeking work and may even drop out of society and begin drifting. On the other hand, having reached the bottom, the view may be adopted that things can only improve. If the family decides to stay together there is the hope that it can reorganise and achieve some success.

5. Readjustment

Many of the studies completed in the inter-war years suggest a depressing prognosis for the very long term unemployed. Zawadski and Lazarsfeld talk about the sombre acquiescence or dumb apathy, and then the alternation between hope and hopelessness, activity and passivity, according to the momentary changes in the material situation. Gatti argues that the individual becomes 'even more apathetic' as unemployment is prolonged. However, Eisenberg and Lazarsfeld suggest a more positive step towards readjustment. They argue that, while he becomes more fatalistic, the unemployed worker 'adapts himself to his new state but with narrower scope'.

Bakke, on the basis of his observations, makes a similar point when he suggests that an important prerequisite of readjustment is acceptance of the fact that achievements of the past can no longer be made standards for the satisfaction of achievements in the present. It is as though the period of disorganisation and crisis unfreezes the family and helps it to search for and find new values and standards better suited to the present.

In terms of the model outlined in chapter 1 the individual has to disinvest himself psychologically of the status of worker; he has to unhook from the past and move forward by tentatively testing new identities and experimenting with new assumptions in order to improve the fit between himself and his environment as it now exists. Instead of constantly looking over his shoulder and clinging to inappropriate assumptions based on past experience he must start living for the present and build his assumptive world afresh.

RETIREMENT

In many cases the individual is suddenly confronted with the prospect of redundancy. It is often completely unexpected. The emphasis in this chapter has therefore been on how people react once they have been made redundant. Retirement, on the other hand, is a process that most people can anticipate, even though the actual transition from being a worker to being retired takes place over a relatively short period of time. Attitudes towards retirement may be developed long before the event, as may plans for coping with retirement. Attention therefore will be focused on the period leading up to retirement as well as on what happens when a person actually retires.

Retirement means different things to different people. For example, Breen (1963) reports a study in which a group of older workers were compared with a matched group of younger workers with respect to their attitudes towards retirement. Considerable differences in their attitudes were noted. It was found that the younger men wanted to retire early, but men old enough to retire completely reversed the young men's responses. It was also found that young men were less realistic about plans for retirement. For example, they said that on retirement they would start businesses of a kind that would clearly require large amounts of capital which they did not have and had no expectation of raising. Plans mentioned by older men tended to be much more realistic and less grandiose.

Age, however, is not the only important variable. Even within the older age group there are many differences, as illustrated by Marrion Crawford's (1971) study of retirement. She asked 99 married couples what kinds of thoughts they associated with the word retirement. Sixteen per cent of her subjects responded with the retrospective comment 'finishing work'. For them retirement meant the end of one life phase rather than the beginning of another. Forty per cent were thinking ahead favourably to retirement and they stressed the rest/ leisure/freedom aspects. Forty-four per cent were thinking ahead unhappily to retirement; for them it meant lack of money or activity or the onset of old age, and a very small proportion said they associated nothing with the word retirement.

She also asked the men in her study what they would miss most about work. Disagreeable aspects of work, the end of which would be welcomed, seemed to centre around getting up early, the journey to work and the pressure of work. Some also mentioned the work itself, the physical surroundings and discipline. Pleasant aspects of work that would be missed included the routine, the physical and mental aspects of work and the money. However, by far the most important aspect of work that would be missed was the company of men at work. This was referred to by well over half of the men in the study. After retirement they saw themselves living in a social vacuum, isolated from male company, seeing the same people every day and feeling cut off from the warmth of a working group.

Crawford did not find the intrinsic aspects of work to be particularly important, but Saleh & Otis (1963) found that those workers who were job-oriented (i.e. those who expressed high satisfaction with the intrinsic aspects of the job) had a less favourable attitude towards retirement than context-oriented workers. A possible explanation being that job-oriented workers anticipated a lack of intrinsically challenging and meaningful tasks to occupy their energy after retirement.

Retirement not only affects the man about to end his work career; it also can have numerous implications for his family. As Crawford points out, one of the major transitions from work to retirement for the married man is the sudden change from spending the day with fellow workers to spending it at home with his wife. This is an equally sudden and far-reaching change for the wife. Consequently their joint experience of retirement is likely to be as much dependent on her attitude and preconceptions as on his.

Crawford found that a number of women associated retirement with ageing. They gave the impression that by retiring their husbands had brought old age closer. This was resented because ageing meant for them that they would be ascribed to a different and lower status group. They would be expected to withdraw from much of their previous participation in society, to disengage.

This attitude towards retirement reflects the basic issues in the debate on 'successful' ageing and retirement. One view is that successful ageing involves maintaining, for as long as possible, the activities and attitudes of middle age (see Havinghurst, 1954). This 'activity theory' assumes that older people should be fully integrated into the social system for as long as possible. Another view, expressed in the 'disengagement theory' of Cumming and Henry (1961) predicts that successful ageing is a process of voluntary withdrawal or disengagement on the part of the individual from his society. Crawford (1972) found that it was possible to identify four major patterns of anticipation of retirement in relation to these disengagement and re-engagement (activity) theories.

(1) One group of men were looking forward to retirement and already had a variety of roles outside the home that could be played more fully after retirement. This group welcomed retirement because it provided an opportunity to *re-engage* in a variety of activities.

(2) A second group of men played few roles outside work and the immediate family and were dreading retirement. They seemed to have depended almost exclusively on their work as a source of satisfactions. Work appeared to be their framework and without it they saw their lives collapsing. They were either unable or unwilling to restructure their existence and consequently they concentrated upon the losses rather than the gains associated with retirement. Retirement implied *enforced disengagement.*

(3) A group of home-centered women looked forward to their husband's retirement. These were women who did not appear to have replaced their central role of mother in the post-parenthood phase. They saw retirement as a legitimisation for their withdrawal into the home and they welcomed the opportunity to draw their husbands more fully into it. Crawford felt this group most closely resembled the *contented disengagers* described in the Cumming and Henry study.

(4) Lastly, there was a group of women involved in activities outside the home who dreaded retirement. Their activities were either split between the home and the outside world or were centered on the community and their friendships. They had re-engaged in outside activities and a wider society after their children left home and had forged a new life for themselves that did not depend on the family for satisfaction. They felt this kind of life threatened by their husband's retirement and they resented the imposition of the status of 'older person'. This group were very *reluctant disengagers.*

Parkes (1971) suggests that gaps between the ideal world and the world as it is represent unfulfilled wishes. A change in the life space may have the effect of closing one of these gaps and will be construed as a gain. Thus when retirement is seen as closing such gaps it is likely to be welcomed, and when the people involved have rehearsed in their minds behaviours and assumptions appropriate to this new, more ideal world the transition may take place smoothly. When retirement is seen to widen gaps between the ideal world and the world as it is (or will be), it will be regarded as a loss. In such circumstances resistance to change is to be expected and internalisation of a new, less attractive assumptive world may be a difficult and even traumatic process.

The terms disengagement and re-engagement may be viewed within this context to reflect different orientations to the status passage from worker to retired person. The re-engager may be seen as someone who welcomes the status passage, quickly separates himself from the status of worker and eagerly assumes the retired status. The change is construed as a gain and the individual is happy to redefine himself and adopt a new set of assumptions about how he should relate to his life space. The disengager may be seen as someone who experiences retirement as the separation from a familiar status rather than the acquisition of a new status. The process is defined in terms of loss rather than gain and even when the disengager has accepted the separation from the previous status he may flounder in a transitional stage before identifying an acceptable and attainable alternative status.

Anecdotal evidence suggests that some reluctant disengagers deny the inevitable and refuse to face up to their status passage until external forces intervene and separate them from the status of worker. There are also accounts of those in the process of transition who find it very difficult to accept the finality of the separation, who yearn for their old work place and lost associates and become depressed with their state of unemployment. In many respects they appear to grieve in much the same way that the bereaved grieve the loss of a loved one (see chapter 9). The emotional response to retirement of both the engagers and disengagers is an area that deserves more attention from re-searchers.

Ritual may have a valuable role to play in the emotional and social adjustment to status passages. Van Gennep (1960) argues that in many semi-civilised societies considerably more attention seems to be paid to changes in status than appears to be the case in our own society. Primitive societies have evolved elaborate *rites de passage* that help people identify status passages and assume attitudes and behaviour appropriate to the new status. They signal the need to modify ideas about how to relate to the world as it has been redefined. The Rapoports (1964) examine the role of ritual in life-cycle transitions in their paper on the honeymoon and find some support for Van Gennep's thesis that ritual helps to smooth transitions.

Ven Gennep identifies three types of rites associated with transitions in semi-civilised societies. He calls them rites of separation, rites of transition and rites of incorporation. Crawford (1973) applies these concepts to the data she collected from fifty-seven retired couples participating in her longitudinal study. She concludes that descriptions of retirement seem to show that retirement includes rites of both separation and transition, but not of incorporation. Rites of separation appear to correspond to the worker's experiences during his last week at work. Often he was expected to leave his task, for part of the time at least, and make a tour of the organisation to make his farewells. Rites of transition and the concept of 'sacred' status mentioned by Van

Gennep seem to correspond to the wearing of 'decent' clothes during some part of the last week and to the position of the retiring man throughout the actual formal ceremony of retirement. The 'typical' ceremony exemplifies the rites of leave taking, which according to Van Gennep typically include 'visits, a last exchange of gifts, a meal in common, a last drink, wishes, accompaniment on the road and sometimes even sacrifices'. Retirement ceremonies often take place within working hours and are attended by representatives of management. The retiring worker occupies a sacred status, in that the ordinary discipline of the work place does not apply to him, and he is often wearing different clothes. Usually the focus of the ceremony is the presentation of a gift, the expression of appreciation and a reassurance that those present will always be ready to welcome the retiring worker if he wants to visit the work place. From this point forward he is in a state of transition while he is still on the work premises, being neither worker nor retired.

There is therefore ample evidence of rites of separation and rites of transition, but what of rites of incorporation? Crawford found that only two men in her study enjoyed anything approaching a rite of incorporation into the family.

This could be important in the light of some of Crawford's findings concerning the influence of ritual on retirement. Forty-three of the fifty-seven men in this stage of her study participated in some kind of leaving ceremony. Although, by her own admission, the data are somewhat limited in quantity and sophistication, they do show that while the absence of separation and transition rituals is not associated with a general maladjustment to retirement, it is related to the men's behaviour in terms of group membership. She found that those who were not ritualised were more likely than those who were to cling to membership of the work group, to return to the work place and to join organisations connected with work. In other words, ritual helped the men cope with the transition from the status of worker to non-worker. It was as though the ritual established a point of reference. After the ritual it was clear that time had to be organised differently, new social relationships developed, new sources of satisfaction sought; in short, the ritual signalled the need for the individual to develop a new series of assumptions regarding his relationship with the world of work. Possibly rites of incorporation could similarly help the family, including the retired worker, reappraise their assumptions regarding family life in the future.

THE PROCESS OF READJUSTMENT

The process of adjustment to loss of employment involves the development of a modified assumptive world (internal changes) and possibly a further redefinition of the life space (external changes) designed to improve the fit between self and environment. Desired transitions are more likely to be associated with smooth adjustment because the individual is motivated to redefine his life space and assumptive world. Undesired change, on the other hand, is more likely to be associated with a reluctance to abandon old assumptions. The redundant worker, for example, may judge his experience against past, inappropriate criteria. It may be some time before he stops looking over his shoulder and develops a here and now or future orientation to life based on new, more appropriate standards. Similarly the enforced disengager may view retirement with dread, cling to old ways, and refuse to reappraise life and seek out new sources of satisfaction.

Retirement and redundancy both involve separation from the status of worker and adjustment to a new status of non-worker. The long-term unemployed studied in the inter-war years appeared to experience five phases in their adjustment to loss of work. These were (1) shock, (2) search and maintenance, (3) threat to identity, (4) disorganisation and crisis, and (5) readjustment. The first three phases were associated with separation from the status of worker, the fourth was a transitional phase from which emerged the fifth phase, adjustment to a new status. With retirement the picture appears to be more complicated. Whereas some people view retirement as a loss, others clearly see it as a gain. Nonetheless, whatever the individual's orientation, the process can still be described in terms of separation, transition and readjustment although a more precise definition of these phases must await further research.

The focus of this chapter has been loss of employment by men, since they, rather than women, have been the subject of most research in this area. Hopefully future research will pay more attention to how this transition is experienced by women workers.

Whatever the attitudes and motives associated with transition it is possible that an experience designed to help and encourage the individual re-evaluate himself within the context of his changing life predicament could greatly facilitate a smooth and satisfactory adjustment to change. The importance of ritual has been mentioned and the apparent absence of rituals of incorporation for the retired into their new status has been noted. Possibly a greater emphasis on ritual throughout society could help people manage transitions more effectively. Personal re-evaluation, described in chapter 11, might also be developed to assist individuals and their families cope with loss of employment. The workshop described by Duckworth in chapter 13 might have applications in this area, as might activities designed to develop achievement motivation and other traits that might influence the job seeking behaviour of those bereft of work.

Many of us will have to withdraw from the world of work more than once in our life-time and, as the age of retirement is lowered and life expectancy increases, a growing proportion of the life span will be associated with unemployment. In our work-oriented society unemployment can be a rude challenge to one's sense of identity. Loss of employment, therefore, is a process that deserves considerably more attention than it has received in the past.

The current economic recession has greatly stimulated research into ways of helping people cope with redundancy more effectively and many employers and retirement associations are experimenting with ways of helping those faced with retirement. Hopefully this activity will add to our understanding of what happens to a person when he or, increasingly, she is deprived of employment and contribute to our knowledge about how to help people cope with this situation.

8. Marriage, Parenthood and Divorce

Barrie Hopson

MARRIAGE

One of the major transitions in almost every person's life is from being single to getting married. More people get married today than ever before in our history (97 per cent of women and 90 per cent of men in the U.S.A. now get married!), in spite of forecasts of doom and gloom, an increase in co-habiting, gay liberationists emerging from their closets, and a few well-known film stars producing children out of wedlock to the accompaniment of magazine photographers' flashbulbs.

This transition is a classic example of a self-sought, *predictable transition*. There is no way someone can wake up one morning and find themselves married — whatever certain Hollywood movie plots may have tried to have us believe.

This discussion has to accept that the transition to marriage is often a different experience for women than for men. Before the arrival of children, a married woman will usually have two roles — housewife and job; the husband — although increasingly 'helpful' in the house — is not a househusband, and usually remains first and foremost an employed worker. For women, the transition to marriage is usually a major career step, with implications for occupational mobility, promotion prospects and long-term career planning. Rarely, as yet, is marriage a career step for a man. Bernard (1972) on the basis of research evidence argues persuasively for not dealing with marriage as one entity in itself, but two — the husband's marriage and the wife's marriage. To attempt to define a theoretical model to encompass the transition to marriage without taking sex differences into account would be as ludicrous as trying to develop a theory explaining occupational choice without taking the same factor into account.

The parallel between occupational and marital choice is an interesting one. Just as it used to be thought that one lived for sixteen years or so and then decided what job one was going to choose, so it was thought (and some people still think) that choosing a spouse happens in the same way. Yet we now know that the process of occupational choice has to be looked at developmentally. A person does not suddenly decide to be a plumber or a lawyer at 18. That decision will be a culmination of a long period of experiences and thinking, all contributing to the shaping of that particular decision. In addition, the process does not stop at the first occupational choice. This may be rejected in favour of others. Most people increasingly make major career changes throughout their lives, which is why vocational psychologists now talk about the *process of career development*. Similarly, I propose that we can discuss a person's *marital career development*.

Ginzberg (1951) and Super (1953) hypothesised that during the early stages of vocational development people pass through the following stages:

(1) *Fantasy*: (approx age 7−10+) This term refers to the nature of the process rather than any specific occupation that children select. Certain adult activities appear pleasurable to them and they know that certain occupations enable one to engage in these activities. Without any awareness of barriers that might stand in the way they choose a job that permits an activity that seems attractive at the moment.

(2) *Tentative*: (approx age 11−18) the child becomes aware of the fact that there is more to a job than simply doing one exciting activity. He realises that there are certain things that give him satisfaction and others that do not. He realises that one needs certain abilities to succeed in different jobs, and finally that some jobs will ask of him things that do not square with his values and beliefs. This stage is one of a growing awareness of the importance of interests, capabilities, and values in choosing a job.

(3) *Realistic*: (age 18+) the person becomes aware of the environmental restrictions and his own restrictions to a completely free choice of a job.

Let us translate this developmental process into the marital context.

(1) *Fantasy*: girls and boys assume that they will be married one day. They usually think they can choose anyone they like, and have little conception of what is involved in living closely with another person.

(2) *Tentative*: they begin to realise that they will not have a completely free choice. Some people are not always happily married — marriages can break up. To be married involves 'give and take'. They can understand the compromises of the marital relationship from the difficulties they are beginning to experience in maintaining their own relationships with peers and significant adults.

(3) *Realistic*: they realise that being married has implications for one's total way of life — traditionally this has been stronger for women than for men. All kinds of freedoms are curtailed, but there is an awareness of some of the very valuable qualities that being married can bring. At this stage the real process of transition begins.

The model of transition presented here has been significantly influenced by theories of vocational development, and in particular that of Tiedemann and O'Hara (1963). Their model traces a person's choice of occupation through three major stages: Anticipation, Implementation and Adjustment. These in turn are broken down into substages of exploration, crystallisation, choice, clarification, induction, reformation and integration. The transition model presented in Fig. 8.1 is adapted from this scheme and is broken down into the stages of exploration, crystallisation, choice, rehearsal, negotiation, and integration. The remainder of this section traces a person's progression through this model.

Stage 1. Exploration

Dating
Dating can serve a number of functions, including pure recreation, acquiring status, conforming to peer pressure to gain acceptance, learning the give-and-take involved in relating to another person, but undoubtedly for most young people dating is in some sense a prelude to marriage. It provides people with practice in making relationships, for unless that social skill is acquired, in a society where people choose their own spouses, eventual marriage is unlikely. It also provides access to a range of 'eligibles'. At some stage when dating a new person, most people will wonder whether this person could be a potential marriage partner.

Fantasising
People imagine what their marriage will be like, sometimes with a particular person in mind, sometimes generally. Their fantasies will be

Fig. 8.1: A model of marital transition

ANTICIPATION		IMPLEMENTATION		ADJUSTMENT	
Exploration	*Crystallisation*	*Choice*	*Rehearsal*	*Negotiation*	*Integration*
Early development	Concepts crystallise about the kind of marriage one wants, and the type of person one wants to live with	Field of eligibles reduced to one	Public commitment	Honeymoon period	There are many forms of integration
Marital 'scripts' develop		Private commitment	Reappraisal	Defining the boundaries	
Dating	Marital readiness		Decisions about future marriage and marital life style are made	Differences between the husband's and the wife's marriage begin to broaden	
Fantasising about married life					
Fantasised role playing					

M A R R I A G E   A C T

This applies to one marriage. Where one marriage ends, a similar cycle will begin again, except that the Anticipation stages will be much briefer.

strongly influenced by their parents' marriage. In our society the married lives of most people are 'invisible' to others. We present images of how we would like to be seen, often even to very close friends. Consequently, many people only experience the interior of one other marital relationship — that of their parents. To use terminology borrowed from Transactional Analysis, people develop 'scripts' that contain many of their parents' marriage 'lines'. How should affection be expressed? How should conflict be resolved? Domestic roles allocated? Where do children fit into an imagined life style? Do they have any separate interests and activities or is it expected that they always do things together? How much and in what ways do relatives fit into their way of life? Is it expected that one's partner should agree on all questions of beliefs and values or is it not too important? Who is supposed to make decisions and about what? What is one's sex life supposed to be like — regular or irregular, what quantity, what quality, who initiates, what is allowable, disapproved of, expected, encouraged? What kind of relationship can one have outside the marital relationship? What will be the relationship between occupational and marital careers?

People are not usually blessed with a great deal of insight into the marriage scripts inherited from their parents. Awareness often comes only by encountering other people intimately and discovering for oneself one's wants and not-wants.

During the exploration phase, relationships will be formed, often abandoned, data will be acquired experimentally regarding what sort of a partner one is looking for, and possible 'matches' will be role-played in fantasy.

Stage 2. Crystallisation

This is the stage at which one's value judgements are becoming clearer. People are in a better position to describe (a) the kind of marriage they want, and (b) the type of person they wish to live with. This stage is not irreversible. People's values and wants will change as a result of new experiences and people encountered, but at least at this stage for the first time there are images of married life, however hazy round the edges.

Ideas will have formed around the most desirable age to get married, if and when one would like to have children. One has approached the stage of 'marital readiness'.

Stage 3. Choice

The field of eligibles is reduced to one. Much has been written about this process in the study of mate selection (see Winch, 1971; Williamson, 1972) so that we know that 'like tends to marry like' when it comes to sociological variables such as nationality, ethnic group, religion, social class and physical proximity. The same hypothesis holds, though less strongly, for personality factors like intelligence, attitudes, and values. It is at the level of personality that there is also some support for the 'opposites attract' or complementary needs school of thought. We know little about the ways in which people develop intimate relationships, but at this point in the model it is appropriate to look at the question more deeply. This is not to imply that only at this stage of choice will people make intimate relationships. For, although we can be certain that almost everyone making a marital choice in Western cultures has established such a relationship at this stage, many people will have established intimate relationships prior to this stage that have not concluded in a marriage choice, either because the other person did not wish to marry them, or because there were some irreconcilable conflicts, or because one or both people were not ready to marry.

Levinger and Snoek (1972) have developed a conceptual framework that plots the transition from acquaintance to superficial to deep relationships. Fig. 8.2 shows the progression of a relationship from awareness (the stage of approach) to the level of surface contact (the stage of affiliation) to the level of mutuality (the stage at which attachments develop). Fig. 8.3 indicates the different interpersonal processes operating at each stage and the conditions that are optimal for transition from one level to another.

Levinger and Snoek propose a filtering process that unfolds as a relationship develops and during which different factors influence attraction at different stages. Physical and social proximity are the first, essential determinants. After these relatively random requisites for attraction are met, they are replaced by more individualistic determinants, such as physical attractiveness, reciprocity of liking, similarity of background, interests and attitudes. Still later, self-disclosure, mutual accommodation and open communication play important roles in fostering attachment. If each of these requisites for attraction is met at its appropriate time, the relationship will have a chance to survive the

Fig. 8.2

No contact	0	
Awareness	1	
		Approach
		1 spatial proximity, climate, and other environmental factors
		2 lack of social distance
		3 person's interest in other people, e.g. affiliation need
Surface contact	2	
		Affiliation
		4 person's time and opportunity
		5 attractiveness of other
		6 perception of other's probable reciprocity
Mutuality	3	
		Attachment
		7 liking for other and satisfaction with prior relationship
		8 circumstances that extend interaction beyond normal role requirements
		9 communication about each other's experiences in interaction
		10 accommodation and the formation of contractual norms
		11 attitude, value, and need compatibility

various filters that can discourage relationships, e.g. if interests or attitudes were to change in ways salient to the relationship, the future of the relationship would be uncertain.

Private commitment
A person will often make a number of deep relationships. It is the development of a private and then a public commitment to live with and share in the life of another person that characterises a marital choice.

Stage 4. Rehearsal

Public commitment
The moment of choice for two people in our society is often, though by no means always, translated into a public statement of their commitment, namely, an engagement. This is a time of testing out the new relationship to see how it fits one's preconceived crystallisations. Increasingly this testing out stage involves a sexual relationship, although for most people it still stops short of a 'trial marriage', i.e. where the two people actually set up home together.

LEVELS OF RELATEDNESS

INTERPERSONAL PROCESSES	1. Awareness	2. Surface contact	3. Mutuality
Communication	Unilateral	Confined to role-required instrumental concerns; no self-disclosure.	Self-disclosure concerning personal feelings and the evaluation of outcomes in the relationship.
Common knowledge	None	Confined to other's public self-presentation.	Much mutually shared information, including knowledge of each other's personal feelings and biographies.
Process of interaction	None	Stereotypic role-taking; trial-and-error responses to novel situations.	Spontaneous and free-flowing; person understands how other is affected by the interaction and has concern for his well-being.
Regulation of interaction	None	By cultural norms; untested implicit assumption that other shares same norms.	By joint construction of some unique pair norms, tested and found appropriate by both persons.
Maintenance of relationship	None	Of little concern; responsibility for maintenance is perceived to be vested in externally derived roles of organisational requirements. Cost of terminating relationship is low.	Person and other both assume responsibility for protecting and enhancing the relationship; cost of terminating relationship becomes increasingly high.
Evaluation of relationship	None	Satisfaction on the basis of self-centered criteria: person compares his outcomes with prior experience and with alternate relationships.	Based on mutual outcomes evaluated against joint criteria, reflecting mutual equity.
Attraction to other	Based on other's reward potential or 'image'	Based on person's satisfaction with experienced outcomes, as well as on other's reward potential. Determined considerably by adequacy of other's role enactment.	Based on affection for other as a unique person and on person's emotional investment, as well as on criteria for surface contact.

In our society approximately 50 per cent of engaged women and 65 per cent of engaged men actually marry the person to whom they are engaged (Burgess & Wallin, 1953). Usually engagement commits the couple to a monogamous relationship; it allows the dyadic relationship of love and associated emotional shadings to develop; it allows people to discover whether they like as well as *love* one another (two different dimensions according to Rubin's research, 1973). Most importantly it allows the couple time to face the reality of sharing a life with one another, discovering areas of agreement and disagreement on some of the issues outlined on page 122. Unfortunately, the research suggests that not every couple is diligent in exploring these issues before marriage, so running the risk of storing up future shocks for themselves. Not that disagreement automatically rules out marriage for those concerned. Indeed, Burgess and Wallin showed that 28 per cent of their sample of 900 couples disagreed in five or more of important areas of married life, namely, in descending order: ways of dealing with the families, matters of conventionality, philosophy of life, religion, and money matters.

Reappraisal

It is common for people to experience doubt at this stage and, as previously indicated, a considerable number of people break off engagements. For many who stay the course, the feeling of mental and physical distress experienced as the wedding day approaches generally signifies the momentous step he or she is taking.

Decision making

Before the marriage can take place a number of issues have to be decided. When are the couple to be married? What kind of ceremony? Where are they going to live afterwards? How will it affect the occupational careers of both? How are they to deal with finances? − in addition to those already mentioned on page 122.

Stage 5. The Marriage Act

The legal or socially appropriate act of public commitment. The line between being unmarried and married.

Stage 6. Negotiation

A new marriage is somewhat akin to the birth of a new culture. Norms will have to be established, although in many instances these will already have been formed during the rehearsal stage. Roles will be allocated. Patterns of interaction in daily living will develop. All of these will come about as a result of consciously and unconsciously made decisions.

A whole series of decisions will have been made, many of them unconsciously, which will determine what the product looks like from outside, and what it feels like from within. He decides to get up first most mornings and make breakfast — she lets him. She decides to cook all the evening meals — he agrees, without a word passing between them. He decides he wants to go out with the boys on two nights a week — she does not agree. He decides to go anyway, and she does not try any harder to stop him (Hopson & Hopson, 1975).

The honeymoon is supposed to provide a breathing space before real 'contract building' begins. However, a couple have already laid the foundations of their new culture before the marriage, and overt and covert negotiations usually continue throughout a honeymoon which, incidentally, many couples find disastrous at worst and tedious at best. A honeymoon often appears like a forced rest period in a contest between opponents who are still highly energised. Many couples cut their honeymoons short (Rapoport & Rapoport, 1964).

It is at this point in the transition model that the difference between the wife's marriage and the husband's marriage becomes increasingly apparent. For example, it appears that the wife makes the greater adjustment in marriage (Burgess & Wallin, 1953).

Understandably so. Because the wife has put so many eggs into the one basket of marriage, to the exclusion of almost every other, she has more at stake in making a go of it (Bernard, 1972).

The husband upon marriage often makes little change in his life routine. The wife has acquired a whole new repertoire of domestic responsibilities.

One of the most poignant adjustments that wives have to make is in the pattern of emotional expression between themselves and their husbands. Almost invariably, they mind the letdown in emotional expression that comes when the husband's job takes more out of him, or the original warmth subsides (Bernard, 1972).

Not surprisingly, the statistics demonstrate clearly that more wives than husbands report marital frustration and dissatisfaction, negative feelings, marital problems, consider separation and divorce, seek marriage counselling, and initiate divorce proceedings. Bernard marshalls statistics to support her contention that marriage is good for men — physically, socially, and psychologically — and bad for women by the same criteria.

Her conclusion is that it is not marriage as such that brings on this multitude of ills to women, but the role of housewife, which in this 'enlightened' age is still perhaps the most significant role transition for a woman on marriage. Dual-career families with equal domestic responsibilities are rare. Even when both spouses subscribe to an egalitarian relationship and agree on the importance of female liberation, the existing research shows that it is still the wife who tends to follow the husband's job, has the major childrearing role, and the ultimate domestic responsibility (Holmstrom, 1972; Veroff & Feld, 1970).

Stage 7. Integration

If negotiation, however low-key, is successful then some degree of integration will ensue. This will not mean for ever, although that does happen. Usually, there will be periods of renegotiation as the partners change and develop different wants and outcomes from the relationship.

The forms of integration are many. Cuber and Cuber (1965) analysed in depth the marriages of 437 American families where the husband had a highly successful career, and they distinguished five distinct patterns of upper-middle-class marriage. These were split into two groups: Utilitarian and Intrinsic. The Utilitarian consisted of three types: the 'devitalised' marriage, where the couple had come from a passionate beginning to a position where they shared few interests, talked little, sex was routinised if, indeed, it existed at all. These couples often felt despair and frustration, but they lacked the motivation, courage and skills to enable them to revitalise their relationship or end it. The 'conflict-habituated' marriage remained stable in spite of persistent nagging, arguing and bickering. Both husband and wife had too much at stake elsewhere to risk the disruption of divorce. The 'passive congenial' couple were 'just good friends'. It differed from the devitalised marriage in that it did not begin with any vitality. It was always amiable and functional, creating a placid home life with a minimum of inconvenience or personal involvement for people whose primary interests were elsewhere. These

Utilitarian marriages accounted for three-quarters of the sample. The Intrinsic marriage consisted of two types: the 'vital', where the most significant characteristic was the exciting mutuality of feeling. Frigidity, impotence, menstrual problems and the like were rare among these couples, who were usually earnestly and fiercely monogamous. The 'total' marriage was one in which the mutual sharing of a vital marriage extended into practically every area of life — leisure, home, career problems, day-by-day accomplishments and almost all thoughts and moods.

The Intrinsic marriages, though more clearly approximating to the Hollywood romantic ideal, were in fact more unstable than the Utilitarian.

Other investigators have arrived at different typologies; for example, Ryder (1970) enumerated 21 types of marriage. The important point here is that there will be numerous forms of integration, and even one marriage can move from negotiation to integration to renegotiation to another form of integration, and so on.

As a marriage develops, if it lasts, there does seem to be a general pattern which traces the transition from one stage of marriage to another. Rollins and Feldman (1970) have defined these stages according to presence of children (Fig. 8.4). This leads us to a discussion of the transition from spouse to parent.

THE TRANSITION FROM SPOUSE TO PARENT

Alice Rossi (1968), in comparing parental roles with those of marriage and work, argues that the parent role is much the more demanding of the three in our nuclear family dominated society. Marriage and work often involve a long period of preparation, with a gradual transition. The transition to parenthood, however, occurs dramatically and totally. The new parent starts out immediately on 24 hours a day duty with full responsibility. Also, in contrast to other commitments, parenthood is irrevocable. Rossi points out that we can have ex-spouses and ex-jobs, but not ex-children.

As with entry into marriage, the experience of parenthood is usually different for women, who in our society are still predominantly the ones primarily responsible for childrearing.

Fig. 8.4: The effect of children on the marriage of parents

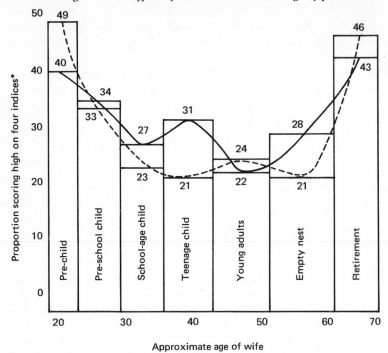

Key: solid line — husband's marriage
         dotted line — wife's marriage

* General marital satisfaction; positive companionship; satisfaction with present
  stage in the life cycle; and absence of negative feeling.

Stage 1. Pre-child

All research studies show that this is the time that most couples recall
as being the happiest of their lives. Feldman (1965) found marital
communication at its high point during the early years.

The first few years of marriage are a honeymoon period which
continues the romance of courtship. With the birth of the first baby,
satisfaction with the standard of living and companionship decline.
In subsequent years, love and understanding lag. These trends do not
involve all couples (90% in this study) but affect a very large

proportion of the total. In the first two years of marriage, 52 per cent of the wives were very satisfied ... and none notably dissatisfied. Twenty years later only 6 per cent are still satisfied, while 21 per cent are conspicuously dissatisfied (Blood & Wolfe, 1960).

At this stage there will be increasing discussion over whether, and then when to have children. Most couples assume that this will mean, at least temporarily, the cessation of the wife's career. Often there is mounting pressure from relatives and friends on a young couple to begin a family, as children are still considered to be a normal transition step in a marriage in our society (as witnessed by the hostility shown to couples who publicly affirm their intentions not to have children — see Peck, 1971).

Stage 2. The pre-school child

Although all researches show a drop in marital satisfaction following the birth of the first child, Lopata (1971) reports a social class difference. In lower socio-economic groups, where the spouses have relatively more segregated lives, she found that children often added a new dimension to the relationship, bringing them closer together. But the opposite was found for college-educated couples.

It is not necessary to invoke esoteric psychiatric mechanisms to interpret the strains introduced by a first child at any age. The sheer fatigue factor, including sleeplessness, would be enough to account for much of it (Bernard, 1972).

Beverley Jones describes the 'tired mother syndrome':

In its severest form it is, or resembles, a psychosis. They complain of being utterly exhausted, irritable, unable to concentrate. They may wander about somewhat aimlessly, they may have physical pains. They are depressed, anxious, sometimes paranoid, and they cry a lot.

Sexual life often suffers, temporarily, and unfortunately the new patterns sometimes persist, so that many couples report a poorer sex life following children. Social activities are curtailed. Hobbs (1968) reports that the stress of the first child is greater for the husband than for the wife, and he commonly feels rejected, left out, and becomes a target for his wife's depression and hostility.

Stage 3. The school-age child

School-age children from 6 to 14 seem to have a particularly distressing effect on marriage, especially for wives. Positive companionship is reported at its lowest level, as is satisfaction with the children. The wife is swamped by demands from all sides, and the husband is probably devoting most of his energies to his career. Some wives too, at about 35, are beginning to achieve some autonomy, overcoming feelings of dependency and inadequacy. The restrictions on personal and career growth imposed by children become very clear. This is the age of the 'drop-out wife', an increasingly common phenomenon on the American scene. The president of a large firm that traces missing persons cited the following statistics from his company: in the early 1960s the number of husbands who ran away compared with the number of wives was about 300 : 1; by the late 1960s it was 100 : 1; in 1972 it was 2 : 1; in 1973 it was equal. He drew a picture of the typical current runaway wife. She's 34 years old, married at 19, first child within a year of marriage, second child eighteen months later. She's intelligent, caring and anxious to elevate herself occupationally.

Stage 4. The teenage child

The situation improves little when the children become teenagers. General marital satisfaction remains low for both husbands and wives; again, the wife's marriage suffers, and she does not find this stage of her marriage very satisfying. Being the father of a teenager is especially difficult ... Fathers and teenage sons are in almost perpetual hassles ... Parent–child difficulties exacerbate any irritations in the husband and wife relationship. It is at the teenage stage that children are more likely to become delinquents, to have troubles in school ... for the first time, the product of the parental input has public exposure, revealing parents' own shortcomings or failures ... Each parent may blame the other.

Bernard's (1972) summary of this explosive stage in a marriage and parenthood makes one wonder how anyone survives. But the majority of marriages do survive and pass into the next stage.

Stage 5. The child as a young adult

This stage has the rewards of adult companionship with one's children, which by no means every family creates, plus the problems of two adult generations trying to live amicably together in the same household. This stage typically coincides with menopause for the wife, and what some psychiatrists have designated the psychological menopause for the husband. This is 'last chance' time. The last chance to make good, to live those dreams, to become excited and exciting, to throw off old harnesses, mortgages are paid up, children are no longer a financial liability.

Stage 6. The empty nest

This is a brand new phenomenon in our history. Most people did not live long enough in the past to reach it, and anyway were probably part of an extended kinship structure. But now, a couple have up to twenty years of marriage left, with the opportunity of encountering one another and living alone again. Small wonder that one-third of all divorces happen after fifteen years of marriage. But any crisis period presents opportunities as well as dangers, and increasingly it looks as if more people are making new starts, individually and together (see chapter 2). This stage begins to register an increase in satisfaction (see Fig. 8.4). Those who are still married are ready to enter the final stage as defined by their parental roles.

Stage 7. Retirement

Parents become grandparents, a privileged role, in which young children can be indulged, played with, enjoyed, without the responsibilities of parenthood setting limits on the relationship, without the physical and psychological tasks of parenthood to physically tire and emotionally exasperate.

This cycle is, of course, too neat. Only two out of three American marriages pass through all of these stages. The other third dissolve at some point, although three-quarters of men and two-thirds of women remarry. However, as three-fifths of the divorced men and two-thirds of the divorced women who remarry do so within five years of their divorces, we might assume that the overall pattern may not be too dissimilar to that described here. The personnel may change at some point in the cycle, and the clock may be put back a stage or two, but one way and another, most of us will pass through these stages.

DIVORCE

If most people in the U.S.A. and the U.K. experience marriage, an increasing proportion of them are also experiencing divorce: 1 in 3 American and 1 in 8 British marriages end in divorce; 1 out of every 9 adult Americans has been through a divorce. The transition into marriage, though certainly a major identity shift, does not necessarily lead to pain. Divorce, on the other hand, almost always does. As with all other transitional experiences, one would expect there to be some discernible stages in the process of ending a marriage. To illustrate this we reproduce some poetry written by someone who recorded her psychological progress through her marital break-up. We reproduce this as there appears to be general agreement on the psychological stages pertaining to divorce, bearing in mind that for some people it is a blessed relief, to others a devastating shock, but to all it means a change of social status, sometimes the acquisition of a social stigma, almost certainly a radical change in life style. As with marriage, the process of divorce usually begins long before the granting of a decree, and continues for long afterwards.

The divorce sequence

"In a recent medical magazine, I found an article quite relevant to my life right now. It was entitled, 'Divorce — Help Your Patient Adjust'. It indicated that, according to studies, four psychological stages of reaction to divorce occurred in a particular sequence. While reading a description of each stage, I realized that, not only had I progressed through each stage, but had written poetry at each one. The sequence is as follows:

1. Denial — '. . . refusal to face reality . . . usually a transient phenomenon . . . .'

    What was once-upon-a-time
    A thick, strong — yet tenderly-woven — cord
    Whose length could accommodate any distance
    Now seems such a thin and fragile thread.
    How painful it is to see it there,
    To feel its delicacy, to ponder its duration,
    And to examine the forces that reduced its size and strength.

What of this frail thread that refuses to be ignored?
If other slender threads are slowly, painstakingly, woven
Onto this one — one by one —
Will it lengthen, strengthen, thicken?
Or will a mere approach
Or an ever-so-careful touch
Cause a final asunder?

At this end — now —
Carefully selected threads are yearning to reweave.
But reluctantly . . . .
Will they be rejected as incompatible, as foreign, as . . . ?
Can this end support the weight
Unless weaving is balanced at the other?
Is the risk of destruction too agonising?
Or the consequence of that risk
Perhaps entirely worth discovery? (January)

2. Depression — '. . . as denial begins to disappear, depression sets in.
This phase is apt to last for weeks or months. The patient lacks energy
and drive . . . .'

I can't rest.
I must constantly watch the light of that lamp.
The light glimmers and my hopes soar; it nears extinction and I
    despair.
The flame began wavering — stubbornly, uncooperatively — some
    time ago
And I have since felt cold, burdened, insecure.
How painful it is to realize what the light is to me —
My warmth, my intimacy, my happiness, my life —
And how close it is to dying.
Oh, God, did it go out? Eyes, don't deceive me!
No! No, there's a flicker! Oh, blessed faint flicker!
Quick, find some more oil!

Could I find other sources of warmth,
Perhaps from another lamp whose flame would burn spontaneously
Or must I always toil, dig, search, for even this meagre warmth?
Is it sufficient — this warmth,
This scant protection from the cold, cruel winds that my lamp now
    gives?

Or, with rest from the search
And with other blankets in which to wrap myself,
Would I be just as comfortable — or no more uncomfortable?

If the light goes out in spite of my efforts,
The light goes out.
Then my hypothetical questions become authentic ones
And will necessarily be answered for me.
I'm so frightened . . . so tired.
I search.   (March)

3. Resignation — '. . . the patient is not particularly happy or optimistic but has reconciled himself to the breakup and usually feels and acts rather drained . . . .'

I don't know where it came from.
I just found it among my possessions.
It was a coat — a coat of hope —
Woven apparently from the toughest and warmest of fibres.
I wore it through the worst winter of my life
When bitter storms filled each bleak day
And howling winds disrupted attempts to sleep at night.
Occasionally I noticed additional tatters on the surface
But the inner lining remained steadfast.
'It will last through this winter,' I concluded.

But no — another storm was yet to come.
It blew in unseasonably late
And raged on for four frigid days,
Ripping my coat finally into a thousand shreds.

The coldness of realization began penetrating my body.
I shivered. I ached. I wept.
It seemed too much to bear.
'I'll surely freeze,' I thought, looking pleadingly towards heaven.
But the sky's appearance suggested the wintry blasts had ended
And more seasonable days were on the way.

Even so, my body is still numb from the cold.
It needs new clothes; spring clothes perhaps.
I'll begin looking as soon as I can move.   (May 22)

4. Acceptance — '. . . psychic energy returns, new acquaintances sought out . . . .'

The statue stood — tall, erect, perfect, strong.
I cherished above all other possessions
This unmerited prize that Fate had granted me.
I polished it faithfully —
Realizing that, even without my efforts,
It would remain just as lustrous
. . . equally as captivating.

Others applied polish too,
Polish of a different quality
That seemed to penetrate the surface
And generate a radiance impossible with mine.
But I was undaunted.
Perseverance, I'd been promised,
Would eventually turn those unmoving eyes
Downward toward mine.
But alas . . . with each new polishing,
I seemed to shrink while the statue heightened.
When I could no longer reach the top
I loathed those who grew tall with it.

Finally I realized . . . .
Those fixed eyes would never reach into mine.

But their message reached my heart:
    'You ask of me . . . .
    An occasional acknowledgement
    A scant show of appreciation
    A meagre demonstration of affection.
    Absurd, impossible demands!'
Forlorn but resolute, I ceased polishing
And my statue was removed.

I still see it on occasion.
Have I grown or has it shrunk?
By looking straight into those eyes
I have made an astonishing discovery.
They could never see me,
Not because they were set straight ahead,
But because they were turned inward.   (October)"

The spectre of divorce haunts most modern marriages. After interviewing hundreds of couples, Lederer and Jackson (1968) learned that approximately 80 per cent had seriously considered divorce at one time or another, and that many of them still thought frequently about it.

Just as the transition to marriage or parenthood can provide an opportunity for personal growth or diminishment, so can divorce. The bookstores have been inundated in recent years with books like *Creative Divorce* (Mel Krantzler, 1973), *The Courage to Divorce* (Susan Gettleman & Janet Markowitz, 1974), and *Uncoupling: The Art of Coming Apart* (Norman Sheresky & Marya Mannes, 1972).

Mel Krantzler's book, alive with his own experience as well as his clients' accounts, describes accurately what he calls 'the promise in the pain':

The Pain

> Divorce is an emotional crisis triggered by a sudden and unexpected loss. The death of a relationship is the first stage in a process in which the death is recognised, and the relationship is mourned and then laid to rest to make way for self-renewal. Intellectually, a newly separated person may deny being in crisis, but it is there to see in everything he or she does. Suddenly normal ways of coping do not seem to work. Overnight the world has changed into a frightening question mark, and everyday life is out of control.

The Promise

> ... [it is] more than just a time for picking up the pieces, divorce is a new opportunity to improve on the past ... *if* you can come to terms with the past, recognise self-defeating behaviour, and be willing to change it.

Marriage, parenthood, divorce, are all potential vehicles for personal growth — like all other transitions, large or small. To understand more about the variety of human experience under each of these labels is to provide people with the opportunity for greater control over their own lives. And a person's marital history, alongside their work histories, takes up most of the variance of living.

9. Death: A Major Life Crisis

John Hayes

Death is a major life crisis because it affects the living: the person approaching death, the person close to someone who is dying and the person who is trying to adjust to life after the death of a loved one. This chapter will examine death from all these points of view.

At some moment in time we all have to pass between the status of living and dead. While death might be inevitable it involves many uncertainties and has a temporally unpredictable character. Glaser and Strauss (1965) refer to dying as a non-scheduled status passage in which it can be difficult to determine when the next transition will occur, where it will take the person in passage and how that person should act and be treated by others at various points in the passage. A scheduled and therefore predictable status passage is likely to create fewer problems of coordination because all involved parties are likely to share a common timetable, and regulate expectations and behaviour accordingly. With dying, however, even though it is possible to map the typical progress of a disease, there can be many transitional sequences in which different patterns of transitional status and different rates of movement between them manifest themselves. Glaser and Strauss refer to a 'lingering' pattern in which a person stays in the 'certain to die but unknown when' status beyond the anticipated temporal limit. There is also the 'short-term reprieve' sequence in which a person seems 'certain to die at a known time' but temporarily reverts back to a 'certain to die but unknown when' status.

For some, death is too terrible to contemplate. For most, it involves a transition from a state of relative security to the insecurity and uncertainty of the unknown. Even those not completely satisfied with life come to know which of their needs and wants can be satisfied and in what ways this satisfaction can be achieved. Life, therefore, provides them with at least some minimum degree of certainty and satisfaction. Only a very small minority actually desire death. Most of those who are unhappy or find life an awful burden seem to prefer the situation and

139

status they know to one completely unknown. Death is irreversible, and when faced with the prospect of this ultimate loss even the most deprived seem to find life preferable.

DEATH AND EGO DEFENCES

The Second World War produced evidence that people in very stressful situations could be pushed beyond their ability to comprehend and manage their predicament. Swank and Marchand (1946) found that some allied troops involved in the Normandy landings reacted with dull, listless and apathetic behaviour. Not the behaviour one would expect from people whose lives were at risk. Numerous studies report that in certain situations the individual can be overwhelmed by massive change and respond by blotting out or denying the reality of the situation.

Many observers have noted that avoidance appears to be a common response to death. It is as though there is a limit to the amount of anxiety a person can tolerate, beyond which he tends to withdraw, psychologically, from the anxiety-producing situation. There is evidence, however, that such 'avoidance' does not necessarily constitute a basic strategy for dealing with the problem but may form part of a broader strategy of attack. In other words, various defence mechanisms can form an integral part of an 'approach' strategy when the change involved is of a potentially overwhelming magnitude.

Parkes (1972) suggests that because repression and other defence processes play a large part in neurotic illness and because psychoanalysis was developed as a means of helping the patient abandon his defences, a somewhat negative view of defences prevails today. There is a tendency to classify defence as a maladaptive response and to underestimate its potential contribution to healthy adjustment. Defences can be employed to regulate the quantity of disabling information an individual can handle at any one time. In those major life changes where almost every facet of a person's identity needs to be reappraised, the task can be tackled bit by bit, so preserving the individual from sudden and total disorganisation. He lowers his defences and deals with as much of the problem as he can handle at any one time. He then withdraws behind his defences until he is able to cope with a little more reality. Avoidance or defensive behaviour is often observed as an inhibitory tendency, which 'by repression, avoidance, postponement, etc., holds back or limits the perception of disturbing stimuli'. This occurs alongside approach or attack behaviour, which is seen as 'a facilitative or reality testing tendency which enhances perception and thought about disturbing stimuli'. Parkes (1972) describes how, for example, intense pining (an approach response) can alternate with conscious or unconscious avoidance of pining (an avoidance response).

GRIEF EXPERIENCED BY THE DYING

Grief is the emotional response to loss. Bowlby (1961) describes it as a peculiar amalgamation of anxiety, anger and despair following the experience of what is feared to be an irretrievable loss. The symptoms of grief, shock, denial, irritability, restlessness, anger, depression, loss of appetite, anxiety, tension and guilt are not only experienced by those bereft. The dying person also experiences grief. She is reluctant to give up life because in doing so she loses spouse and children, her roles in the working world, the places she knows so well and the things she enjoys doing. Her loss is complete, and because it seems inevitable she experiences grief in advance.

Elisabeth Kübler-Ross (1969) has made an important contribution to our understanding of the grief process experienced by the dying patient. Through her seminars and continuing contact with the terminally ill at the University of Chicago Billings Hospital she was able to observe the emotional reactions of patients as they approached death.

She found that people knew they were dying. Even those who had not been told explicitly knew it anyway from the implicit messages or altered behaviour of relatives and staff. John Hinton (1967) also found that, regardless of what they had been told, the majority of terminal patients knew they were going to die at some time before the end came.

How patients cope with this knowledge and come to terms with the inevitability of death is described by Kübler-Ross (see Fig. 1.3, p. 14) as follows:

Denial
All patients reacted to the news that they were dying with shock and disbelief. This denial reaction functioned as a buffer after the shocking news, allowing the patient to collect himself, and, eventually, to

mobilise other less radical defences. Of the 200 terminally ill patients interviewed only three attempted to deny the approach of death to the very last. For the majority, denial was replaced by partial acceptance.

Anger

When denial could no longer be maintained it was replaced by feelings of anger, rage, envy and resentment. The 'No, it cannot be me' response was replaced by the question 'Why me?'. This stage is very difficult for others to cope with because anger is displaced in all directions. Particular difficulties were created when people took personally anger that originally had nothing to do with them. When these others, medical staff and family, were able to tolerate this anger the patient was greatly helped to cope with his grief.

Bargaining

Kübler-Ross describes bargaining as the third phase of coping. It appears to be a form of defence reaction that gave hope to patients for brief periods. Most bargains were made with God and were usually kept secret or disclosed only to the chaplain. Others were made with the medical staff. Bargaining was an attempt to postpone pain and death. It offered a prize for good behaviour, set a self-imposed deadline, and included an implicit promise that the patient would not ask for more if this postponement were granted. Fulfilling this promise was difficult because it demanded acceptance and the abandonment of hope. Kübler-Ross describes a patient whose son was about to be married. She made all sorts of promises if she could only live long enough to attend the wedding. On her return, tired and exhausted, her first words were 'don't forget I have another son'.

Although not explicitly mentioned by Kübler-Ross, this phase may also be associated with the patient's tendency to make sense of his predicament. Schoenberg and Senescu (1970) reported that the patients viewed their disease as a punishment visited upon them for past sins, although usually they could not identify what they had done that was so bad.

Depression

When the patient could no longer deny the terminal nature of his illness because of prolonged hospitalisation, further surgery or visible deterioration in his physical condition, his numbness, anger and stoicism were replaced by a sense of great loss and a feeling of depression. This depression appeared to take two forms. The first was reactive depression. This refers to the depression a patient experiences as a result of past loss. He may have lost various capacities and functions, which meant that he could no longer partake in certain pleasurable activities, fulfill the requirements of his job, or function as an effective member of the family. His wife may have had to assume the role of breadwinner, or, if the terminally ill patient were a woman, she may have had to observe her husband's attempts to manage the children while maintaining his job and visiting her regularly in hospital. The second kind of depression was preparatory depression. This did not occur as a result of past loss but reflected the patient's preparation for impending loss. It was an important step on the path towards acceptance — a silent phase during which the patient experienced much sorrow in anticipation of losing everything and everybody he loved.

Acceptance
This was not a happy period but one void of feeling. The patient was not depressed, afraid or angry about his fate. He had expressed his previous feelings of envy and anger and had mourned the impending loss of all that was important to him. He was, therefore, able to contemplate his death with a certain degree of quiet expectation. He was peaceful.

THE ANTICIPATORY GRIEF OF OTHERS

Dying involves a withdrawal from the ongoing life of social groups and produces numerous changes in the role status and interaction patterns of surviving members. In the family, death of the husband involves the status passage from wife to widow for the spouse, and from two-parent to one-parent child for the offspring. When the family are told that a patient is certain to die, even though it may not be possible to predict the time of death with any accuracy, they are provided with a period of anticipation in which members are able to carry out some grief work in advance of the loss.

Fulton and Fulton (1972) suggest that over an extended period of time the family may (i) experience depression, (ii) feel a heightened concern for the ill member, (iii) rehearse his death, and (iv) attempt to adjust to the various consequences of it. There is, however, some confusion as to the effects of this anticipatory grief. Fulton and Fulton argue that by the time death occurs the family will, to the extent that they have anticipated the death or dissipated their grief, display little or no emotion. This view, however, does not seem to receive universal support and research evidence fails to demonstrate any clear link between intensity and duration of anticipatory grief and the intensity and duration of conventional grief.

Aldrich (1974) argues that such contradictory findings as those reported by Parkes (1970, 1972), Clayton *et al.* (1968) and Maddison *et al.* (1968) may be explained by the existence of opposing factors, of which some operate to increase and others to decrease the intensity of conventional, post-loss grief. The intensity of conventional grief may be increased because the period of anticipation not only allows others to come to terms with death, but also gives the hostile component of ambivalence a heightened destructive potential. For example, if the dying patient lingers, the anticipatory mourner may increase his guilt by committing what he later sees as the unforgivable sin of expressing a death wish.

While the effects of anticipatory grief may be uncertain, it is without doubt an important phenomenon. Those experiencing it may be involved in a major transition, the like of which they have never experienced before. This transition involves the abandonment of a familiar and relatively secure past and the prospect of an uncertain and potentially threatening future. It is not surprising, therefore, that the news that a loved one is dying is difficult to come to terms with.

CONVENTIONAL GRIEF

The strict ritual of mourning is being eroded in our society and there appears to be less support for the bereaved and an expectation that they should maintain a stoic and controlled posture in the outside world. We must not, however, be misled into underestimating the possible undesirable consequences an individual may experience after losing a loved one.

Death is a major life change for all involved. This fact is demonstrated by the Social Readjustment Rating Scale, developed by Holmes and Rahe (1967), which attributes mean values to the degree of adjustment required after a series of life events. The scale was originally constructed by telling 394 subjects that marriage had been given an arbitrary value of 50 and asking them to attribute a score to 42 other life events indicating whether each event would require more or less adjustment than marriage. The mean values attributed to the 43 events ranged from 100 for death of a spouse to 11 for a minor infringement of the law. Fig. 9.1 illustrates how mean values were distributed over 8 of the 43 life events included in the Social Readjustment Rating Scale, and underscores the relatively high level of social readjustment required by the death of a spouse or other close family member.

Subsequent studies have demonstrated remarkable consensus in the importance people attribute to life events in widely different cultures. It would seem, therefore, that death is experienced as a major life change by all those immediately involved.

Death rarely occurs as an isolated life change but is usually accompanied by a whole series of associated life changes. For example, the widow might be forced to go out to work, move house, develop new circles of friends and in many other ways reorganise the pattern of her life. Thus death frequently precipitates a major life-change sequence.

There exists a large body of literature documenting the association between life changes and subsequent illness (see chapter 2, p. 38) that supports the observation by Holmes and Masuda (1973) that the magnitude of life change is highly significantly related to the time of onset of disease. There is also evidence that there exists a strong positive correlation between the magnitude of life change and the seriousness of the illness experienced.

It should come as no surprise, therefore, to discover a statistical relationship between bereavement and illness, and even bereavement

Fig. 9.1: Selected life events from the Social Readjustment Rating Scale

Rank	Life Event	Mean Value
1	Death of Spouse	100
2	Divorce	73
5	Death of close family member	63
7	Marriage	50
8	Dismissal from Work	47
10	Retirement	45
23	Son or daughter leaving home	29

and an increase in the death rate among survivors. Young, Benjamin and Wallis (1963), writing in the *Lancet*, found an increase of almost 40 per cent in the death rate of widowers during the first six months of bereavement. Parkes (1972) reports a study in which he established a link between bereavement and mental illness. He compared the number of spouse bereavements that had actually occurred in a psychiatric population with the number that could have been expected to occur by chance association (based on data from the Registrar General's mortality tables for England and Wales). He found considerably more spouse-bereaved patients than would have been expected by chance alone (significant at the 0.001 level). This finding supports earlier work by Stein and Susser (1969) which showed an abnormally large proportion of widows and widowers among people coming into psychiatric care for the first time. There is, therefore, strong evidence that bereavement and associated life changes can cause a breakdown in the healthy functioning of the human organism.

Fortunately, major breakdowns of this kind are not typical. Colin Murray Parkes, at the Tavistock Institute, London, has conducted a thorough and enlightening study into the way twenty-two widows under the age of 65 coped with the stress of bereavement (Parkes, 1970). He interviewed each widow five times over a twelve-month period; after the first month and again after the third, sixth and ninth months. The final interview was conducted after the thirteenth rather than the twelfth month in order to avoid the 'anniversary' reaction. Like Kübler-Ross, Parkes found that the majority of subjects seemed grateful for the opportunity to talk freely about the disturbing problems and feelings that preoccupied them. These interviews enabled him to collect some extremely rich data relating to the sequential progress of grief. The phases of grief he describes are, in many ways, similar to those experienced by the dying patient, as reported by Kübler-Ross.

Numbness

Although sometimes preceded by an expression of great distress, the most frequent reaction to the announcement of death was a state of numbness. This was reported by ten of the twenty-two widows interviewed and lasted for 1 to 7 days in five cases and for more than two months in two cases. One widow described how this period was a blessing because it helped her cope with the children and arrange the funeral. There was evidence, however, that the longer and more complete was this period in which all feelings were inhibited then the more severe were the feelings when they finally emerged. Seven widows who expressed little or no effect in the first week displayed a steady increase in effect so that by the third month they all showed evidence of being moderately or severely disturbed. On the other hand, a group of nine widows who were severely disturbed in the first week showed considerably less effect later. In fact, only three of the nine showed more than mild emotional disturbance by the third month.

There was considerable variation in the precise nature of the immediate reaction, but brief periods of intense feelings were not uncommon. Episodes of panic or distress tended to punctuate the periods of numbness. Even though this numbness was usually short lived, some form of denial of the full reality of what happened tended to persist. Parkes reported that a year later thirteen widows still said that there were times when they had difficulty in believing their husbands dead.

Yearning and protest

The phase of numbness gave way to a period in which the bereaved experienced pangs of intense pining for the dead person. These pangs of grief were an expression of severe anxiety produced by the separation from a loved one. They gave rise to a strong urge to recover the dead person, and even those who recognised the futility of this behaviour still experienced a strong urge to search.

It was during this phase that the interplay between approach and avoidance strategies could be observed. The desire to search occurred alongside a tendency to deny, inhibit or avoid such behaviour. Parkes identified four components of search behaviour.

(i) *Pining and a preoccupation with thoughts of the deceased person.* These thoughts tended to be painful because they were associated with a persistent wish for the person who was gone. The widows tended to go over in their minds events of the past in which their husbands had taken part, and experienced extremely clear memories of the dead person, not only his face but also his voice and even his touch. Some also experienced haunting memories of the final illness or death.

(ii) *Direction of attention towards places and objects associated with the lost person.* Many of the widows described feelings of being drawn towards places that they associated with their dead spouse and most of them treasured possessions that had previously belonged to him.

However, some of the widows reported that old haunts and intimate articles could evoke such intense pining that they tended to avoid all such reminders. Gradually such objects and places tended to lose their hold as the widow accustomed herself to her loss.

(iii) *Perceptual set.* After reviewing a number of studies of searching behaviour in animals, Parkes (1972) observed that when seeking behaviour was evoked at high intensity, finding behaviour tended to occur even in the absence of the object sought. This phenomenon tended to manifest itself in his London study in cases where widows misinterpreted sounds around the house as their husband's presence, or when they momentarily misidentified people in the street. Ten widows reported that they thought they heard or saw their husbands sometime during the first month, and sixteen reported some sense of presence during that same period. Twelve of the widows still experienced some sense of presence a year later.

(iv) *Calling for the lost person.* When infants are separated from their parents they cry and call out for the lost object. This behaviour is an important part of searching and increases the likelihood of finding the lost parent. A similar tendency could be observed in the searching behaviour of the bereaved. They called out for the dead person or burst into tears.

In addition to Yearning this phase is also characterised by Protest. The widows in the London study exhibited anger, irritability, restlessness and tension. Thirteen of the twenty-two widows expressed general irritability and bitterness, which was often associated with feelings that the world had become an insecure and dangerous place. Sometimes this anger was directed at a specific person. Four widows directed their anger at the dead spouse, blaming him in some way for leaving them, but most anger was directed at the living: other members of the family, the clergy, the doctor and even local government officials.

Some guilt was also evident and many widows reported going over the events of the death in order to seek some reassurance that they had done all that could be done. Parkes reported that several widows felt they had failed their husbands in some way during the terminal phase of their illness, 'I seemed to go away from him', and seven expressed self-reproachful ideas centered on some act or omission that might have harmed the dying spouse or impaired his peace of mind.

This phase of yearning and protest tended to pass its peak after the fourth week, although many of its components were still evident for many months. Bowlby (1961) suggests that the painfulness of mourning may be accounted for by 'the long persistence of yearning for the lost object and the constant repetition of bitter disappointment on not finding it'.

Disorganisation

As these disappointments mounted the bereaved gradually faced the reality that reunion was impossible; consequently it declined as the object of behaviour. Parkes describes his widows as aimless and apathetic and commented on their disinclination to look to the future or see any purpose in life. He reported that two-thirds of the widows in the London study were still disinclined to look ahead at the end of the first year.

This slide into aimlessness might be compared to the culmination of Lewin's (1947a) unfreezing phase. The widow's failure to find the object of her search finally produced a disconfirmation of her old identity. This was a painful process but it was an indispensable preliminary to successful readjustment. Bowlby makes this point by suggesting that just as a child playing with meccano must destroy his construction before he can use the pieces again, so must an individual, when he is bereaved, accept the destruction of a part of his personality before he can organise it afresh towards a new object or goal.

Gaining a new identity

Parkes (1972) argues that where someone had relied on another person to act in many ways as an extension to himself then the loss of that person could be expected to have the same effect upon his view of the world and his view of himself as if he had lost a part of himself. In other words, the loss of a loved one on whom he had depended was accompanied by a loss of part of the self. There is, therefore, a need to rebuild a complete identity and re-establish a purpose in life.

Especially in the early stages of grief the bereaved tended to be preoccupied with the business of searching for the lost one and little energy was left for other interests. The newly bereaved often showed little concern for food, sleep, personal appearance, work or the family. Establishing a new identity began when an awareness of an interest in the outside world re-emerged.

Re-establishing oneself in the outside world involves exploring the implications of the new status of widowhood, seeking out an acceptable place in the social hierarchy, finding out how one is viewed by the rest of the world and assessing one's ability to define and solve problems. In the early stages of bereavement the first response when faced with a new problem tended to be 'What would my husband have done about this', but, as Parkes pointed out, the answer to this question was not always apparent and the use of the remembered husband as the ever present referee tended to diminish with time. It appeared that as old assumptions about how to relate to the life space were proved ineffective and as a fresh set of assumptions was developed, so the old identity dissolved and was replaced by a new and different one. The London widows reported that new friends and new workmates provided useful role models, and several of them remarked how they had been helped by talking with other widows with whom it was easy for them to identify.

Parkes postulated that widows who had fully accepted bereavement and made a good adjustment would look back on the past with pleasure and to the future with optimism. He found, however, that only three widows in the London study satisfied both these criteria after thirteen months. Six of the widows still found the past too painful to think about, although nine were able to look back with some degree of pleasure. The future was viewed optimistically by five widows, pessimistically by a further five and the rest preferred not to think about it.

If we accept Parkes' definition of readjustment, together with an assumption that grief work will continue until readjustment has been achieved, then it would appear that for most people grief work tends to extend over a considerable period of time.

COORDINATION THROUGH THE PASSAGE FROM LIFE TO DEATH

Dying has often been described as a lonely process, but, as we have seen, it is a process that affects a number of people simultaneously. Rarely does a person with a terminal illness reach death without knowing that he is about to die. Similarly, few close survivors are taken completely by surprise. Towards the end all involved usually know that one of their number is dying. It often happens, however, that each makes the assumption that the others involved do not know and that even if they did they probably would not want or be able to talk about it. It also happens that the various parties often become aware of impending death at different moments in time and in different ways.

There are, therefore, a number of issues about the sharing and coordination of knowledge about death that deserve discussion. For example, what are the implications of knowing that one, or somebody close, is dying, and what are the rights of the various parties involved to this knowledge?

Glaser and Strauss (1965) argue that an essential element in shepherding the patient through the dying status passage is coordination of the definitions of the passage held by the parties involved. The doctor is a potentially central figure in this process, especially so when the patient is hospitalised. At the point in time when the doctor diagnoses a terminal illness he is the only person who knows, with any degree of certainty, that the patient is going to die. He must decide how much of this information to give to which parties and when this information should be disclosed. Other members of the medical team are usually informed immediately because in this area coordination of knowledge is imperative if consistent treatment is to be maintained. The doctor's need to coordinate his and the dying patient's family's perceptions of the patient's status is more ambiguous. It could be argued that the sharing of information could avert a situation in which the patient's spouse might inappropriately assume that death was imminent. Communication to the patient of this premature conclusion could cause him to lose hope and give up the fight to live even when the doctor was confident that indefinite remission was a possibility. It could also be argued that the unexpected death of a patient could endanger the health and even the life of the survivors or could provoke angry attempts from them to press charges of negligent medical attention. Whatever the cause, custom and practice would seem to indicate that the medical profession and hospital authorities take great care to keep the patient's family fully aware of his dying status through the issue of formal bulletins and 'sick notes' allowing round the clock visiting.

This coordination of views and sharing of information within the medical team and between the doctor and the patient's family does not appear to extend to the patient himself. What evidence there is seems to indicate that the doctor rarely tells a patient that he is going to die. The reasons for this are rather unclear, but could be associated with (a) a fear that the news might make it more difficult to manage the patient — he may refuse to accept the diagnosis and resist the proposed treatment offered by the doctor or even cease treatment altogether and go elsewhere in search of another more acceptable prognosis; (b) a fear of difficult, emotionally charged, interpersonal situations — breaking the news of a fatal diagnosis is something many doctors might prefer to avoid; (c) a belief that knowledge of a fatal diagnosis is likely to be depressing and a desire to withhold this painful news and not to disturb unduly the patient's peace of mind. An additional complicating factor might be (d) the trend towards hospitalisation of the sick and dying so that the attending physician, at this important status passage, is unlikely to be the family doctor with intimate knowledge of the patient and a well-established rapport. Consequently, the doctor rarely tells the patient that his illness is fatal but abdicates this responsibility to the family, if and when they feel the patient should be told.

Often there is little deliberate coordination of definitions of the dying status held by the patient and his family. The family frequently demonstrate a reluctance to share their knowledge with the patient because (a) they themselves find the news difficult to cope with, tend to deny it and hang on to unrealistic hopes for recovery; (b) they desire to protect the patient; (c) they fear that they will not be able to face the patient with the news or manage the emotional consequences. As a result they may try to mislead the patient and maintain an optimistic and encouraging posture. This can be difficult, particularly between close relatives who are used to sharing their hopes and fears. The patient, aided by observations of unnatural behaviour, stilted conversation or altered time frames may see through this ruse and conclude that others are trying to deceive him.

The doctor and immediate family are not the only ones confronted with the dilemma about whether or not to share information with those faced with impending loss. The patient may also hesitate to share his knowledge with loved ones. He may have been told by one of the hospital staff, by a visitor or may have 'discovered' his prognosis indirectly through observation and inference. Given this knowledge he might want to deny the truth and avoid thinking or talking about it, he may want to protect his family, particularly his spouse, and he may feel inadequate to deal with the emotional consequences of disclosure.

It is interesting to note, however, that both Kübler-Ross and Parkes found that the patient and those close to him or her frequently welcomed the opportunity to discuss their grief, and, on a more practical level, discuss the various loose ends they wanted to tie up and the formal arrangements they needed to make. Kübler-Ross also observed that such discussions were welcomed not only with neutral outsiders; she reported cases where she was able to facilitate communications between patient and spouse and help them coordinate their status definitions. For example, Mrs W. (Kübler-Ross, 1969, pp. 115—19) said that the only reason for staying alive was her husband's unwillingness to accept her death. He wanted to prolong her life at any cost. They both perceived her status differently. Once they began to share and discuss their perceptions the husband realised that his wife had reached a point where she was ready to accept her death and wanted to detach herself slowly from all the meaningful relationships in her life. She needed him to let go, to help her to die. In this example coordination helped both the patient and the spouse to face death.

Even where such coordination would be unwelcome or too painful, there may still be a case for somebody, probably the medical adviser, to inform the patient, so giving him time to set his affairs in order, giving him the opportunity to prepare for his passing and giving him continued reason for confidence in his medical advisers. This last point refers to the likelihood that he will find out that he is dying before the end. Coordination of status definition between the patient and doctor will tend to maintain the patient's confidence in him.

THE PHASIC NATURE OF THE PROCESS OF GRIEF

A number of similarities can be observed in the phasic progress of grief described by Kübler-Ross and Parkes.

(1) The departure from the initial stable status of living and entry to the transitional status of dying or being deprived of spouse is marked by a phase of denial.

(2) Partial acceptance of this status passage stimulates yearning for all that was good and valued of the initial status and attempts to regain that status. Parkes refers to searching behaviour and Kübler-Ross describes bargaining and hope. Both Parkes and Kübler-Ross observed anger and protest in this phase.

(3) A more complete acceptance of the inevitable loss of the initial status leads to an apathetic and depressed phase in which, after some floundering, the implications of the new status slowly begin to emerge.

(4) The process ends with adjustment to the new status. The dying reach a state of acceptance of the impending status of death and the survivors adjust to a different status of living (e.g. widowed).

The anticipatory grief experienced by the family and others close to the dying has not been thoroughly researched but there is no reason to believe that this process should follow a different sequence or display fundamentally different characteristics to the patterns of grief so far described. It is possible that anticipatory grief work could ease the burden of conventional grief but, as already mentioned, there is always the chance that it could complicate the process of conventional grieving. Anticipatory grief work, then, might best be seen as an important, integral, preparatory phase in the total process of grieving rather than a potential substitute for conventional grief.

No matter how long or successful is the process of grief, it is unlikely that the bereft will ever completely replace that which was lost; they will never find a substitute. As Freud (1929) wrote 'No matter what may fill the gap, even if it be filled completely, it nevertheless remains something else. And actually this is how it should be.'

PART THREE

The Management of Transitions: Preparation and Help

10. Self-Management

John Adams

So far in this book, the transition process has been described as a sequence of identifiable phases. It has been suggested that personal growth is inherently possible as an outgrowth of any significant transition (even negative ones) and some of the more common major transitions have been described in some detail. The stress response has also been reviewed and it has been shown how transitions create stress and strain. Chronic strain, it was pointed out in chapter 3, eventually leads to illness.

This chapter is the first of several that describe ways of seeking or capitalising upon the opportunity values of life's necessary transitions. However, if one's 'equipment', one's body-mind, is not kept in good working order, one may eventually fall prey to debilitating or fatal stress-related diseases and lose out on one's maximal opportunities. This chapter provides some insights into how to get one's equipment into top shape and/or how to keep it there. It is about habits, techniques and attitudes each of us can develop, which have been demonstrated to be effective in reducing the reactions to chronic strain, as described in chapter 3, such as hypertension, psychological frustration, anxiety, uncertainty, dissatisfaction and changes in skin resistance and temperature, cholesterol levels and heart rate. Whether or not changing these reactions actually maintains one's stability and prevents the onset of serious diseases is not yet established conclusively. I think, however, this linkage will be made in the not too distant future.

The Chinese word for 'crisis' consists of the merger of their words for 'danger' and 'opportunity'. I cannot emphasise too much that I see both in the experience of major transitions. There is growth *opportunity* and there is *danger* of strain leading to illness.

How does one equip oneself to take advantage of transition opportunities (through buffering oneself against strain, the impact of stress)? An absolute plethora of suggestions is presently available. Some of them are good; some, probably not. Among the most common suggestions are: exercise, rest, good nutrition, psychotherapy/ counselling, encounter groups, regular medical check-ups, talk to a friend/colleague, consciousness raising, balance work and leisure activities, reduce unpredictability in the environment, develop a commitment to your 'God', seek the support of others, avoid too many big changes at once, take frequent breaks and holidays, take megavitamins.

While I am generally in agreement with most of these, they don't immediately suggest a programme for taking care of ourselves. They do tell us a lot of things we already know but probably do not practise. It is my belief that an integrated approach to self-management and body management is needed. Further, there are probably many alternative ways to engage in such integrative approaches and each individual should be encouraged to develop one tailored to his or her particular situation and interests.

Basically, six different components need to be considered in an integrated approach to self-management and body management: (1) work setting; (2) support systems; (3) self-awareness; (4) exercise; (5) nutrition; (6) letting go. These reflect the potpourri of suggestions listed above. This chapter attempts to provide some order to them. The first component, work setting, is only briefly dealt with here since this was introduced at the conclusion of chapter 3. The bulk of this chapter is devoted to a review of some of the research findings related to the other components.

1. Work setting

It is now clear that much of the stress caused at work is due to organisational factors and norms such as ambiguity, chronic unaddressed conflict, too much or too little work to do, poor interpersonal relationships (see chapter 3), and boundary problems (see chapter 6). In this enlightened age, no one should tolerate working in settings where these conditions exist in great magnitude (they will always exist to some degree). Organisation development consultants have worked on such factors as these for over fifteen years without demonstrable effect in most instances. The primary reason for this is that most people in organisations are willing to tolerate these stress inducers rather than enter into the sometimes tough arena of confrontation and conflict resolution. This is partly because the symptoms of strain are not immediately apparent and partly because we are taught not to make waves. When people take responsibility for themselves and refuse to tolerate such conditions, both work and health will improve. Organisation development consultants and practitioners can then become the resources they are trained to be.

2. Support systems

It was pointed out in chapter 3 that Western society does not encourage us to develop networks of reasonably intimate or close friends. As a result, most people have few others they trust well enough to talk their problems over with in times of stress.

Charles Seashore, a consultant in Washington, D.C., works with his clients to help them become aware of and develop their support systems. He distinguishes between six different support systems that can help us satisfy different needs in a transitional situation (see Fig. 10.1).

> The composition of support systems ought to be looked at in terms of what kind of difficulty or problem situations you find yourself in at any given moment. I look at a support system as pulling together a small group of people from a large population to suit my needs at a particular time. My support system when I left Washington D.C. this morning is quite different than the support system I need to operate comfortably here in Chicago . . . .
>
> The function of the support system is to help you move from left to right when you are in difficulty on any of these dimensions [see Fig. 10.1]. If you are experiencing social isolation and you feel a need to be part of a larger group of people – where are the people like me? You want to look for people who share common concerns with you. On the other hand, you might be feeling very vulnerable and out of touch and you want to move towards a place where you can get assistance and in that sense you may want to look at people

Fig. 10.1: Support systems composition

What you feel	What you need	What you want to feel
Social isolation	Share concerns	Social integration
Vulnerability	Depend on in crisis	Assistance
Emotional isolation	Close friend	Intimacy
Powerlessness	Respect competence	Self-worth
Stimulus isolation	Challengers	Perspective
Environmental isolation	Referral agent	Access-resources

you can depend on in a crisis. For that function, new parents of a new child might want to look for a pediatrician as opposed to other parents who are having the same trouble with colic on that given night. If you are feeling not social isolation but emotional isolation, you know that there are lots of people like you but your primary feeling is one of aloneness and you are looking for some kind of intimate warm contact. You would be looking for people you can count on as close friends. You can depend on a person but never want to play golf with him. Close friends may be the most irrational people going but they are close and they are warm. You may be feeling a sense of powerlessness and wanting to get some additional feelings of self worth. One of the most frequently left out categories of people in support systems as I've analysed them, especially with people who are not employed, has to do with locating people who respect your competence. It's a kind of gratification that a craftsman gets from a returning customer. That reaffirmation of one's self worth can be an extremely important aspect of a support system. (Seashore, 1974).

He identified two other kinds of isolation: stimulus isolation and environmental isolation. If you put a person in a situation without any auditory or visual stimulation, within a short period of time (48—72 hours) he will begin hallucinating and experience extensive anxiety.

Some of you may experience that right on the job with a lot of noise around you. The opposite of that is to build into your support system, somebody who is bumping up against you, somebody who is pushing and abrasive to you. Abrasive in the sense that you get a perspective of how you might be different. It's generally asking you things you may not want to think about . . . . I call this the seeking of challengers. You will find that some people systematically leave out of their support system any notion of abrasion. Their notion of abrasion is a headon collision between a dripping can of mollasses and a razor sharp marshmallow, it doesn't have a whole lot of impact. And lastly, to the degree that you feel disconnected from what is available in the environment to you and you want to have access to other resources, what you are looking for is people who can be good referral agents. They don't have to know how to do it themselves. You will find that kind of person floating through a lot of organizations. They know exactly where to have something mimeographed. They know where the toilet paper is stored (ibid.).

In his work, Seashore finds that most people's support groups are too small and homogeneous to accomplish these shifts 'from left to right' effectively. He also finds that many people who do use support systems actively become overly dependent upon them, and even collude with them to maintain their problems. However, Seashore participated in many of the French *et al.* research studies, wherein the use of support systems (quality of relationships) was found to reduce strain (see, for example, French & Caplan, 1972).

3. Increasing self-awareness

A basic pre-requisite for self-management is the drive to learn more about oneself. This self-awareness is not something that is accomplished once and for all. The process can be begun, for example, in attending an encounter group, EST group, therapy group, consciousness raising group, or in an honest discussion of feelings, problems, and personal hang-ups with one's friends. After this start, regardless of the actual setting or mode of discovery, two things can happen. The quest for continued self-awareness can become a never-ending process of personal inquiry and growth. Or, it can be allowed to atrophy and die, leaving one with only the memory of an exhilarating experience of how life could be if one were willing to work at it. A great many descriptions of these groups have been published (see, for example, Rogers, 1971), so they will not be discussed here.

Many workshops on increasing self-awareness frequently involve the use of standardised instruments to provide participants with easily grasped concepts to use in understanding their needs, peculiarities, values, strengths, weaknesses, and habits. In addition to the ideas developed in chapters 11 and 13 a brief sampling of other instruments is presented here.

Life Style Orientations (LSO)

This instrument, developed by Frank Friedlander at Case Western Reserve University, is based on the thesis that everyone, to some degree, looks to authority, to their peers *and* inside themselves for direction, guidance, value setting, and so on. The Life Style Orientation instrument measures one's *formalistic* (looking to authority, tradition, precedent), *sociocentric* (looking to friends, colleagues), and *personalistic* (looking introspectively) orientations or tendencies. Some groups, like military officers, tend to have relatively high formalistic scores and relatively low sociocentric scores. Scientists, on the other hand, tend to score highest on personalistic and low on the others. Human relations specialists tend to score highest on the sociocentric dimension.

Once a person has his scores, he can check them against the population norms that have been calculated and compare them with others in a discussion group. If a person has a relatively low formalistic score for his or her age, sex or occupational group, for example, and is working in an authoritarian setting, that person may decide it is time for a job change or time to look in new places for supportive friends (Friedlander, 1970).

Firo—B

These letters stand for Fundamental Interpersonal Relationship Orientation—Behavior. It is the name of a widely known instrument developed by William Schutz when he was at Harvard. Like the LSO above, the FIRO—B measures orientations or tendencies. It measures the degree of strength of six orientations that every one of us has: our *expression* of *inclusion, control* and *affection* towards others and our *desire* to be *included, controlled* and *receive affection* from others (Schutz, 1958).

As was the case with the LSO, one's FIRO—B scores can be compared with population averages or with the scores of others in a discussion group as a means towards increased self-awareness. Many people, for example, discover that they have a high need to be included by other people and feel easily left out. Many of these people also have a low desire to include others in their own activities. One result of such a balance is that after a period of not including others in their own activities, the others begin to feel the person is not interested in them and they stop including that person in their activities, leaving the person feeling lonely or isolated much of the time. In organisations, such people frequently complain about not being in the chain of command, but take few initiatives to get the information they feel they are not receiving. They are irritated easily by this left out feeling, but nothing management attempts seems to resolve their irritations.

Parallel consequences can be projected for imbalances on the expressed and desired control dimension and the expressed and desired affection levels.

Peter Smith, a social psychologist at the University of Sussex, has done extensive research on the composition of self-learning groups (eg. T-groups) based on FIRO—B scores. Put most briefly, he found that members of groups that are composed of a maximum mix of FIRO–B scores learn more and have more durable learnings than do the members of groups composed of homogeneous FIRO–B scores (Smith, 1964).

Strength Deployment Inventory (SDI)
This instrument is relatively new, but is being widely used in America by trainers and consultants in the human relations movement. It has been developed by American consultant Elias Porter (1973) and, as with the LSO and FIRO–B, provides scores along three types of dimensions present to some degree in each of us: *Altruistic-Nurturing* (helpful, concerned, harmonising), *Assertive-Directing* (powerful, challenging, competing), and *Analytic-Autonomising* (self-sufficient, judicious, planful). It can be used in the same manner as the FIRO–B and LSO, but has two additional features. It provides a score on each of these dimensions for when things are going well for us and a score for when we are under stress, conflict or opposition. This makes it a particularly useful instrument in helping people relate their inter-personal styles and the ways in which they handle stress. Secondly, Porter has developed a list of strengths and weaknesses attendant upon high scores along any of the dimensions.

Work Motivation Inventory (WMI)
This instrument has been developed by Jay Hall, a Texas consultant, and is based upon the late Abraham Maslow's hierarchy of needs (Hall & Williams, 1973). After completing the inventory, the individual's score reflects the degree to which five motivating forces actually serve to motivate his or her behaviour. These motivating forces are basic (survival), safety (psychological and physical), belonging (acceptance by others), ego-status (recognition of one's worth), and actualisation (achieving one's potential). Population averages are again given and people can compare their scores with the population at large. When one learns that some of one's scores are out of line with the base population or with those of one's work group, one has increased choices about where to focus one's attention to get one's needs met.

Whether or not a person's scores on the above (or other) inventories are in line with the averages is immaterial. The important point is that the person's self-awareness of his needs, orientations, peculiarities and so on is increased. With this increased self-awareness, one has a much greater chance of making choices that will remove one from strain-inducing situations and allow one to find more opportunities for self-fulfilment.

4. Exercise

There are a great many exercise plans available. For example, nearly everyone has at least heard of Aerobics and the Royal Canadian Air Force routines. Increasingly, adults are jogging, golfing, playing tennis, hiking, or otherwise engaging in active pursuits. Modern conveniences have removed the necessity of using one's body very much and the resurgence of vigorous exercise during leisure time seems to be an indication that, for whatever inborn or media-produced reasons, people are concerned about the sedentary lives society has made available to them.

Organisations are beginning to respond as well. The U.S. Government has placed signs next to the lifts in many of its buildings advising people to walk up one flight and down two flights rather than using the lift. Large corporations such as Exxon and General Foods have hired trainer-coaches and equipped exercise rooms for the use of their personnel. Most also require their personnel to undergo regular physical examinations and have full-time medical staffs to provide these examinations.

As I pointed out in chapter 3, the autonomic nervous system is largely independent of our wishes to control it. Yet, we will always have disruptions and surprises intruding upon us. There will always be things that make us angry. Even the calm people we all know who say that nothing angers them are likely to have hypertension or an ulcer beginning to form. If we cannot find ways to fight these intrusions or escape them, we begin to fight ourselves.

Exercise provides release for pent up energy and feelings and, through toning and strengthening our bodies, helps us to resist the gradual wear and tear of the stress response. In addition, being fit is a pleasant feeling. Those who keep themselves fit can tell the difference in their bodily feelings when they are compelled to miss only a day or two of their exercise routine. They report that they feel tired and less fluid. Many studies have shown that exercise *creates* energy and that those who exercise very little feel chronically fatigued.

In their discussion of how carefully planned exercise reduces the impact of stress, McQuade and Aikman (1974) point out that nearly all of the exercise 'professionals' insist that the only way exercise significantly improves the body is through a programmed approach to physical exhaustion. They stress endurance activities that increase conditioning and oxygen intake, thereby increasing one's ability to face stressful situations. As one becomes more fit, one's lungs become more efficient in taking oxygen from the air and getting it into one's bloodstream.

The London School of Hygiene and Tropical Medicine (cited by McQuade and Aikman, 1974) studied the exercise habits of heart attack patients and of those who had not had heart attacks. It was found that 11 per cent of the heart attack patients had been in the habit of exercising strenuously, while 26 per cent of the control group did so. Light exercise did not seem to make any difference. Furthermore, exercisers who did suffer heart attacks had a better recovery rate.

In general, vigorous exercise reduces the impact of stress by increasing oxygen in the blood, decreasing blood pressure, decreasing the production of stomach acid (thereby assisting in the remission of ulcers) and increasing the supply of blood through the growth of capillary routes and strengthened arteries.

There need to be some cautions. In addition to having periodic physical examinations, one should not overextend one's physical capabilities or move too quickly through a limbering up period to strenuous activity. The type A person as described in chapters 2 (p. 38) and 3 (p. 46) tends to exercise in ways that enhance his or her risk of a coronary. They are the ones, for example, who go jogging with a stopwatch in their hand, ever attempting to complete their run faster than the previous day. As a general homily, I would encourage exercisers to acknowledge that they have normal body rhythms of higher and lower physical and emotional energy levels. If one 'listens' to one's natural rhythms and avoids trying always to outdo yesterday's achievements, one's exercise will have the greatest enhancing effect.

As a lead-in to the next section, I want to point out that exercise alone does not lead to weight loss. A good exercise plan combined with a good nutrition plan will both improve one's fitness and reduce one's waistline.

5. Nutrition

There are even more diet plans than exercise plans. Every bookstore has dozens of different diet books to sell. It often seems that each month's edition of 'your favourite family magazine' introduces a new diet. Most of them do not work and many of them have been shown to be dangerous.

It takes approximately 3500 calories to maintain one pound of weight. Whenever one consumes fewer calories than it takes to keep one's weight stable, one loses weight. For example, assume that your weight stays the same when you consume an average of 2500 calories per day. If you average 2000 calories per day for a week, you will lose one pound (7 days x 500 calories = 3500 calories). That diet plan does work.

Probably, most of the people reading this book are overweight because most people in the English-speaking world are at least a little overweight. If you gently pinch your waist at the side and find that there is more than an inch of you (or two and a half centimetres) between your thumb and forefinger, you are overweight. Being overweight is a major factor in hypertension and heart disease. At the same time, overeating is one popular but dangerous way of coping with stressful situations.

Researchers are now learning that *what* we eat is at least as important as how much we eat. Most people, for example, are now aware that red meats, egg yolks, bacon and many cheeses and so on are high in cholesterol. Cholesterol is now thought to be a major factor in heart disease and a substance whose level is increased by the stress response. Some people seem to absorb cholesterol from the food they eat more readily than others (type A's in particular).

More recently, nutrition researchers have begun to write about the vast amount of food value lost in the processing that produces white flour and white sugar. Pastries, cakes, sweets and commercial bread are among those foods consumed in enormous quantities in our society that are almost entirely made of sugar and white flour. Nutrition experts call these foods 'empty calories'.

Processed foods have all but taken over the diets in a majority of households. With both parents often working and with the ease and convenience of these foods (e.g. canned soups, vegetables and fruits; T.V. dinners; processed meats; prepared gravies and sauces, etc.), the home preparation of natural foods seems headed towards the category of a lost craft in many sectors of our society.

What happens in processing foods? Preservatives and artificial colourings and flavourings are added (linked to hyperactivity and cancer). So are great quantities of salt (linked to hypertension). For example, processed meats (bologna, salami, bacon, ham, etc.) contain sodium nitrate and sodium nitrite, which cure, colour, preserve and flavour the meat and sometimes mix with other body chemicals to form nitrosamines which are carcinogenic.

A recent book called *Psychodietetics: Food as the Key to Emotional Health* by Cheraskin, Ringsdorf and Brecher (1974) provides an excellent review of the effects of these inessential additives on our functioning, emotional stability and abilities to handle and survive stress. Cheraskin *et al.* relate all of the additives mentioned above to emotional instability, schizophrenia, hypoglycemia, sexual inadequacy, hyperactivity, allergy, senility, alcoholism and strain.

Their major contention is that the intake of these additives is one of the major sources of drug abuse in our society. In discussing the Holmes and Rahe Social Readjustment Rating Scale (see chapters 2, 3 and 9), they argue persuasively that proper nutrition that avoids these additives and minimises the intake of white flour and refined sugar and contains a balanced input of vitamins and minerals will protect one from the illnesses predicted by a high social readjustment score.

6. Letting go

So far it has been argued that healthy organisation settings, the use of support groups, self-awareness, exercise and diet can all contribute to reducing the effects of stress. These are necessary but not sufficient, however. It was pointed out in chapter 1 that realising the growth potential in transitions involves 'letting go' of the pre-transition state of affairs, and in chapter 7 and elsewhere the need to abandon inappropriate pre-transition assumptions and unhook from the past was emphasised.

Likewise, learning to let go of one's usual conscious world and to turn inward is necessary to reduce the strains created by chronic stress. The mystics may refer to joining a 'cosmic consciousness'; Elmer Green of the Menninger Foundation refers to it as 'Passive Volition', or willingly being passive to allow desirable things to happen.

K. Lamott, in *Escape from Stress* (1975), has reviewed investigations into the effectiveness of a whole range of letting go techniques. With due acknowledgments, this section includes a summary of the findings he has pulled together regarding the way letting go techniques reduce strain symptoms. The following paragraphs will consider yoga, Zen, transcendental meditation, hypnosis, acupuncture, autogenic training and biofeedback.

Yoga

Most Westerners picture yoga as a tortuous set of body postures that some people think is good for them for something. This yoga is called

Hatha Yoga and is but one of several forms of yoga. In some schemes, it is used as preparation for the more advanced (and to Westerners, more esoteric or mystical) yogic forms which have *Samedhi*, or union with the One, as their goal. Some elements that are present in all forms of yoga are concentration, focus on breathing and acute body awareness.

In the U.S.A., the most prominent researchers on the strain-reducing effects of yoga are Elmer and Alyce Green who are research workers at the Menninger Foundation in Topeka, Kansas. Their work with Swami Rama, who travelled to the U.S.A. to bring Eastern and Western traditions closer together, is widely known. Swami Rama showed that by using his knowledge of yoga he could increase, decrease or stop his heart rate.

Indian scientists B. K. Anand, G. S. Chhina and B. Singh demonstrated that yogic meditation was accompanied by increased alpha brainwave activity, and eventually theta brainwave activity, which indicate deep and total relaxation and reverie respectively.

In Bombay, K. K. Datey of K.E.M. Hospital uses a form of rhythmic yoga breathing, called *Shavasan*, to treat hypertensives. Shavasan, Datey reports, reduces headaches, nervousness, irritability, insomnia and systolic blood pressure (by an average 27 mm).

Zen

Zen is a Japanese word which means 'state of absolute calmness and abstraction'. It was originally related to yoga in India, and was taken to China and then to Japan several centuries ago. Zen is much more ascetic and 'severe' and becomes a total way of life for its adherents whose goal is, through a form of meditation, to achieve *Satori*, or the attainment of internal peace, a state of 'nothingness'.

Kasamatsu and Hirai of Tokyo University have used similar techniques to the Green's in Topeka — E.E.G. recordings and measurements of Galvanic Skin Response (electrical resistance of the skin is a stress indicator) — on Zen masters in meditation. They found increased alpha (relaxation) and theta (reverie) brainwave activity. G.S.R. and respiration rates are also lowered in meditation.

Transcendental meditation

TM has taken on the characteristics of a panacea in Great Britain, the U.S.A. and the West generally. It is of recent origin, having been developed in the early 1950s by Mahareshi Mahesh Yogi. His mentor, Guru Dev, instructed Mahareshi to develop a form of yogic meditation simple enough to be practised by anybody, which he did. Obviously, such a process has great commercial value in our society and this has detracted somewhat from its power. Literally hundreds of thousands of people in America and Europe have learned TM. Basically it involves sitting in a relaxed position and quietly repeating one's 'mantra' (a syllable that has no meaning to Westerners, but may be an important word in yogic tradition) to oneself, allowing thoughts to come and go at their discretion. Mahareshi claims that each thought intrusion is strain being relieved somewhere in the body. It is generally recommended that one do TM twice a day, for 20–30 minutes each session.

Bensen and Wallace of Harvard have had remarkable success in using TM with drug addicts and alcoholics. For these people TM is an alternative trip to escape the stressors in their lives.

Several research efforts, by Bensen, Wallace and others, have consistently found that TM lowers respiration rate, increases alpha brainwave activity and reduces heart rate and blood lactate (which is a part of the stress response). Blood pressures were not shown to be lowered, but the average blood pressure of the participants in the research is very low to start with (106/57). Others have experienced lowered blood pressure as a result of TM.

Hypnosis

Hypnosis is more familiar to most of us than the meditative arts arising from yoga, because it is of Western origin. Franz Mesmer, an eighteenth-century Austrian, created a great deal of excitement in medical circles in Vienna and Paris with his demonstrations of how 'animal magnetism' (later called mesmerism and then hypnosis) could treat hysterical symptoms such as stress-induced blindness and paralysis. The medical establishment rejected Mesmer, however, and the respectability of hypnotism as a medical tool has never been widely established, although it is used effectively by a great many practitioners to help people lose weight, stop smoking or drinking, relax, and so on.

Medical hypnosis revived for a period during the nineteenth century and was used as an anaesthesia for tooth extractions, child birth and surgery. The British surgeon J. Esdaile reportedly performed over 3000 operations in an Indian prison hospital using hypnotism as the sole anaesthetic. He noted that not only did hypnotism reduce or eliminate pain, but it drastically reduced post-operative mortality as well. When Esdaile returned to England, he was tried for malpractice because of his interest in hypnotism and lost his licence.

Later in the nineteenth century, Jean Charcot, a neurologist, became interested in hypnotism and taught Sigmund Freud how to do it.

Hypnotism formed the basis for the free association aspects of psychoanalysis eventually developed by Freud. When he dropped it from his practice because it covered up the all important resistances and transferences Freud chose to deal with, hypnosis again fell into disrepute.

At last, in 1955, the British Medical Association permitted doctors to use hypnotism in their practice. In 1958, the American Medical Association followed suit. Even so, there are still disagreements about whether or not hypnosis is in any way different from a meditative trance and even whether or not there is such a thing as hypnosis.

In Toronto, E. H. Doney practises hypnosis as a part of his therapy with heart attack patients. In comparing the benefits to those patients who actually run and exercise with the benefits to those who, under hypnosis, are asked to imagine they are running and exercising, there were no differences in physiological changes recorded between the two groups.

C. Harding of Portland, Oregon uses hypnosis to cure migraine. T. P. Hackett of Boston uses hypnosis to treat the stress-related sexual complaints of impotence and premature ejaculation.

Acupuncture

Acupuncture has recently become a widespread practice in the West, although it has been known in China for untold centuries. While no one can fully explain how acupuncture works in terms acceptable to the rational Western mind, its capabilities as an anaesthetic and pain reliever are now known to nearly everyone who reads magazines or newspapers with any regularity.

The Chinese claim that it works because it promotes harmony between Yin and Yang. Relatedly, Looney and Kroenig of Los Angeles argue that acupuncture is a precise method for promoting balance between the sympathetic and parasympathetic nervous systems. Therefore, it is a useful procedure for intervening in the processes of the autonomic nervous system to restore homeostasis to the body.

While great feats of surgery have been performed with acupuncture as the anaesthetic, it seems to many investigators that one has to believe in it to make it work.

Acupuncture, like hypnosis, would seem to have great potential in reducing or removing stress-related ailments. A great deal is yet to be learned about each.

Autogenic training

Autogenic means self-generated, and autogenic training is primarily an application of the principles of hypnotism to stress and the related diseases. In the 1890s, Berlin brain physiologist Oskar Vogt learned that he could teach his patients to hypnotise themselves through a system of simple mental exercises. Vogt's patients reported that the experience left them feeling heavy and warm and that their tensions, headaches, and so on had disappeared. They also found it easier to cope with their daily problems.

A few years later, Berlin psychiatrist J. H. Schultz combined Vogt's system with what he knew of yoga and wrote a book called *Autogenic Training*. The methods Schultz developed are widely applied in Europe and Japan and are beginning to attract a great deal of attention in the U.S.A. As one might expect, the Greens of the Menninger Foundation are strong supporters of autogenic training.

Schultz and Luthe have made great claims for autogenic training. They say that three ten-minute training periods a day can, after two to eight months, improve or cure bronchial asthma, constipation, cardio-spasm, sleep disorders, anxiety, phobia, indigestion, ulcers, ulcerative colitis, angina, hypertension, diabetes and many more stress-related diseases. These claims have not all been substantiated by research, but many appear to be valid. Since it is nearly as easy to learn as TM, consisting of repeating simple suggestive phrases to oneself, it deserves further investigation as a way to reduce or avoid the ravages of chronic strain.

According to Lamott:

> As ways of letting go, Zen, yoga, hypnosis, and autogenic training are remarkable more for their similarities than for their differences. All are based on the principle of passive concentration, whether on a meaningless phrase or on a specific suggestion. All can cause measureable changes in the functions of the body that respond to stress. All work. (1975, p. 136.)

Biofeedback

Biofeedback uses an electronic device to show the individual attached to it how certain of his body functions are changing. For example, if a person can see his heart rate, he can raise or lower it consciously.

Once again, the Greens of the Menninger Foundation are involved actively with biofeedback. In one experiment they showed that with feedback from an electronic monitoring device subjects could learn quite quickly to reduce their muscular tensions, increase their alpha brainwave activity, or increase their skin temperature. The Greens have also had excellent results in combining autogenic training with the feedback capabilities of biofeedback.

To date, biofeedback seems to offer Westerners the quickest and most effective way to alleviate strain. Each of the methods described earlier in this section is still useful and effective, but biofeedback can shorten the process by providing immediate and direct feedback on the specific function or symptom being treated. Westerners love short-cuts and scientific gadgets, making biofeedback more readily acceptable as well. So far, research into the effectiveness of biofeedback has been uniformly encouraging and there is, as yet, no end in sight to its applicability.

Biofeedback is now widely and successfully used to treat chronic tension headaches, migraine headaches, phobias, high blood pressure, arrhythmia, high heart rate. As an added extra, it appears that the state of mind reinforced by biofeedback is often uncharacteristically high in alpha brainwave activity, indicating a general, deep relaxation.

In order to engage successfully in any of the seven means for letting go described in this section, one needs to make a serious commitment to learning how to let go regularly. The potential benefits are well documented. This brief section does not teach the reader *how* to do any of them, or even describe any of them in sufficient detail.

Different people, upon further study, will find different ones of the approaches to be more appealing and more successful for them. It is hoped that this chapter will encourage those who want to learn how to let go to seek out professional assistance in learning a method for doing so.

All of the various ways of letting go work. If the individual believes one will work for him or her and makes a commitment to incorporate that approach into the daily routine, it is now clear that strain reactions can be significantly reduced.

SUMMARY

This chapter has looked at how one can manage one's self so as to be able to take maximum advantage of transition opportunities. The work setting, support systems, self-awareness, exercise, nutrition and letting go have been identified as components in an integrated approach to self-management and body management.

11. Personal Re-Evaluation: A Method for Individual Goal-Setting

Barrie Hopson

In previous publications (Hopson & Hough, 1973; Hopson & Hopson, 1975; Hopson, 1973) we have discussed numerous uses of a technique known generally as *Life Planning*. This is an approach to personal problem-sharing and goal-setting that has been used by a number of applied behavioural science professionals in a variety of settings. Perhaps the major contributor to this approach has been Herbert A. Shepard, although many people have contributed new techniques and exercises. Indeed, one of the strengths of this approach is its flexibility. We have used it in relation to career development for managers, scientists, and administrative staff at a variety of levels; helping married couples to reassess their relationships; helping prospective school-leavers to map out career and life objectives; assisting final-year undergraduate students to prepare for the transition from university to non-university life; and training residential staff of hostels for ex-offenders, drug addicts, and alcoholics in its application for them. We have used it on American, British and Swedish populations.

As we have used this approach throughout these different situations with a wide variety of people, one of the most commonly encountered criticisms has been concerned with the title 'Life Planning', and more specifically, with the implications of the word 'planning'. Some people have said that they do not like the idea of 'planning their lives away'. Others discover that they are the kind of person who only likes to look ahead for the next few months of their lives, and possibly not at all. These are all quite legitimate objectives as one of the goals of life planning is the clarification of one's own needs. The term 'need' is not strictly appropriate here. What we are really concerned with are 'wants' or 'wishes'. There is an important difference in emphasis. A need is imperative — 'I *need it* = I *must* have it'. The implication is that without it one would not survive. Later in this chapter I discuss the rationality of 'needs', where the main point is that many people think they have 'needs', i.e. they must satisfy these at all costs, whereas in fact they are only 'wants' or 'wishes', i.e. they would like such and such to happen, but if it does not they will not be destroyed. A major educative function of the trainer in Life Planning is to convince the participant that most of his *needs* are only *wishes* and objectives. There is no imperative from the trainer to plan ahead in the best traditions of 'rational man'. It is the process of clarification and the opportunity for re-evaluation that are of primary importance. Consequently, it is with some reluctance that we have recently been using the term 'Personal Re-Evaluation'. We decided that the risk of confusing people with old wine in new bottles was better than misleading them with a culturally loaded title.

PERSONAL RE-EVALUATION (PRE)

Personal Re-Evaluation is concerned with providing a structured opportunity for individuals, working alone and in mutual support groups, to answer the following questions for themselves:

(1) Who am I and where am I now?
(2) How did I get here?
(3) How satisfied am I with who and where I am?
(4) How would I like to change my life and myself?
(5) How rational are these desires?
(6) How do I accomplish these changes?

Allen (1975) has described the desirable outcomes from PRE very succinctly:

(1) Changes in internal *cognitive* functioning, e.g. understanding one's behaviour and the reasons for it better.
(2) Changes in internal *affective* functioning, e.g. coping with negative feelings more effectively, feeling more positively about the self, etc.
(3) Changes in externally observable *behaviour*, e.g. creating or taking opportunities, etc.

The time period used for working through a complete Personal Re-Evaluation programme has varied from one day to five days.

Typically there have been two trainers to a group of 10–12 participants, although we are experimenting constantly with new designs, especially those that can increase the cost-effectiveness of the trainer, i.e. just how many clients a trainer can effectively manage at one time.

A TYPICAL PERSONAL RE-EVALUATION LABORATORY DESIGN

Contract building

The clients, who will usually have seen a brochure or handout describing the broad aims of Personal Re-Evaluation, will be asked to participate in a contract building exercise. They share their expectations, personal and professional (if appropriate), and discuss any anxieties or fears they are experiencing around the workshop. They also present data to the trainers as to what they expect the trainers' roles to be. At each stage, the trainers also share their expectations and anxieties. As with any contract building the trainers make very clear what is and what is not negotiable. These data are collected on flip-charts which are displayed prominently for the duration of the course. If no one refers to them again it is the responsibility of the trainers to do so as the course nears its end so that a check can be made to see if the contract is being kept. Once made the contract can be renegotiated at any point. It is not inviolable.

The objectives of Personal Re-Evaluation are restated and the value assumptions underlying the programme are discussed openly (these are examined in the next section).

The workshop begins. It often commences with an exercise to accelerate getting to know one another. This is usually some form of self-disclosure device, such as Otto's 'Depth Unfolding Experience' (1970). It is essential to the development of the appropriate learning climate and mutual trust that trainers participate equally in an exercise of this kind.

The participants then complete a series of exercises. These are done alone, but at appropriate points the data are shared — with the large group, a subgroup (4–6), in trios or pairs, depending on the size of the group and the trainers' objective at that point. Inputs may be given by the trainers formally or informally as discussions progress. Generally the workshop moves from exploring 'who am I?' and 'how did I become what I am?' to considering how satisfied the participant is with his current predicament and deciding how he/she would like to develop.

Who am I and where am I now?

A variety of exercises exist to generate data around this question. Typical examples are:[1]

Lifeline: each person draws a line to represent his life and places a mark at the point he has reached.

Who am I?: ten statements that sum up oneself.

Peak and trough experiences: the events and experiences that have caused one the greatest satisfaction and the most despair in one's life.

How did I get here?: a number of exercises have been developed primarily based on transactional analysis.

Script analysis: responses to a number of questions about one's family and culture are analysed to see the impact on the person's script development.

Circle of satisfaction: drawing a circle and splitting it up according to the sources of one's life satisfactions.

Obituary: writing one's own obituary as it would probably be written, and then as you would like it to be written.

How would I like to change my life and myself?

Fantasy day: how one would spend 24 hours if money were no object.

Fantasy working day: each person keeps a log of his ideal working day.

Fantasy life: what one's fantasy life would look like now and in the future.

How rational are these desires?

What are my needs?: a 'trick' exercise which makes the point that the only 'needs' one has are physiological.

What are my irrational beliefs?: a check list of commonly held irrational beliefs that often act spuriously as motivators for personal goal achievement.

How do I accomplish these changes?

Life investment record: how does one presently invest one's time and energies?

Developing action plans: each person makes plans for however far ahead he wishes to look. He is encouraged to sensitise himself to the personal, interpersonal and community resources at his disposal. He constructs a series of behaviourally specific action steps that must be taken in order to achieve each specific personal objective.

A more detailed description of a PRE programme, one developed for British school-leavers and to be run by teachers in the classroom, is to be found in Hopson and Hough (1973).

ASSUMPTIONS UNDERLYING PERSONAL RE-EVALUATION

These are always discussed in the programme, and indeed we are continually discovering more of our own assumptions and values as we conduct training programmes:

(1) Everyone is free to make changes in their lives;
(2) a belief in self-autonomy can sometimes be threatening;
(3) the ability to create change in one's life is influenced by sex, age, class, ethnic group, but this ability is teachable;
(4) experienced powerlessness generates depression and alienation;
(5) a highly effective way of re-evaluating oneself is with the help of other people;
(6) certain 'needs', however they are defined, are irrational.

(1) Everyone is free to make changes in their lives

We live in an age where many people bemoan the fact that they are not free to make the changes they would like to make. Rollo May (1969) makes the point that we have forgotten how to make an impact on a malleable world. We are hypnotised by our feelings of powerlessness and use this as an excuse for doing nothing.

    ... the central core of modern man's 'neuroses', it may be fairly said, is the undermining of his experience of himself as responsible, the sapping of his will and ability to make decisions. The lack of will is much more than merely an ethical problem: the modern individual so often has the conviction that even if he did exert his 'will' — or whatever illusion passes for it — his actions wouldn't do any good anyway. It is this inner experience of impotence, this contradiction in will, which constitutes our critical problem.

The social sciences, with their deterministic orientation, have provided us with too many excuses about why we are in such an unhappy job, marriage or mood.

Man is distinguished by his capacity to know that he is determined, and to choose his relationship to what determines him. He can and must, unless he abdicates his consciousness, choose how he will relate to necessity, such as death, old age, limitations of intelligence, and the conditioning inescapable in his own background. Will he accept this necessity, deny it, fight it, affirm it, consent to it? (May, 1969).

Rotter's (1966) work suggests that undoubtedly not everyone feels themselves to have power to control what happens to them. He has developed the Internal—External Control Scale, which distinguishes between people who believe that events occur as a consequence of their personal actions and are under their personal control (Internals) and those who believe that events are unrelated to their personal behaviour and therefore beyond their personal control (Externals). He has provided evidence to show that American college students felt more powerless as the sixties decade progressed. I would define powerlessness like Seeman (1959) as an 'expectancy or probability held by the individual that his own behaviour cannot determine the occurrence of the outcomes, or reinforcements he seeks'.

Tiffany and Tiffany (1973) have felt that control actually has four components and is *experienced* rather than expected:

(a) control *from internal* organismic states, e.g. impulses (FI)
(b) control *over* these *internal* states (OI)
(c) control *from* the *environment* (FE)
(d) control *over* the *environment* (OE)

Self-determined individuals feel they have a high degree of control *over internal* and *external* forces (OI/OE) and non self-determined people experience little control over these factors (FI/FE). Their scales of experienced control do not correlate with Rotter's Internal—External Control Scale (Ingram, Tiffany, Markley, Tiffany & Smith, 1971; Tiffany, Salkin & Cowan, 1970).

Gurin *et al.* (1969) found difficulty with the Rotter scale when administered to black students. They discovered that the scale was better regarded as two separate scales — *personal control* and *system blame.* The personal control scale items referred to the sense of personal control in one's own life, e.g. 'When I make plans, I am almost certain that I can make them work', is contrasted to 'It is not always wise to plan too far ahead because many things turn out to be a matter of good or bad fortune anyhow'. However, a *system blame* item like, 'Leadership positions tend to go to capable people who deserve being chosen', when contrasted with the External alternative, 'It's hard to know why some people get leadership positions and other's don't — ability doesn't seem to be an important factor', tends to support the status quo in society. Gurin found that for black students, internality of personal control may indeed aid individual minority group members to move up the social scale, but internality of system blame would not help one's minority group to improve its status as a whole.

The Tiffanys' (1973) work supports this conclusion, which implies that a feeling of personal control over oneself and one's environment is not always enough, certainly to create social change, and, they argue, even for individual change. They believe that many social action programmes fail when they emphasise only self-directing control mechanisms (OI/OE). The reason for failures is that no attempt is made to alter environmental conditions (FE) which, subsequently, militate against actualisation of personal aspirations and lead to withdrawal and apathy, or, when manifested in social unrest, are evident in impulsive, acting out behaviour (FI). Conversely, changes only of environmental conditions with little or no attempt at increasing the person's feeling of control will also end in failure.

The implications for Personal Re-Evaluation and transition training from all of these researches are:

(i)   that everyone can make some changes in their lives;

(ii) not everyone *feels* that they have control over what happens to them;

(iii) in training people to define and achieve their goals, only limited results can be obtained by concentrating solely on developing a person's feeling of self-direction;

(iv) for a transitional event to be most productive, the organisation, social system, individuals, etc. that constitute the situational element in the transition must itself or themselves make a positive contribution to the transitional experience of the mover.

(2) Belief in self-autonomy can sometimes be threatening, which is why people need support from others

To know and believe that what happens to you is the combined result of what you make happen and how you react to external events outside your sphere of influence, is an alarming concept to many people. Erich Fromm (1942) outlined this 'fear of freedom' very clearly and emphasised that the feeling of being alone and self-determining before the universe was sufficiently threatening to many people that they immediately surrender their freedom into the welcoming bosom of mother church or mother party. For people to feel alone and cut off from their environment can lead to psychological disintegration, as demonstrated by sensory deprivation experiments (Vernon, 1965). Fromm anticipated this in social terms twenty years earlier:

> To feel completely alone and isolated leads to mental disintegration just as physical starvation leads to death. This relatedness to others is not identical with physical contact. An individual may be alone in the physical sense for many years and yet he may be related to ideas, values, or at least a social pattern that gives him a feeling of communion and 'belongingness'. On the other hand, he may live among people and yet be overcome with an utter feeling of isolation.

Eric Hoffer (1951) advanced this thesis further with his discussion of the true 'believer' — the ardent supporter of mass movements political, social and religious, which are a refuge for the frustrated and the ontologically despairing. Walter Kaufmann (1973) has even invented a word to describe people who fear autonomy — *decidophobics*. In his book he describes a number of ways in which people protect themselves from autonomy. Consequently we have a picture in which some people are afraid of autonomy, others experience alienation. The answer for many is to seek self-validation and meaning in causes and people external to themselves, rather than validating themselves from within.

*(3) The ability to create change in one's life is partly dependent upon
      sex, age, class and ethnic group, but this ability is teachable*

It is quite clear from our day-to-day experiences that some people seem
more willing and able to create change in their lives than others. I have
discussed the basis for some of these differences already at the
individual level (under (1)). But there would appear to be a number of
social factors that influence people's feelings of power or lack of it,
which must be taken into account by trainers.

Women in our society have typically been more conservative than
men in politics, religion and, it is not too unreasonable to hypothesise
generally, in the practice of taking personal risks. For the cause of this
we need look no further than our socialisation process.

Similarly, the older people get the more resistant they appear to be
to change (Botwinick, 1966). But there is no reason to suppose that
this is determined by anything more 'natural' than expectations of how
one should live in one's later years, plus the fact that one often has
self-imposed family responsibilities that are demanding in a different
way from the responsibilities of youth. The former, of course, do not
operate once children have left home, when middle-aged couples are
suddenly faced with a wide range of possible alternatives. The fact that
many couples are very disturbed by this freedom is well documented,
and that many people cling on to what they know best is more evidence
of Kaufmann's 'decidophobia'.

However, socio-economic groups have reported feelings of powerlessness (Irelan 1967; Leibow 1967) which often result in hopelessness,
fatalism, and apathy. Seeman (1971) describes intercultural differences
in experienced powerlessness between the U.S.A., France and Sweden:

> There is a sharp contrast in the social structure of the two European
> nations: Sweden is a country with strong labor organisations and a
> history of stability in government, while France is notoriously
> unstable in politics and relatively weak in its structure of internal
> organisations. Though a simple comparison of the level of power-
> lessness was not the main burden of our interest, we did find some
> differences between these two countries. For example, on the item
> concerning work success, Frenchmen showed greater feelings of
> powerlessness. Among the better educated manual-workers 46% of
> the French sample stated that getting a good job was a matter of
> luck; among the Swedes, the comparable figure was 17%. Americans

were closer to the Swedes — 24% of the American sample chose the luck answer. We found the same pattern on questions about exerting influence on governmental policies. On the whole, the French expressed a strong sense of impotence.

An overall generalisation from these studies would appear to be that groups with more actual access to social rewards are more internally oriented, i.e. it is highly difficult for some people to control their environment. The only thing they can control is their reaction to it.

The implication for trainers here is that they should not encourage people to believe that they can become complete masters of their own destiny. There are ways of achieving more environmental control but this can never be guaranteed. What can be promised is greater internal control (Tiffany's OI component).

Seeman's (1971) research indicates that experienced powerlessness is clearly related to access to information. His experiments in Sweden and the U.S.A. were designed to discover whether powerlessness produces poor learning, or whether people who lack information tend to feel powerless. His data support the former hypothesis. The implication for trainers is that unless people feel that they can have some control over what happens to them, any information that could help them make plans, discover resources, etc. is likely to fall on deaf ears.

Coleman's (1966) research also underlines the importance of feelings of powerlessness in learning situations, in demonstrating the association between internal orientation and school success. His team showed that pupil achievement was more deeply affected by the pupil's sense of powerlessness (what Coleman called the sense of 'fate control') than by objective advantages such as teacher qualifications, access to counselling, the character of the library, parental income and the geographical location of the school. Evidently, internally oriented students seem to feel that they can get ahead by trying; and they devote themselves energetically to the job. Externally oriented students seem to feel that their efforts make little difference and therefore do not seem to try very hard.

All of these behavioural tendencies must be closely linked with socialisation processes and consequently one should be optimistic about the possibility of teaching people to have greater control over themselves and their reactions to their environments, and to attempt to exercise more control over their environment, the latter, naturally, being the more difficult objective, often requiring political or social change.

(4) Experienced powerlessness generates alienation and depression

By some definitions, everyone in Western society must be alienated, which makes the concept analytically useless. It is a term used in a number of different ways and Seeman (1971) has distinguished between six very common uses:

(i)   *Individual powerlessness:* I have no control over my own life. It is not within my power to decide my own future. Destiny is in the hands of external forces such as luck, or fate, or the government.

(ii) *Meaninglessness:* My life is absurd, incomprehensible. Nothing I do seems to make any sense. Even if I would like to change society, I don't understand how or why things happen. Somebody must have an answer, somewhere.

(iii) *Normlessness (cynicism):* Normal methods don't produce results. If you want to get anywhere in this life you're going to have to cut a few corners. Hard work never made anybody rich or famous.

(iv) *Cultural estrangement:* There must be something more to life than money. Whoever set up the priorities in our society ought to have his head examined, or his books audited. I pity the kid who has to grow up in this country.

(v)   *Self-estrangement:* I haven't lived up to my own expectations. I'm not all that I would like to be or ought to be. I'm not really involved in anything I do.

(vi) *Social isolation:* I feel so lonely, excluded. I'd like to call some friends but I'm not sure I have any. I don't really feel accepted as a person.

Seeman's own preference is self-estrangement in the Marxist sense, i.e. alienated as a result of carrying out unfulfilling or uncreative work. Certainly trainers in Personal Re-Evaluation will be spending a considerable amount of time attempting to help the person discover the areas of his life in which he can work creatively, preferably looking for a balance between work in employed and non-employed activities. However, many trainers will also be concerned with reducing feelings of individual powerlessness, meaninglessness and social isolation, if the latter two are indeed experienced as problems by participants.

Seligman (1975) has shown that feelings of helplessness are learned and that they have the same symptoms as depression. His studies with animals and people show that depression is a belief in one's own helplessness. This applies whether the things that happen to one are rewards or punishments. If the reward or punishment bears no causal relationship to one's actions, there is a feeling of resigned helplessness or powerlessness. Seligman's work in treating 'learned helplessness' demonstrates the difficulty of extricating a depressed person from his depression. His experiments suggest that the most effective way of doing this is to ensure that people find out and come to believe that it is their responses that produce the gratification they desire. Only then can they believe that they can be effective human beings. Belief in internal control may thus be necessary for avoiding depression.

(5) A highly effective way of re-evaluating oneself is with the help of other people

The process of re-evaluation involves firstly an assessment of one's present position, including one's past history, plus a projection into the future. To do the former involves collecting considerable data on oneself, and this will be more comprehensive if other people are enjoined to provide feedback. Reality testing follows self-disclosure in ways not consonant with individual self-analysis. In terms of the Jo Hari window (Luft, 1970),[2] feedback is required to provide data on the blind area and the area of unknown activity (see Fig. 11.1).

To project oneself constructively into the future requires a belief that one has some control over the future. It is more likely that such a belief will be established via a group setting than in a one-to-one situation. One clear finding about attitude change is that it is always more effectively done through a group than through private persuasion (Lewin, 1947b).

Fig. 11.1

		Known to self	Unknown to self
D I S C L O S U R E	*Known to others*	Public area	Blind area
	Unknown to others	Hidden area	Unknown area

FEEDBACK

Belonging to a small group or organisation in which one participates in decision making and to which one is attracted is a powerful antidote to estranged alienation. Seeman (1971) found that active members of work organisations who reported more attendance and participation in organisational affairs felt more control than inactive members. He also found that membership in purely social or leisure-time groups did not decrease feelings of powerlessness. Successful re-evaluation, therefore, requires:

(i)   a group setting with a clearly defined work task (e.g. Personal Re-Evaluation workshop);
(ii) self-disclosure, which by definition involves at least two people;
(iii) feedback from others to provide reality testing opportunities.

(6) Certain needs, however they are defined, are irrational

Some techniques of helping people to solve problems more effectively and make decisions are limited in that they only (i) help people to discover their needs (we prefer to say 'wishes' or 'wants' as explained earlier), or (ii) teach them how to satisfy those wishes.

Personal Re-Evaluation adds a vital intermediary step: evaluating the rationality of these wishes. As trainers we are not interested in spending a great deal of time helping someone to develop and achieve an elaborate action plan to become a great financial success if the only reason that he wishes to do this is that he thinks that he will only be of value as a person if he is validated in this way.

Our thinking here has been profoundly influenced by Ellis's system of rational-emotive therapy (1973b), which holds that many people tend to believe in several unrealistic ideas which pattern their lives and dictate behavioural objectives. They hold to these ideas often with dreadful results in terms of their emotions and behaviours. In Ellis's terms, 'They consist of unqualified demands and needs, instead of preferences and desires. Consequently, they have nothing to do with reality.'

Ellis believes that there are perhaps 10—15 supreme 'necessities' that people commonly impose on themselves and others, but that these can be reduced to what he calls the 'irrational trinity':

(i)   'Because it would be highly preferable if I were outstandingly competent, I absolutely should and must be; it is awful when I am not; and I am therefore a worthless individual.'

(ii) 'Because it is highly desirable that others treat me considerately and fairly, they absolutely should and must, and are rotten people who deserve to be utterly damned when they do not.'

(iii) 'Because it is preferable that I experience pleasure rather than pain, the world absolutely should arrange this and life is horrible, and I can't bear it, when the world doesn't.'

Rational-emotive therapy is concerned with directing the client to examine the basis for his belief systems, and to realise that the way anything affects him in this world depends not on the 'real' world but his construction of it. Change that construction and the effect is different. I am not suggesting that during Personal Re-Evaluation a trainer takes his participants through intensive therapy — that is not the aim of the programme and there is not usually sufficient time. But the trainer should be helping participants to focus on questions like:

'Who really "owns" my wishes and values — me, my parents, spouse or someone else?'

'Do I really *need* this, or only *want* it?'

'How rational is it to want the things that I want — in other words, why do I want them?'

'How do I react when things don't go my way — am I disappointed or shattered?'

'Am I worthwhile as a person? What sorts of criteria do I use to answer this question?'

PERSONAL RE-EVALUATION: THE FUTURE

Apart from subjective evaluations from trainers and participants, there has been little systematic evaluation of Personal Re-Evaluation! (see Allen, 1975; Wilson, 1975). Although subjective assessment, if carefully structured, provides some validation, nothing convinces the sceptic more than externally measured behavioural changes which follow on from a programme like Personal Re-Evaluation. This is something that we want to endeavour to do next, as well as experimenting with new laboratory designs, exercises and client populations. Mencke and Cochran (1974) have assessed one life planning workshop in this way, which implies that perhaps we too can have cause for optimism, for we remain convinced that each of us carries with us an enormous potential to change and grow. Our task as trainers is to help people to make contact with that potential. Personal Re-Evaluation, we believe, is one effective method of doing this.

NOTES

1. None of these exercises are described in detail. Those who want more specific instructions and details of similar exercises can consult Birney *et al.* (1970); Hopson & Hopson (1975); Hopson & Hough (1973); Pfeiffer & Jones (1970); Crystal (1974); Ford *et al.* (1972).
2. This scheme for looking at aspects of the self was developed by Joe Ingrams and Harry Luft, who cutely named it after themselves!

12. Dealing with Personnel Changes in a Working Team

Michael D. Mitchell

Transferring a manager or employee across the country, across town, or perhaps even into a new job across the hall may provoke considerable personal strain for the individual involved; this strain has been well described by Toffler in *Future Shock* and Packard in *A Nation of Strangers*. Organisations, too, are frequently confronted today with the disruption accompanying personnel moves. Particularly when it is the manager of an organisational unit who is replaced – which occurs, predictably, all too often today in many large organisations – the problem is likely to be both acute and costly.

Management transition is often accompanied by considerable trepidation among the incoming manager's new subordinates. Often the reasons for the change of management are not known, and, in the absence of information, fears surface that the previous manager (and by association his subordinates) may have been unfavourably evaluated. Often, when reasons *are* given, doubts as to their authenticity linger. What are the new manager's values, strengths and weaknesses? How will he evaluate me? How must I adapt to him? What are the rules of the new ball game?

At such times, the incoming manager arrives to find suspicious and fearful subordinates who are strangely reluctant to advance opinions on important issues or to act without his specific direction. Staff meetings are marked by little discussion and awkward silences. Programmes and projects begun before his arrival appear to show little progress and now seem to be in limbo. Discussions with his subordinates take on the air of cat and mouse games that seem designed to force him to take positions on a variety of issues. At a time when he truly doesn't know where he stands on many of the crucial problems of the new organisation and most needs help and decisive action from his subordinates, he finds that he must help himself and make many of the decisions with insufficient information. He discovers that, while he is the leader of the management team, he is also very much alone.

Many managers ride out this uneasy transition by:

Calling frequent staff meetings to find out what is happening.
Holding long individual interviews with each subordinate.
Taking frequent tours of the organisation's facilities.
Poring over historical files of correspondence and operational reports.
Waiting with impatience for subordinates to resume making decisions and taking risks as they tire of 'lying in the weeds'.

This method of making a transition clearly has its frustrations for the incoming manager, but it is often the only means he can see available to him.

There is, however, another approach, one which I devised several years ago to facilitate what promised to be a very difficult management transition. It is quite straightforward, requires very little time — no more than a day for the management personnel involved — and seems to yield significantly positive results. I refer to it as a 'transition meeting'. While this approach is of my own design, various elements of it have undoubtedly been utilised by organisation consultants many times in the past.

The transition meeting seems particularly relevant when:

The incoming manager is unknown to most of his subordinates.
Considerable anxiety exists because of the forthcoming change of managers.
Breaks in continuity are unacceptable for important, ongoing programmes or projects.
Little time is available at the time of transition for sorting out problems, team-building, etc.
The relevant personnel are willing to be candid.
The capability exists for following up on any action plans developed.

CASE HISTORY

The following case history may best explain how the transition meeting approach can facilitate the management transition process (see the Appendix, pp. 199–200, for an outline of this approach). The initial use of the transition meeting approach occurred several years ago in a large manufacturing plant. Business conditions in one company location dictated the almost immediate transfer to another location of the highly capable and well-liked plant manager. His only possible replacement was a manager who, rightly or wrongly, had developed a reputation as a 'poor' manager of people and resources. His new staff were aware of that reputation. None of them, however, had ever met him. Moreover, he was being transferred from a plant that was currently viewed by his new staff as 'failing'. As a result, his announced appointment was greeted with considerable anxiety, hostility and a staff decision to communicate these concerns to the senior management person responsible for the transfer, and the one to whom the incoming manager would report. (Since the outgoing manager had launched an OD (Organization Development) 'programme' at the plant a year earlier, this concerted action by the staff might be laid at the feet of the team-building and openness-enhancing effects of the OD programme.)

The incoming manager's 'style' appeared inimical to the recently-inaugurated OD efforts, which had proved highly successful both in improving organisational performance and in improving the inter-personal and managerial skills of the plant's management personnel. Anxiety about the incoming manager's potential non-support of the OD programme added to the trepidations of his staff. Moreover, the outgoing manager was 'a hard act to follow'. He was well-liked in the plant and in the community, and under his leadership the plant had recently attained peak production and efficiency. He had also been extremely successful in dealing with explosive labour matters in the past, and the union contract was shortly due to expire.

Clearly there were many factors pointing to a potentially disruptive transition and the need for some sort of facilitative effort:

An unknown incoming manager whose reputation inspired little confidence among his subordinates.

An outgoing manager whose performance was viewed as highly successful.

Apparent 'style' differences between outgoing and incoming managers that appeared to threaten the prevailing organisation climate and methods.

High anxiety among management staff members.

An impending labour contract negotiation.

Very little time to make the transition.

Awareness of these conditions and concern for the transition resulted in the senior manager requesting my consultation, which led to the formulation of the three stages of the transition meeting.

Stage I: Pre-meeting discussions

Before any action could be taken on such a meeting, however, it was critical that the senior, incoming and outgoing managers be convinced of the need to act decisively to make the transition successful and that they be willing to 'experiment' with a novel approach. The senior manager was agreeable. He and I had worked together in the past, and he was convinced that something did in fact need to be done. Moreover, it was important to him that the OD programme at the plant should proceed without difficulty and that the new manager should also succeed. The senior manager had personally backed him and was convinced that, with help, the incoming manager could both be a significant resource to the organisation and make a success of his new assignment. The outgoing manager (because of concern for the organisation and confidence that I could help) agreed to experiment. The new manager agreed as well, particularly with the support and encouragement of the senior manager. As a result, a series of discussions was planned with the various participants of the forthcoming transition meeting, designed to bring them into the meeting with a positive frame of mind and a commitment to the success of the transition.

Outgoing manager
In the first discussion with the outgoing manager, an effort was made to elicit his concerns about the transition and his hopes for the future of the organisation, and to develop support for openness and collaborative behaviour in the meeting. I also tried to help him to surface and thus neutralise any subconscious desires he had for the incoming manager to fail. I sought to overcome any negative feelings he had about leaving 'his' organisation in someone else's hands by underscoring his concern for the people in the organisation and for the continued high performance of the people and the organisation alike.

These efforts were most productive. Like most managers who have been instrumental in moulding and creating organisational patterns and practices, he was reluctant to see them change with his departure. He was also able to admit that he had had some not-so-subconscious thoughts and wishes that involved his replacement having organisational difficulties. Bringing these issues into the open and contrasting them with his desires for the continued success of the organisation supported his succeeding positive efforts on behalf of the transition.

Manager's staff

The second meeting, with the manager's staff, was more difficult in that it was necessary to spend considerable time helping the group to voice its anxiety, fears and concerns so that it would be possible for the group to develop empathy for the incoming manager and the problems that he was facing. The time set aside for developing empathy was well spent and yielded a willingness on the part of the staff to take action to facilitate the transition. As a result, the group compiled a list of actions it could take in the transition meeting to make for success. A very useful by-product of this meeting was the staff group's discovery of the obvious — that it had considerable power which it could levy in support of success or failure of the new manager. This recognition emerged in a discussion of the incoming manager's ability to destroy the plant's effectiveness; as one staff member said: 'Yes, he could really make a mess of things, but he can't be successful without our help.'

In this way, then, the staff prepared themselves to enter the transition meeting with a willingness to discuss their concerns, fears, anxieties and commitments candidly. It was realised that in order for the meeting to be a success, the staff would have to be careful not to threaten the incoming manager's perceived prerogatives. Furthermore, the group members would need to focus attention on being maximally supportive of the incoming manager's efforts to understand them and their organisation. They recognised that they had considerable ability to make the transition meeting extremely uncomfortable for him and his subsequent job extremely difficult if they chose to do so. To do so would, of course, jeopardise the success of the organisation and make it difficult to incorporate the new manager's considerable technical expertise into the organisation's resource pool.

The staff also discussed the need to maintain support for each other in the meeting, for while there was considerable enthusiasm for supporting the transition, there was also an awareness that some of the group members might, through ambition, fear, preference for avoiding risks, or whatever, tend to be less than candid and thus undermine the meeting. A discussion of all these factors resulted in a commitment (by the end of the meeting) to work together to make the transition meeting a success.

Incoming manager

The third and last meeting, with the incoming manager, was critical. Since we had no previous experience in working together, it was first important to build trust between us. We devoted all the available time we could to that process and I then 'walked' him through the forthcoming meeting, and explained how each of the various phases would work.

I encouraged a positive outlook on his part by emphasising the positive orientations of the outgoing manager and his staff. I also worked to help him develop empathy for the outgoing manager and the staff and encouraged him to speculate as to the transition concerns that they were likely to have and to express to him in the meeting. From that discussion, we developed a meeting plan for him that involved being candid, trying to listen well, avoiding implications of threat or the use of power, encouraging candidness by all the other participants and supporting their efforts to learn about him and to learn about his values and techniques. The final product of our discussion was his list of the following objectives for the transition meeting:

(1) To get people to express what they are committed to.
(2) To get to know them as people.
(3) To know what the group is trying to do and why.
(4) To discover what their fears are with regard to interruptions in what they are trying to accomplish.
(5) To gain their confidence that [I] can work with them without being destructive to their present system of management.

By the end of that meeting, the incoming manager was not only willing to view the transition meeting as an experiment, but saw it as a logical and useful approach for entering the organisation with a minimum of disruption.

Stage II: The transition meeting

My role in this stage was that of both a facilitator and a stage manager. Thus, after a short period of informal conversation and introductions of the new manager to the various staff members, I formally began the first of the five phases of the meeting.

Phase 1: Introduction

I began the meeting by listing for all participants my understanding of the objectives of the meeting and requesting their suggestions for modifications of that list. The objectives were:

(1) Getting to know each other.
(2) Clarifying concerns and commitments.
(3) Identifying problems and difficulties.
(4) Identifying factors necessary to facilitate management transition.
(5) Planning for action.

After testing for acceptance of these objectives, I next restated the factors that I felt would facilitate meeting those objectives:

(1) An exercise of candidness in the discussion.
(2) Efforts to empathise with the concerns and commitments of all the other participants.
(3) A willingness to confront difficult issues.
(4) A recognition that all participants shared a common concern for the success of the organisation.

The last part of the introduction was devoted to explaining the general structure and phases of the rest of the meeting.

Phase 2: Sharing of concerns and commitments

Outgoing manager — An open recitation of his hopes for the future success of the organisation, regrets at leaving and concerns for the continuation of a number of 'pet' projects such as the OD programme, set the stage for the sharing of the other participants.

Manager's staff — Obliquely at first, and then with greater candour, the staff listed the concerns and anxieties that they were experiencing in anticipation of the change of managers. They also listed the various programmes and projects to which they were committed and their hopes for the continued emphasis upon these programmes, prime among which was the OD programme.

Incoming manager — He was placed last on the agenda so as to minimise the pressure on him, since he was the participant most likely to feel threatened by the content of the meeting. His professed desire for the future success of the organisation and for seeing the commitments of the group met led to an explanation of his preferred style of management. He capped his comments by assuring the group that he could support their efforts to meet the goals to which they were committed.

Phase 3: General discussion

The purpose of this portion of the meeting was to examine the previous sharings of commitments and concerns, to allow the incoming manager to address himself to the expressed issues and to unearth other issues that would be of importance during the remainder of the meeting and in their future work together. As the discussion of the various concerns and commitments proceeded, I pointed up commonalities and encouraged the group to focus on the high degree to which the various parties were in agreement. This, in concert with the incoming manager's expressions of willingness to support the commitments of the staff and to continue the various programmes designed to improve the organisation, tended to build trust and raise a feeling of optimism in the group.

As the discussion progressed, a number of important issues emerged. One in particular (which was discussed and resolved) is especially noteworthy. The group began to discuss management style, and in that discussion it became clear that the incoming manager's experience, habit and preference was to manage his staff as a group of individuals. The staff group, on the other hand, had over the preceding year moved significantly away from this form of management under the outgoing manager, and had become both in favour of and adept at operating as a team. The new manager's awareness of the extent to which the group truly operated in this fashion was heightened when he asked the production manager to 'suppose' that a particular piece of production equipment had broken down, and what he would do about it. When the manager hesitated, the new manager responded with, 'Well, what are you going to do? You've got a problem.' At this point, the maintenance manager responded by saying, 'It's not *his* problem, . . . it's *our* problem!'

Phase 4: Identification of issues needing to be explored to facilitate the transition

The group began by identifying and listing the various issues that could affect the success of the transition. They next selected those issues that required discussion and assigned priorities to them. The last step was to discuss the issues and to explore the various ramifications, methods of coping with problems and various alternatives available.

Phase 5: Action planning

The last phase of the meeting involved a listing of all the various actions that the group members would take in order to facilitate the management transition. Some of the work was done in subgroups. When this phase of the meeting was complete, the group had developed a plan complete with timetables, action steps and responsibilities. The plan covered such objectives as helping the new manager to become acquainted with the technical operation, introducing him to management personnel, facilitating closer working relationships between him and his staff members, planning for his involvement in the forthcoming labour contract negotiation and continuing and supporting ongoing programmes and projects.

Stage III: Post-meeting follow-up activities

A number of meetings with various participants were held subsequent to the transition meeting in order to capitalise on the work already done.

Outgoing manager

In this meeting we discussed the process and content of the meeting, his role in it and his resultant learnings. I encouraged him to list and commit himself to subsequent behaviours which he could take to maximise chances for a successful transition and to try to avoid unconscious, counter-productive behaviour that would destroy the potential success of our efforts. His list included: statements to the staff supportive of continued candour and cooperation with the new manager, expressions of optimism regarding the new manager, suppression of expressions of pessimism about the success of the transition and maximum candour with the new manager regarding subsequent transition details and issues.

Incoming manager

In this meeting I gave him feedback and support on his role in the meeting, and coached him on actions he could take to follow up and support the work on the action plan that had been generated. I suggested, for example, that he attempt to provide positive support for team effort, avoid 'one-to-one' management, maintain candour with and among his subordinates and permit his staff to 'help' him make the transition. I also encouraged his continued use of his staff OD consultant for feedback and consultation, and encouraged him to view both the meeting process and content (some of which had been quite uncomfortable for him to experience) as a high-risk endeavour that he and his new staff had successfully undertaken together.

Senior manager

In this meeting I asked him to list the difficulties the incoming manager would be facing. (Examples: uncertainty about the senior manager's expectations as to his management style and behaviour, and an unconscious tendency to fractionate the staff team by dealing with subordinates in a one-to-one style.) Once we had discussed the list and I felt he had empathy for his new subordinate, I then asked him to examine and list the means available to him for supporting the new manager's endeavours to make the transition successfully. His list included such actions as clarifying his expectations for the new manager, frequent counselling and discussion, and sitting in on plant staff meetings.

Manager's staff

I discussed with the group the content, process and learnings in the transition meeting and congratulated the staff on their success in living up to their pre-meeting plan. I also strongly encouraged the group to work together to meet its commitment to maintaining openness and forward progress on the action plan.

POSITIVE RESULTS

Several years have passed since the meeting described in the case history. The success of the transition and the continued and increased success of the organisation are now matters of record. The incoming manager moved into the organisation smoothly (the labour contract was settled without incident) and effectively supported and facilitated work on key programmes. His management approach blended well with the approach of his subordinates, and he was able to offer both management direction and technical expertise to the organisation. When he left for a new and desirable company position after two years, he was considered to have been highly successful. Under his leadership, the plant had attained a record climb in production combined with the lowest production costs it had ever had.

As for the outgoing manager, he moved into his new assignment with optimism and energy, and at the end of two years had achieved wide recognition for his skilful marshalling of resources to effectively 'rescue' a plant in crisis.

Experience with this approach and follow-up data convince me that it can be a powerful and successful tool to facilitate the transition of managers into other organisations. There seem a number of reasons why, in other organisations, such an approach will be successful:

(1) The fear of the unknown is removed. Key personnel have more information about each other and know what to expect.
(2) A new manager's move into an organisation is strengthened without threatening his managerial prerogatives.
(3) All parties involved experience a reduction in anxiety.
(4) Key people can have a success experience as they work together to tackle and resolve a high-importance, high-risk task.
(5) Subordinates are involved in helping a new boss rather than in second-guessing him.
(6) Subordinates can avoid the anxiety and negative self-image that arise from 'lying in the weeds'.
(7) Meaningful programmes and projects requiring priority are allowed to proceed without interruption.
(8) New skills and resources are quickly incorporated into the organisation.
(9) Everyone involved ends up with immediate plans for action.

There is no question that a number of specific factors facilitated the success of the meeting described in the case history. The support of the senior manager, the high-stakes 'need to succeed' for the incoming manager, the previous trust-building in the organisation, and the ongoing efforts of an on-site OD consultant all served to yield positive results.

POTENTIAL PROBLEMS

A number of factors can work against the success of such an approach. An incoming manager can fear that his prerogatives as a manager will be weakened or lost, various participants in the meeting can fail to be candid and honest, and participants may respond with counter-productive behaviour to the tension that such a meeting can evoke. Additionally, if the action plan contains unrealistic and unattainable goals and deadlines, failure to accomplish those goals can be a negative experience for the participants. Even more destructive would be the failure to carry out the action plan through lack of support by the incoming manager.

SUMMARY AND CONCLUSIONS

In times of major personnel changes, the transition meeting can be a helpful approach to avoiding the disruptions that follow such changes. It is particularly appropriate when:

The incoming manager is unknown to most of his subordinates.
Considerable anxiety exists because of the forthcoming change of managers.
Breaks in continuity are unacceptable in important, ongoing programmes or projects.
Little time is available at the time of transition for sorting out problems, team-building, etc.
The relevant personnel are willing to be candid.
The capability exists for following up on any action plans developed.

While the transition meeting can be particularly helpful when a new top manager moves into an organisation, this general approach can be utilised whenever any individual joins an organisation. The need to understand individual and group concerns and commitments, to cement group membership, to examine values, to avoid unproductive time expenditures, to utilise new skills and resources quickly, and to develop plans for facilitating transition can make some modification of this approach a worthwhile consideration. Moreover, the transition meeting can be conducted without professional help, which makes it a useful tool available to the results-oriented manager.

APPENDIX. OUTLINE OF THE TRANSITION MEETING

Stage I: *Pre-meeting discussions*

>   Develop positive attitudes among participants
>   Build empathy for other participants
>   Support commitment to a successful transition
> Discussion 1. Outgoing manager (1 hour)
> Discussion 2. Manager's staff (1—2 hours)
> Discussion 3. Incoming manager (1 hour)

Stage II: The transition meeting

Phase 1: Consultant* introduction (15—30 mins)
    Restate meeting objectives
    Focus on facilitative behaviours
    Preview meeting agenda
Phase 2: Sharing of concerns and commitments (30—45 mins)
    Outgoing manager first
    Manager's staff next
    Incoming manager last
Phase 3: General discussion (1—2 hours)
    Examine sharings
    Respond to important issues
    Identify additional issues
Phase 4: Identification of issues needing to be explored to facilitate the
         transition (1—1½ hours)
    Set priorities
    Problem solve
Phase 5: Action planning (1 hour)
    Develop timetables and responsibilities

Stage III: Post-meeting follow-up activities

Phase 1: Discussions with participants
      Support constructive behaviour
      Maintain positive attitudes
      Maintain empathy for participants
   Discussion 1. Outgoing manager (1 hour)
   Discussion 2. Manager's staff (1 hour)
   Discussion 3. Incoming manager (1 hour)
Phase 2: Progress review (two hours)
      Evaluate progress after six to eight weeks
      Plan next steps

---

* Although the term 'consultant' is used here, this role can successfully be filled by anyone not directly involved with the transition: other line or staff managers, personnel, industrial relations and organisation development specialists, or anyone else who can take on the role of an objective third party.

13. A Training Programme for the Modification of Coping Processes

Douglas Duckworth

In chapter 4 some features of coping processes were examined, on the grounds that coping is a salient issue when considering transitions. Coping was portrayed as a series of control activities where an individual was endeavouring to operate in such a manner that his various learned and innate requirements were catered for. Some of the possible consequences of deficits in control skills were explored, and an approach for helping a person to increase the general effectiveness of his control activities was outlined, together with some possible training strategies. This chapter describes a training programme designed to implement that approach. Since it could be implemented in a number of different ways, and using any of a range of different teaching techniques, this training programme is seen as one of a *family* of possible implementations. A variety of measures were taken of the impact of the training, and some of the general findings that are emerging from an analysis of these data will be described.

THE DESIGN OF THE TRAINING PROGRAMME[1]

Subjects, training groups, and overall design

A population of approximately 230 undergraduate students was approached with information about the training programme (TP), during class-time. The TP was described as a course in problem-solving and decision making, designed to help a person increase his control over himself and his environment. They were told that the course was to enable research into ideas and techniques that were going to be used in a Management Development Workshop. The group of students came from a wide variety of parent disciplines, and consisted of all those reading some Management subjects as part of their degree course. Of the 76 who indicated interest, 64 were eventually selected for the TP. Since the personality dimension of locus of control (Rotter, 1966) was relevant to the study, the volunteers completed the Internal—External (I—E) Scale (see chapter 11, p. 178) (M = 11.48; SD = 4.29). A comparison of these scores with those collected from the rest of the students at a later date showed that there was no evidence that the volunteers differed in locus of control from the non-volunteers.

In order to permit an evaluation of some of the effects of the TP and an examination of the moderating influence of the locus of control dimension, the volunteers were first divided into two sets of 32 on the basis of I—E scores. Those with a score of 12 or more were designated 'externals', and those with 11 or less 'internals'. Then, four externals and four internals were randomly selected for each of four training groups and four equivalent control groups. The latter were informed that for reasons connected with the research they would receive the TP at a later stage. Training groups of this size were formed so that participants would have the benefit of some individual attention from the trainer, together with the opportunity for sharing and comparing their experiences with their peers. From the trainer's viewpoint, group sessions as opposed to individual sessions enabled some economy of time.

Each of the four training groups attended five sessions in a room on campus. The sessions were spread over five weeks, and each lasted for one and a half hours. In any particular week, therefore, the trainer conducted four equivalent sessions. The TP was scheduled in this way so that the ideas and techniques to which participants were exposed could be examined and tested by them in settings quite distinct from the training situation. This would not have been so possible if the activities and content of the TP had been accommodated to, for example, a day or a residential weekend. To facilitate these processes further, a series of assignments was completed by participants between the sessions. Toward the end of the TP, the trainer provided written comments on the first three assignments completed by participants. Each session had a warm-up period of about ten minutes during which time a liberal supply of tea and coffee was served, and discussion was not restricted to the task in hand. An orientation sheet was distributed during this period, which had a space for personal notes. Synopses of the ideas from sessions were also given out when appropriate.

The structure and content of the first session

In attempting to create some realistic expectations, provide adequate background information, and begin to place responsibility for change firmly in the hands of the participants, the following points were elaborated:

(a) Although people receive an extensive education in academic and practical subjects, they are given relatively little instruction in how to manage their lives and solve their problems. One purpose of the TP was to reduce this learning deficit.

(b) The TP would not be like studying another academic subject. The emphasis would be on developing skills, not just on accumulating more facts. It would be concerned with the process of living: helping individuals to exercise more control in their lives and to manage them more satisfactorily.

(c) The TP was not a form of therapy, in the ordinary sense of the word. In addition, the aim was not primarily to help participants solve any current problems that they happened to have, but to help them become independent problem-solvers, so that they would be better equipped to manage future problem situations on their own.

(d) The trainer would be seeking to arrange a learning situation in which participants had the opportunity to change some of their ideas about problems, their approaches to problems and their skills for dealing with them.

(e) The responsibility for learning and changing would be almost entirely upon the participants. The trainer would endeavour to exert only minimal pressure upon individuals. It would be quite possible, and fully permitted, for a person to attend the TP and not gain much benefit. If a participant wanted to change in any of the ways described in the TP, it would involve him in a great deal of self-imposed hard work and practice.

(f) A major purpose of the exercise from the trainer's viewpoint was to conduct research into any effects the TP had upon people. This would involve participants in such things as filling out questionnaires at various points, and would necessitate the sessions being tape-recorded. Also, it would mean that the continued attendance of all participants at the sessions was highly desirable, even if some were to find that the TP was of little value to them.

This introduction was concluded with a preview of the TP in which the next four sessions were briefly described. Attention was then turned to the first theory module. The aim was to introduce participants to the concept of a difference between a state of affairs that exists (or, that might exist in the future) and a state of affairs that is required. Any observed, non-trivial difference was to be termed a *discrepancy*. The nature, recognition and articulation of discrepancies, possible reactions to them, and a discrepancy-based definition of what constituted a problematic situation were considered. A participant was encouraged to describe a required state of affairs in terms of what *he wanted*, so that the responsibility for any action tended to rest upon himself. The sequence of ideas was:

(a) If a person wishes to cope more effectively with the various problems, difficulties and unsatisfactory states of affairs in his life, it is useful to start in any particular case by articulating and then probing the discrepancy between:

(i)   the state of affairs that exists (or, that may exist)
(ii) the state of affairs that he wants.

(b) The states of affairs described in discrepancies can be articulated at the level of specific situations (e.g. that person spoke sharply to me at the meeting), or at progressively more general and abstract levels (e.g. people never seem to treat me with respect).

(c) A discrepancy can arise through either of two kinds of change: a change in a person's mind about the state of affairs that he wants, or a change in some existing (or, potential) state of affairs. In both cases, the state of affairs in question can be something to do with the person, or something to do with his situation.

(d) Some discrepancies can be perceived immediately, but others are implicit, evidenced by feelings of dissatisfaction and sometimes definite emotional states (e.g. irritation, anxiety, depression, and so on).

(e) Implicit discrepancies usually can be inferred and made explicit after the thoughts and events have been recalled that took place immediately before any feelings or emotions arose.

(f) When experiencing any kind of discrepancy, a person has three alternative ways of responding open to him: doing nothing, exacerbating the situation, or reacting constructively. The latter, even if it leads to the decision to do nothing further, is the only logical alternative for a person who wishes to exercise more control in his life.

(g) When a discrepancy is considered, it may be that only routine planning and activities are necessary in order to cope with it. But there are occasions when it is not possible to see what actions will resolve a discrepancy. This state of affairs would be referred to as a problematic situation.

(h) The remainder of the TP would be concerned with the question of how to probe a discrepancy with a view to deciding what was the most useful kind of action to take.

After this theory module, the assignment for the coming week was distributed. Part of it was concerned with a procedure for facilitating assimilation of the theory, but the main part was an exercise in which participants were requested to produce a list of up to ten current discrepancies from their own experience. The aim here was to promote the development of relevant perceptual skills, and the tendency to respond constructively to discrepancies. It was suggested that they should compile the list using two methods: firstly, by surveying the various areas of their lives and working on anything that was definitely unsatisfactory, and secondly, by paying attention to their feelings as they experienced the various events of the week. For each discrepancy in the list, they were requested to consider what feelings, thoughts or observations led them to notice it, whether it constituted a problematic situation for them, what they felt like doing when they noticed it, and what they actually did about it.

The structure and content of the second session

The experience of the previous week's assignment was discussed and related to the theory covered in the first session, and then attention was turned to the second theory module. In the short term, the aim in considering the theory and techniques in this session was to help participants gain some control over the kinds of emotional responses that can lead to avoidance behaviour, or disruption of coping responses in the face of a discrepancy. The longer-term aim was to facilitate the gradual removal of potentially self-defeating irrational requirements, and the substitution of corresponding rational requirements. In practice, this entails a person moving from a position where he implicitly or explicitly believes that something (to do with himself or his environment) *should, ought,* or *must* be different from the way it is, to a position where he simply *prefers* or *wants* something to be different. The consequences of holding irrational requirements have been fully explored by Ellis (e.g., Ellis, 1973a), and I developed the theory and techniques used in this session from the theories underlying his rational-emotive therapy. The sequence of ideas was:

(a) For many people a significant proportion of discrepancies (routine or problematic) have negative (unpleasant, undesirable) feelings associated with them. Such feelings can increase the apparent significance of a discrepancy and make it more unpleasant to experience and difficult to resolve.

(b) Feelings can be regarded as inner responses to the way a person is thinking at any particular time, so if a person wishes to experience less negative feelings one strategy he can adopt is that of making explicit, and then changing, some aspects of his thinking.

(c) Two kinds of thinking can be isolated that play a particularly important role in determining a person's experience of negative feelings. The first kind is related to how a person thinks about himself, and the second to how he thinks about the various components of his world.

(d) In the first case under (c) it is as if the person thinks: (i) It is essential that I am a good, adequate, and acceptable person: it would be awful to be anything else; (ii) in order to be such a person I must, in my own judgment and that of significant others, behave in particular ways and possess certain attributes (e.g. be competent in my profession; be liked by people that I choose; be achieving something in life).

(e) If a person matches up to these demands upon himself, he will feel satisfaction; if he fails and begins to conclude that he must therefore be inadequate in some ways as a person, he will tend to feel depressed and maybe indulge in self-recrimination; if he anticipates encountering a situation in the future in which he may fail, and thus prove that he is in some ways inadequate as a person, he will tend to feel apprehension and anxiety.

(f) People vary in how strongly they believe in the relationship between their behaviours and their goodness, adequacy, and acceptability. This will partly account for differences between people in the intensity of feelings they experience in particular types of situation.

(g) If a person wishes to avoid the experiences and inefficiencies generated by this kind of thinking, he can do it by systematically eradicating it and consciously adopting a more realistic alternative. For example, he can work toward the position that any act of classifying himself as good or bad, and so on, on the basis of his behaviours and attributes is rather meaningless. He can accept himself as a fact of life and can decide (on any grounds that he chooses) what personal qualities he prefers, and work toward them. If he cannot achieve his goals he can either seek to devise a more sophisticated strategy or decide that his time and energy would be better spent in the pursuit of some other goals.

(h) In the second case under (c) it is as if the person thinks: (i) the various components of my world should be good, proper and acceptable; (ii) in order to be like this, they must meet certain conditions that are laid down (e.g., people should be punctual; my car should start each morning; life should not create too many problems for me).

(i) If the various components of a person's world measure up to his expectations, he will feel satisfied. But if any do not, he will tend to become indignant or angry, implicitly (or, explicitly) demanding that they change and become as they should be. Since demanding in the first instance does not amount to doing anything, the person frequently is left without the change that he wants.

(j) If a person wishes to avoid the experiences and inefficiencies generated by this kind of thinking, he can do it by systematically transforming his various demands into action-oriented personal preferences. This process will be aided when cases present themselves by recollection of these two facts: (i) there is no law (except a person's own arbitrary and obviously ineffective ruling) that dictates that the world should be anything other than it is at any point in time, and (ii) apart from fortuitous changes, the only thing that will cause the various components of a person's world to be as he wants them to be is his own constructive action to that end.

After the theory module, the assignment for the coming week was distributed. The main part of this was an exercise in which participants were required either to choose a minimum of two discrepancies from the list produced during the first assignment, or to specify two or more other cases of current concern. Either way, the discrepancies were to be examples that had associated negative feelings, preferably different kinds of feelings. A *Scheme of Questions* was included with the assignment. It was devised by me to help a person to work back from a specific discrepancy to a meaningful explication of the thinking that lay behind his negative feelings. It included some worked examples to illustrate the process. The *Scheme* first of all asked a person mentally to simulate the limit of the discrepancy, that is, the situation where he could not bring about the state of affairs that he wanted, and then very carefully to identify the feelings or emotions that he would be experiencing. Next, the person was asked to state why he would feel this way, in order to help him gain an entry into his own implicit theory of the situation. From this point on, although the principle of the questions was fairly straightforward, they became more difficult to answer in a useful way. Practice was needed for a person to elicit new information from himself, as opposed merely to repeating the same information or going off at a tangent by getting into a rationalisation. The principle behind the questions was that any reasonably complete account of why a person feels a certain way will indicate at least one thing that he is wanting or demanding which is of a more general kind than the specific goal articulated in the discrepancy. Further, if a person gives an account of why he wants or demands this state of affairs, it in turn will indicate some still more general state of affairs that he wants or demands. At this stage, many people will have gone as far as they can. Some people, though, may find it necessary to repeat these steps several more times in order for their theories/explanations to be exhausted. Once the process has been completed, a person has before him a meaningful illustration of the theoretical ideas: he can see either a chain of reasoning that links his specific behaviours to self-evaluations, or a chain of demands that links his specific demands to his more general demands on the world at large. This puts him in a position from which he can systematically modify his thinking. If the person mentions two different types of feeling in his original statement (e.g., anger and anxiety), in order to get a more complete picture he will need to apply the technique to each feeling in turn. This is because the theory suggests that in such a case both kinds of thinking are operative.

The process can be illustrated by considering a student who predicts that he may fail an examination, and very much wants to pass it. As he contemplates this discrepancy, he feels unpleasantly anxious and apprehensive in a way that cannot be accounted for by the objective consequences of failing. If it turns out that he thinks he would feel very ashamed should he fail, he might come to realise that his shame would be partly due to the fact that certain significant others were thinking that he was not in fact very competent. If he examines this account, he will be able to see that in wanting to pass the examination he is also wanting these other people to think that he is competent. If he pursues the question of why he wants others to think that he is competent, he will probably find that to be considered academically competent makes him feel in some senses adequate and acceptable as a person, and that this is one of the most general and pervasive things that he wants. In fact, 'needs' is usually a more appropriate term. A person has little choice in the matter until he performs a reconstruction that brings all this to light. Part of the reason, then, why the anticipation of failing an important examination can be anxiety-provoking to a person, is that it immediately raises disturbing, and in the first instance largely uncontrollable implications about his adequacy, acceptability, and status as a person. If, after the above type of analysis, the person persists in modifying this chain of reasoning (as in (g) above) and so obviates his self-administered threat, then both the anticipation of the outcome of the examination and the outcome itself — even if it is a failure — will be less unpleasant. In terms of constructive problem-solving, it is likely that both the preparation for the examination and post-examination coping will be more adaptive and less disrupted by emotional activation. This may be particularly true if the person is emotionally reactive in Eysenck's (e.g. 1967) sense.

The structure and content of the third session

It was considered that by this point in the TP it was appropriate to review progress, and spend a longer period dealing with any difficulties or confusions that participants had experienced with the assignments, theories and techniques. So each person was invited to say something about his experience with the previous assignment, and to raise any other issues that were concerning him. This led into a general discussion in which the trainer took up any issues where there was lack of clarity, and also introduced a few new ideas when relevant. The main topics discussed were:

(a) Although problematic situations by definition involve discrepancies, and can sometimes be difficult to resolve, this does not mean that they always generate unpleasant experiences. If strong negative feelings are associated with them, until these are dealt with the experience may be unpleasant. But there is not any necessary connection between difficulty and unpleasantness. The resolution of a problematic situation can be a challenging and enjoyable process.

(b) The first kind of thinking described in Session Two can militate against the identification and probing of unpleasant problematic situations. A person can think that if he is normal he should not really have this kind of thing in his life, and therefore he may be unwilling to perceive the facts and do anything about them.

(c) To probe the thinking behind the negative feelings associated with a discrepancy, and even to change it, does not automatically resolve the discrepancy. It will only do this in cases where the discrepancy becomes insignificant once the negative feelings have been dealt with.

(d) At one extreme, the *Scheme* can be used for probing the thinking that lies behind negative feelings associated with long-standing and difficult problematic situations. At the other extreme, it can be used for probing relatively transitory problematic situations (e.g., feeling uncomfortable in the presence of another person). It can also be used for gaining a retrospective understanding of reactions and feelings in situations in the past that still remain enigmatic, and for helping other people to understand some of their difficulties.

After the discussion, the assignment for the coming week was distributed. The main part of this was an exercise in which participants were requested to use the *Scheme* to probe three recent occasions (no matter how trivial) when they experienced negative feelings, as a way of reinforcing their understanding of the theory and their skill in using the techniques.

The structure and content of the fourth session

The experience of the previous week's assignment was discussed and related to the ideas and techniques covered up to that point, and then attention was turned to the third theory module. This theory, together with ideas added to it in the fifth session, was largely concerned with the resolution of discrepancies through the alteration of existing states of affairs, and/or the alteration of specific requirements. In this fourth session the theory consisted of an exposition, with illustrative examples, of the principles embodied in *A Guide For Resolving Problematic Situations* that was distributed to participants. This *Guide* was devised by me and took the form of a programme designed to lead a person from his statement of a discrepancy through to an evaluation of his implementation of specific tactics for resolving it. For the purposes of the *Guide*, the discrepancy that was considered to be at the core of the problematic situation was termed the central discrepancy. Clearly, since discrepancies can be articulated at various levels of abstraction (see Session One) it would be useful for a person to experiment until he found the most fruitful level in a particular case. The techniques for generating and evaluating the consequences and utility of alternative resolution strategies and tactics were adapted from the approach suggested by D'Zurilla and Goldfried (1971) for training clients to solve problems. They will not be described here in any detail. The recommendations for how to use the *Guide*, and the main principles underlying it were:

(a) The *Guide* was intended to be a flexible tool, adapted to suit specific needs. Following a detailed exploration to see what could be involved in the resolution of problematic situations, it was recommended that participants should aim simply to incorporate some of the principles into their everyday thinking (e.g., considering indirect, as well as direct resolution strategies).

(b) In approaching a problematic situation, it is highly advisable first to deal with any associated negative feelings, in the manner previously described.

(c) Although all problematic situations have the same basic structure, subjectively they seem to take two major forms, which can be designated *Type A* and *Type B* problematic situations, respectively.

(d) In a *Type A* problematic situation, an unsatisfactory state of affairs has arisen and the person wishes to make it more satisfactory. For example, a teacher finds that he can no longer control his class, and wishes to regain control. (The ideas can be transposed for a state of affairs that is anticipated in the future.)

(e) In a *Type B* problematic situation, a person has decided, on what feels to be his own initiative, to try and create a particular state of affairs in the future. For example, a person decides that he would like to apply for a particular job he has seen advertised, in another part of the country.

(f) For each type of problematic situation, two kinds of resolution strategy can be investigated, one direct and the other indirect. In any particular problematic situation, both may have application.

(g) In *Type A* problematic situations, a direct resolution strategy would focus on influencing the unsatisfactory state of affairs. In terms of the example given, this might involve using more powerful social-influence techniques in order to regain control in the teaching situation. In contrast, an indirect resolution strategy would focus on reducing or removing any undesirable consequences of the state of affairs. This approach would be particularly relevant in cases where the significance or importance of the central discrepancy stemmed primarily from the undesirable consequences associated with the unsatisfactory state of affairs. It would also be relevant where the probability of achieving a direct resolution was low (e.g., when a friend is dying). In terms of the example, the teacher might notice that some of his colleagues were having similar problems, and this could lead to him convincing his superiors that the lack of control was not attributable to a deficit in his pupil-management skills, but rather to organisational factors beyond his control. In this way, he might be left without the control that he initially desired, but with increased assurance that some of the important consequences of not exerting control, such as incurring the displeasure of his superiors and so failing his probationary period, would not materialise. In a very real sense, therefore, this kind of problematic situation can be substantially resolved by an indirect approach.

(h) In *Type B* situations, a direct resolution strategy would focus on causing the desired state of affairs to materialise. In terms of the example given, this might involve the person in a variety of activities calculated to maximise the probability of him securing the new job. These could range from taking professional advice on the structure of a curriculum vitae to initiating a preliminary interview with an appropriate person. In contrast, an indirect resolution strategy would focus on achieving as completely as possible each of the components that contributes to the attractiveness of the specifically desired state of affairs. In terms of the example, this could lead to the person applying for a local job that would give him the extra money that he wanted, together with sufficient flexibility to enable regular trips into the kind of countryside that he enjoyed.

(i) The *Scheme* can usefully be applied to the analysis of *Type B* problematic situations, to check the thinking that lies behind the intentions for the future, and to ensure that the choices are as much under the control of the person as he assumes.

(j) For a specific *Type A* or *B* problematic situation, both direct and indirect strategies need to be generated and evaluated, and then some final mix of strategies selected. After this, operational tactics for implementing the chosen strategies need to be selected in a similar fashion. Finally, after an attempt has been made to implement the resolution strategies, their efficiency needs to be examined, and if necessary, further plans devised and implemented.

After the theory module, the assignment for the coming week was distributed. This consisted of an exercise designed to help participants implement the ideas outlined in the *Guide*. They were requested to list two discrepancies that constituted problematic situations for them, and to use the *Guide* in an attempt to resolve them.

The structure and content of the fifth session

The experience of the previous week's assignment was discussed and related to the material in the *Guide*, and some additional theory points were integrated into this discussion:

(a) In *Type A* problematic situations a particular kind of strategy can sometimes be useful: it involves the person simply moving out of the situation that is unsatisfactory into another where the discrepancy no longer exists. For example, a teacher with a pupil-control problem might be able to get a post in another school where pupils were generally more docile.

(b) In *Type B* problematic situations, it can be useful for a person to change his mind about the specific thing he wants, and seek out some other state of affairs that generates a broadly equivalent experience for him. For example, a person who fails in his application for a particular job can look for another job with similar characteristics.

(c) In these cases, and in other cases of indirect resolution, the reason such strategies can be entertained is that any particular state of affairs a person wants is invariably an expression of more basic or more general wants. These can in fact be at least partially satisfied by more than one specific state of affairs.

(d) The outcomes of a person's interactions with his environment, as he resolves problematic situations, provide him with information that is invaluable when it comes to formulating strategies on subsequent occasions. Also, useful information is generated when a person tests his assumptions and experiments with novel strategies.

After discussion, a sheet was distributed which re-stated the aims of the TP, briefly summarised the three major theory modules, and outlined the final assignment. The latter requested participants systematically to sort through the materials that had been given to them, arrange them in a logical order, and check their understanding of each of the ideas and techniques. This concluding assignment was not followed up.

THE EVALUATION OF THE TRAINING PROGRAMME

In order to gain some insight into the impact of the TP, various categories of data were accumulated. From the participants, information was gathered about their reactions to the different aspects of the TP. From participants and control subjects, measures were taken of individual attributes that might be expected to change as a result of the training. Information was also collected after the TP about how participants and control subjects responded in some real-life situations, and what grades they gained in their examinations.

Reactions to the TP were gathered in order to understand more about how the ideas, techniques and assignments were perceived and reacted to by participants. They wrote about their expectations before the TP; after each session they rated such things as its usefulness and difficulty; at the beginning of each session they rated their experiences with the assignments; and eight weeks after the completion of the TP they were interviewed concerning their overall evaluations of it. Some of this information is being used to provide a basis for a detailed study of how selected individuals responded to the TP.

One objective of the TP was to increase a person's belief in the efficacy of his own control processes, as a means of supporting constructive response tendencies as opposed to passivity. Rotter's (1966) scale for measuring locus of control was therefore administered. It was used before the TP, as already described, to give a basis for an initial categorisation of subjects. It was administered again, immediately after and then eight weeks after the TP, in order to examine any differences between participants and control subjects that might emerge as a result of the TP. Another objective of the TP was to help a person gain more control of certain of his potentially malfunctional emotional reactions, and in the longer term to change some of the irrational beliefs that contribute to such reactions. Form A of the Eysenck Personality Inventory (Eysenck & Eysenck, 1964) was therefore administered immediately after and then eight weeks after the TP, and interest centered on differences in emotional stability that might exist between participants and control subjects. An attitude questionnaire was also completed by all subjects at the same intervals. This was to assess any differences in expectations regarding the possibility of personal change and the quality of daily experience, and also any differences of attitude towards activities such as examining personal thoughts, feelings and motivations. It was anticipated that the experience of the TP might lead to changes in some of these attitudes. Immediately after the TP participants and control subjects provided written answers to questions about the kinds of strategies they would employ in four types of problem situations. Differences in approach were once more expected.

Eight weeks after the TP, participants and control subjects returned written responses to an assignment given to them at the close of the TP. This assignment requested each person to report some of his observations and responses on two occasions when he experienced negative feelings, and on one occasion when he faced a definite problem. Differences in approach and level of insight were expected between the two groups. Finally, in order to move away from self-reports, examination performance was examined. Grades obtained by participants and control subjects in their year-end Management examinations were collected. Also, the final degree performance was investigated of all who graduated during the fifteen-month period after the TP. Examinations are a major task facing students. They call forth an array of coping processes, and the grades gained by a person tend to play an important role in his future affairs, both within the university and elsewhere. Examination grades therefore provided a useful, unobtrusive (cf. Webb *et al.*, 1966) measure of coping activities.

THE RESULTS FROM THE EVALUATION

So far, the results from the evaluation are very encouraging. A full account of the results will be given in a forthcoming publication. In general, comparisons between participants and control subjects show that the TP had a range of definite effects upon the participants, and that changes were relatively stable over the eight-week period after the TP. For example, after the TP the participants evidenced a considerably higher level of emotional stability than the control subjects ($p < .01$).

Eight weeks later this difference between the groups was maintained at an almost identical level. Examination performance also showed the impact of the TP. It was predicted, for example, that during the fifteen-month period after the TP, participants would gain higher grades than control subjects in their final degree examinations. This prediction was confirmed ($p < .02$), thus supporting the idea that the TP was capable of generating quite far-reaching changes in a person's ability to manage his control activities.

In conclusion, therefore, it would seem that training of this kind holds considerable promise as a means of augmenting the skills necessary for the successful management of transitions. It has relevance to the personal management of *affective* responses to transitions, for example, and also to the management of a very important feature of transition situations: their relative *novelty*.

NOTES

1. At present, all materials used in the Training Programme are in the form of unpublished manuscripts. Further details can be obtained from Douglas Duckworth, Department of Management Studies, University of Leeds, Leeds LS2 9JT, England.

PART FOUR

Transition Dynamics: A New Area for Study

14.   Signposts for the Future

John Adams and John Hayes

The intention throughout this book has been to establish the fact that personal transitions represent a potential new area of inquiry. Whether the changes and disruptions each of us faces in the course of our lives are intentional ones, ones brought on as a total surprise, or attendant upon natural life stages, we have to make some adjustments or adaptations. While there are costs involved in these changes in the form of physical and emotional stresses and strains, they also carry opportunity value with them. The thesis has been that when one understands the transition process, one can make personal choices that will reduce the costs and enhance the prospects for personal learning and growth.

PHASES OF TRANSITIONS

One of the ways transition processes have been described is as a rather predictable sequence of phases. Various phase models are presented in this book and it is interesting to note that while these models are drawn from a broad array of social science sources their phases have a great deal in common.

The general model of transition presented in chapter 1 identifies seven stages in the transition cycle. However the various studies referred to in this book emphasise different phases of this cycle. It would appear that where the transition is seen primarily in terms of a loss, for example death or redundancy, then the major concern for the person in transition is often seen as one of disengagement from the past. Consequently attention tends to be focused on the early stages of immobilisation, minimisation, depression and letting go, and the later stages, concerned with finding and adjusting to a new identity, tend to receive less detailed attention. On the other hand, where the transition is seen primarily in terms of a gain, e.g. starting work, promotion, marriage, then attention tends to be focused on finding and adjusting to a new identity, and the process of disengagement from a past identity is given only passing attention.

One of the major characteristics of the models presented in this book is that the early phases of transition involve periods of uncertainty, denial, anger and depression. These feelings, and especially uncertainty, tend to occur as an early part of one's adjustments to a transition even when the transition is a pleasant one or one that has been entered into intentionally. But even long and eagerly awaited transitions take the person into new areas of experience that require new kinds of responses, which may include denial, anger and depression. Pleasant and expected or otherwise, the early experience of any transition involves reacting to the unknown with at least some motivation to maintain as much as possible of one's self-image and behavioural repertoire. In some circumstances, as pointed out in chapter 6, this initial maintenance of an inappropriate self-image can result in the experience of identity strain.

In order to move beyond these reactive and often unconscious responses to transition and enter into the later phases, where the individual becomes more aware of and responsible for his or her readjustment, it seems necessary to let go of that which one is in transition from. This process of unhooking from the past state empowers or enables the person in transition to take command more fully of how he or she is adapting and responding. As Van Gennep (1960) has described it, we have developed specific rites for many of the most widely experienced transitions to assist with one's 'letting go'. Examples of these rites are the academic degree granting ceremony, the marriage ceremony, the funeral ceremony and house warming parties.

Van Gennep observed that in many societies the passage process involves three steps: (1) social disengagement, wherein the person relinquishes his or her former status; (2) isolation, wherein the person enters into a neutral zone (the letting go period); and (3) rebirth, wherein the person is reintegrated into society with a new status. Perhaps the clearest examples of these stages are the rituals used for admitting boys to adulthood in most aboriginal African and American tribal groups.

It seems to us that our modern Western society provides many of the rites for disengagement, but that people are largely left to their own devices in finding the appropriate 'neutral zone' and in reintegrating. In Parts II and III of this book, an attempt has been made to provide some directions to these latter two stages of passage through rather detailed descriptions of transitions and of means presently available for learning and growing from them. The remainder of this final chapter reviews some of the gaps in our knowledge of transitions and some of the as yet unaddressed needs for learning to manage and grow from one's transitions.

RESEARCH NEEDS

New fields of study evolve from research discoveries more rapidly than they do from theorising that is not empirically tested or based. To date, insufficient research has been done to substantiate or refute the theories and models advanced in this book. It is our belief that new kinds of research are needed in order to facilitate the development of transition dynamics as a field of study.

The social research that has been done on the processes of transitions and, more generally, on individuals' coping and adaptation responses, is far from adequate. Most of these efforts involve the subjects' self-reporting of their experiences. It is well known that individuals' perceptions and recollections are highly subjective and personalised. Further, it has been pointed out repeatedly in earlier chapters that the transition experience itself distorts the individual's perceptions. In other words, a man's description of his emotions and behaviour fifteen minutes after his wife has asked him for a divorce is likely to be quite different from his description of the same phenomena looking back after a year or so. An independent observer might well describe these phenomena in yet a third way. Thus, longitudinal studies are needed which are based on independent sources of data.

From a second standpoint, additional research is needed to determine whether or not strain reduction techniques as described in chapter 10 actually do reduce the incidence of stress-related diseases. We do not yet know, for example, if those who have learned to let go do in fact live longer, happier and healthier lives than the rest of the population. Here again, long term medical and social research is needed.

Third, we must keep in mind the tremendous differences between individuals. We need to understand why a given situation or type of transition affects one person in one way and a second person in a totally different way. In a related way, we have yet to determine the extent to which people's responses to transitions are biologically programmed and the extent to which they are socially learned. Also to be considered is the role of factors such as previous experience, complex technologies, economic levels, verbal skills and so on in the transition experience. As we learn more about the relative impact of all of these factors, we can begin to do a better job of helping people manage their transitions effectively.

Fourth, there are differences between transitions as well as between individuals. Studies are needed that will investigate the differing impacts of and learning potentials inherent in positive and negative transitions and also in transitions under our control and beyond our control.

Overall, there has been relatively little research on how adults experience life, and our society does not encourage us to share our personal experiences. Thus, feelings that may be widely shared and a normal part of adult life remain private, self-induced stressors. In order to change this situation, studies are needed that focus on specific transitions and associated specific stresses. Effective and ineffective coping strategies need to be catalogued. More knowledge is also needed as to what individuals in transition experience as helpful or as hindering within any given phase and in the movement from one phase to the next.

THE APPLICATION OF TRANSITION DYNAMICS

As additional research findings accumulate and new techniques are developed, means for reaching the public need to be developed as well. Usage of the term 'transition' has become widespread over the past few years. There has been a rapid growth in the number of counsellors, consultants, teachers and so on who are working with people in transition. The next step in the development and application of transition dynamics might be a series of conferences of those who are professionally involved in the field. The general public, however, remains unaware generally of the increasing number of transitions in everyone's lives and of the physiological and psychological costs and opportunities. This calls for education to increase the public's awareness of transition and the provision of help for those who experience difficulty coping with transition.

Conferences

In May 1975, the first professional conference dealing specifically with transitions was held in California. At the time we are completing this manuscript, additional such conferences are being contemplated. We believe that several such conferences should be held as the next step in developing transition dynamics as a field of study. Each conference could have a different focus. One conference, for example, could bring together experts from each of the six components identified as being necessary in an integrated approach to strain reduction in chapter 10: work setting, support systems, self-awareness, exercise, diet and letting go. The participants in such a conference could pool their resources to develop a more integrated approach to strain reduction and self-management.

Another conference might focus on a particular type of transition. As the Lakes pointed out in chapter 2, many people are making intentional life-style changes. The knowledge to be gained from a conference that examined life-style changes from several in-depth points of view would be of great use to social science professionals.

If such working conferences were well documented, further books on transitions would be forthcoming and new areas of research and application would evolve.

Educational systems

Future-oriented academic programmes have been established in a few universities. Most of these focus on life in the future from economic, technological or sociological points of view. In these programmes, little attention is given to the magnitude of personal change individuals will have to undergo to live in the future as it is being forecast. It would appear that most of the futurist planners feel that those who cannot cope with the transition to the future will be considered to be casualties and will be treated medically or psychiatrically. Preventive treatment does not receive much attention because we are not yet knowledgeable enough about the relationships between transitions, stress, strain and stress-related illnesses.

It is our belief that future awareness and transition training should be built into the educational experience of children from a very early age. We want students to grow up anticipating and understanding personal change processes as naturally as they learn to expect to work for a living.

Stress and transition clinics

We would like to see multiple-purpose interdisciplinary clinics established to work with various aspects of stress and transitions. A clinic that brought together doctors, psychiatrists, counsellors and consultants could develop a diverse programme for the public. In addition to serving patients who are under stress, anticipating major life transitions, or recovering from a stress-related illness, such a clinic could develop public education programmes, conduct transition-related research, and teach social science and medical professionals how to deal with their clients' transitions more effectively.

As we finish this manuscript, such a clinic is being discussed in Washington D.C., but concrete plans have yet to be developed. In London, the Tavistock Institute continues as one of the few centres actively researching and consulting with clients on transition problems at both the individual and the system level.

The time has come to draw together the work being pursued by the various specialists in the field with a view to integrating and developing further study of transition dynamics. This book is an initial step. We hope it might stimulate others to continue along the same road.

Bibliography

Adams, J. D. (1969) 'Phases of personal and professional development', unpublished doctoral dissertation, Case Western Reserve University, Cleveland, Ohio.

Aldrich, K. C. (1966) *An Introduction to Dynamic Psychiatry*, New York: McGraw-Hill.

Aldrich, K. C. (1974) 'Some dynamics of anticipatory grief' in B. Schoenberg *et al.* (eds.) *Anticipatory Grief*, New York: Columbia University Press.

Allen, C. A. (1975) 'Life planning: its purpose and position in the human potential movement', unpublished M.A. thesis, Dept. of Management Studies, University of Leeds.

Archibald, H. C., Long, D. M., Miller, C. & Tuddenham, R. D. (1962) 'Gross stress reactions in combat − a 15 year follow-up', *American Journal of Psychiatry*, **119**, pp. 317−22.

Aries, P. (1962) *Centuries of Childhood*, New York: Alfred Knopf.

Arning, H. K. (1965) 'Cultural differences affecting international business', American Management Association Seminar, July, 14.

Bakke, E. W. (1960) 'The cycle of adjustment to unemployment' in N. W. Bell & E. F. Vogal *A Modern Introduction to the Family*, New York: Free Press.

Beales, A. L. & Lambert, R. S. (1934) *Memoirs of the Unemployed*, London: Gollancz.

Becker, H. S. & Strauss, A. L. (1956) 'Careers, personality and adult socialisation', *American Journal of Sociology*, **62**, 3.

Bennis, W. S. & Slater, P. E. (1968) *The Temporary Society*, New York: Harper & Row.

Bernard, J. (1972) *The Future of Marriage*, New York: World Publishing Co.

Bier, T. E. (1967) 'Contemporary youth: implications of the personalistic life-style for organizations', unpublished doctoral dissertation, Case Institute of Technology.

Birney, D., Thomas, L. E. & Hinkle, J. E. (1970) 'Life planning workshops: discussion and evaluation', *Student Development Reports*, **8**, Colorado State University.

Blood, R. O. & Wolfe, D. M. (1960) *Husbands and Wives: The Dynamics of Married Living*, New York: Free Press.

Botwinick, J. (1966) 'Cautiousness with advanced age', *Journal of Gerontology*, **21**, pp. 347−53.

Bowlby, J. (1961) 'Processes of mourning', *International Journal of Psycho-Analysis*, **44**, 317.

Breen, L. Z. (1963) 'Retirement − norms, behavior, and functional aspects of normative behavior', chapter 47 in R. H. Williams, C. Tibbits & W. Donahue (eds.) *Processes of Ageing*, Vol. II, New York: Atherton Press, pp. 381−8.

Brooke, J. W. (1960) *Arthritis and You*, New York: Harper.

Brown, J. A. C. (1954) *The Social Psychology of Industry*, London: Penguin Books.

Buhler, C. (1968) 'The general structure of the human life cycle' in C. Buhler & F. Massarik *The Course of Human Lives*, New York: Springer, pp. 24—5.
Burgess, E. W. & Wallin, P. (1953) *Engagement and Marriage*, Philadelphia: Lippincott.

Cain, L. D. (1964) 'Life course and social structure' in R. E. L. Faris (ed.) *Handbook of Modern Sociology*, Chicago: Rand McNally, pp. 272—309.
Carnap, R. (1953) 'The two concepts of probability' in H. Feigl & M. Brodbeck (eds.) *Readings in the Philosophy of Science*, New York: Appleton-Century-Crofts.
Cheraskin, E., Ringsdorf, W. M. & Brecher, A. (1974) *Psychodietetics: Food as the Key to Emotional Health*, New York: Stein & Day.
Clayton, P. L., Desmarais, L. & Winokur, G. (1968) 'A study of normal bereavement', *American Journal of Psychiatry*, 125, 168.
Coleman, J. S., Campbell, E. Q., Hobson, C. J., McPartland, J., Mood, A. M., Weinfeld, F. D. & York, R. L. (1966) *Equality of Educational Opportunity*, Washington, D.C.: U.S. Government Printing Office.
Crawford, M. (1971) 'Retirement and disengagement', *Human Relations*, 24, 3, pp. 225—78.
Crawford, M. (1972) 'Retirement and role playing', *Sociology*, 6, 2.
Crawford, M. (1973) 'Retirement: A *rite de passage*', *The Sociological Review*, 21, 3.
Crites, J. C. (1969) *Vocational Psychology*, New York: McGraw-Hill.
Crystal, J. & Bolles, R. N. (1974) *Where do I go from here with my life? The Crystal Life Planning Method*, Virginia: Crystal Management Services Inc.
Cuber, J. F. & Cuber, P. (1965) *Sex and the Significant Americans*, Baltimore: Penguin.
Cumming, E. M. & Henry, W. (1961) *Growing Old*, New York: Basic Books.

Dailey, C. A. (1971) *Assessment of Lives*, Washington, D. C.: Jossey-Bass.
D'Zurilla, T. J. & Goldfried, M. R. (1971) 'Problem-solving and behaviour modification', *Journal of Abnormal Psychology*, 78, pp. 107—26.

Eisenberg, P. & Lazarsfeld, P. F. (1938) 'The psychological effects of unemployment', *Psychological Bulletin*, XXXV, pp. 358—90.
Ellis, A. (1973a) 'Rational-emotive therapy' in R. Corsini (ed.) *Current Psychotherapies*, Illinois: Peacock.
Ellis, A. (1973b) *Humanistic Psychotherapy: The Rational-Emotive Approach*, New York: Julian Press.
Entine, A. D. (1974) 'Mid-life careers: new strategies for emerging needs', keynote address at University of Southern Florida, symposium of New Careers at Mid-Life, Tampa, Florida.
Erikson, E. H. (1963) *Childhood and Society*, 2nd edn., New York: W. W. Norton; 1st edn. 1950.
Eysenck, H. J. (1967) *The Biological Basis of Personality*, Springfield, Illinois: Thomas.
Eysenck, H. J. & Eysenck, S. B. G. (1964) *Eysenck Personality Inventory*, London: University of London Press.

Feldman, H. (1965) *Development of the Husband—Wife Relationship*, Ithaca, New York: Cornell University Press.
Fink, S. L. (1967) 'Crisis and motivation: a theoretical model', *Archives of Physical Medicine and Rehabilitation*, 48, pp. 592—7.

Ford, G. A., France, A. M. & Gamewell, B. (1972) *Personal Planning Workshop*, 2nd edn., Washington: Mid-Atlantic Training Committee Inc.

French, J. R. P. & Caplan, R. D. (1972) 'Organisational stress and individual strain' in A. J. Marrow (ed.) *The Failure of Success*, New York: AMACOM, pp. 30—66.

Freud, S. (1961) Letter to Binswanger in *Letters of Sigmund Freud*, ed. E. L. Freud, London: Hogarth, p. 386.

Friedlander, F. A. (1970) 'Congruity framework for organizational diagnosis and change', Interim Report, Case Western Reserve University, June.

Friedman, M. & Rosenman, R. H. (1974) *Type A Behavior and your Heart*, New York: Alfred Knopf.

Fritz, C. E. (1957) 'Disasters compared in six American communities', *Human Organization*, **16**, 2, pp. 6—9.

Fromm, E. (1942) *Escape from Freedom*, New York: Holt, Rinehart & Winston.

Fulton, R. & Fulton, J. (1972) 'Anticipatory grief' in B. Schoenberg *et al.* (eds.) *Psychosocial Aspects of Terminal Care*, New York: Columbia University Press.

Futurist, The, magazine published by the World Future Society, 4916 St Elmo Avenue, Washington, D. C. 20014.

Gatti, A. (1937) 'La disoccupazione come crisi psicologia', *Arch. ital. di psicol.*, **15**, pp. 4—28.

Gellerman, S. W. (1968) *Management by Motivation*, American Management Association.

Gettleman, S. & Markowitz, J. (1974) *The Courage to Divorce*, New York: Simon & Schuster.

Ginzberg, E., Ginsberg, S. W., Axelrad, S. & Herma, J. L. (1951) *Occupational Choice: An Approach to a General Theory*, New York: Columbia University Press.

Glaser, B. G. & Strauss, A. L. (1965) 'Temporal aspects of dying as a non scheduled status passage', *American Journal of Sociology*, July, pp. 48—59.

Goffman, E. (1952) 'On cooling the mark out', *Psychiatry*, **15**, 4.

Goffman, E. (1959) *The Presentation of Self in Everyday Life*, Garden City, New York: Doubleday.

Gould, E. & Sheehy, G. (1974) 'Catch 30 and other predictable crises of growing up adult', *New York Magazine*, pp. 32—51.

Gullahorn, J. T. & Gullahorn, J. E. (1963) 'An extension of the U curve hypothesis', *Journal of Social Issues*, **19**, pp. 33—47.

Gurin, P., Gurin, G., Lao, R. C. & Beattie, M. (1969) 'Internal-external control in the motivational dynamics of Negro youth', *Journal of Social Issues*, **25**, pp. 29—53.

Hall, E. T. & Whyte, W. F. (1963) 'Intercultural communication: a guide to men of action', *Practical Anthropology*, **10**, pp. 216—99.

Hall, J. & Williams, M. (1973) *Work Motivation Inventory*, Teleometrics, P. O. Drawer 1850, Conroe, Texas 77301.

Hampshire, S. (1965) *Thought and Action*, London: Chatto & Windus.

Harré, R. & Secord, P. F. (1972) *The Explanation of Social Behaviour*, Oxford: Blackwell.

Harvey, O. J., Hunt, D. E. & Schroder, H. M. (1961) *Conceptual Systems and Personality Organization*, New York: Wiley.

Havinghurst, R. J. (1954) 'Flexibility and social roles of the retired', *American Journal of Sociology*, **59**, 4, pp. 309—11.

Hayes, J. & Hopson, B. (1971) *Careers Guidance: The Role of the School in Vocational Development*, London: Heinemann.

Hendrick, I. (1943a) 'The work and pleasure principle', *Psychoanalytic Quarterly*, 12, pp. 311—29.

Hendrick, I. (1943b) 'The discussion of the instinct to master', *Psychoanalytic Quarterly*, 12, pp. 516—65.

Hinton, J. (1967) *Dying*, Harmondsworth, Middx: Penguin Books.

Hobbs, D. (1968) 'Transition to parenthood', *Journal of Marriage and the Family*, 30, pp. 413—17.

Hoffer, E. (1951) *The True Believer*, New York: Harper.

Holmes, T. H. & Masuda, M. (1970) 'Life change and illness susceptibility', paper presented as part of Symposium on Separation and Depression: Clinical and Research Aspects, annual meeting of the American Association for the Advancement of Science, Chicago, December.

Holmes, T. H. & Masuda, M. (1973) 'Life change and illness susceptibility', *Separation and Depression*, American Association for the Advancement of Science, pp. 161—86.

Holmes, T. H. & Rahe, R. H. (1967) 'The Social Readjustment Rating Scale', *Journal of Psychosomatic Research*, 11, pp. 213—8.

Holmstrom, L. L. (1972) *The Two-Career Family*, Cambridge, Mass.: Schenkman.

Hopson, B. (1973) 'Career development in industry: the diary of an experiment', *British Journal of Guidance and Counselling*, 1, pp. 51—61.

Hopson, B. & Hayes, J. (1968) *The Theory and Practice of Vocational Guidance*, Oxford: Pergamon.

Hopson, B. & Hopson, C. A. (1975) *Intimate Feedback: A Lovers Guide to Getting in Touch with Each Other*, New York: Simon & Schuster. Published in Britain with the title *Twosome Plus: A Guide to Co-habitation*, London: Blond & Briggs, 1973.

Hopson, B. & Hough, P. (1973) *Exercises in Personal and Career Development*, Cambridge: CRAC.

Ingram, C., Tiffany, D., Markley, R., Tiffany, P. & Smith, R. (1971) 'The effect of experienced and expected control on verbal operant conditioning', paper presented at a meeting of Kansas State Psychological Association, Overland Park, April.

Irelan, L. (ed.) (1967) *Low Income Life Styles*, Washington, D.C.: U.S. Department of Health, Education and Welfare.

Jones, B. (n.d.) *Towards a Female Liberation Movement*, Boston: New England Free Press.

Kaufmann, W. (1973) *Without Guilt and Justice: From Decidophobia to Autonomy*, New York: Peter Wyden.

Keleman, S. (1974) *Living Your Dying*, New York: Random House.

Kelly, E. L. (1955) 'Consistency of the adult personality', *American Psychologist*, 10, pp. 659—81.

Keyes, R. (1973) *We, the Lonely People*, New York: Harper & Row.

Kiel, E. T., Riddell, D. S. & Green, B. S. R. (1966) 'Youth and work: problems and perspectives', *Sociological Review*, 14, 2, pp. 117—37.

Kierkegaard, S. A. (1967) *Stages on Life's Way*, New York: Schocken.

Kohlberg, L. (1969) 'Stage and sequence: the cognitive-developmental approach to socialization' in D. A. Goslin (ed.) *Handbook of Socialization Theory and Research*, Chicago: Rand McNally, pp. 347—478.

Kolb, D. A. & Plovnick, M. S. (1974) 'The experimental learning theory of career development', paper presented at the MIT/ILP Conference on Career Development, Cambridge, Mass., May 22.

Krantzler, M. (1973) *Creative Divorce*, New York: M. Evans.

Kübler-Ross, E. (1969) *On Death and Dying*, New York: Macmillan.

Kübler-Ross, E. (ed.) (1975) *Death: The Final Stage of Growth*, Englewood Cliffs: Prentice-Hall.

✕Lamott, K. (1975) *Escape from Stress*, New York: G. P. Putnam.

Lang, P. J. (1969) 'The mechanics of desensitisation and the laboratory study of human fear' in C. M. Franks (ed.) *Behavior Therapy: Appraisal and Status*, New York: Pergamon.

Lederer, W. J. & Jackson, D. D. (1968) *The Mirages of Marriage*, New York: W. W. Norton.

Leibow, E. (1967) *Tally's Corner*, Boston: Little Brown.

LeShan, L. (1966) 'An emotional life-history pattern associated with neo-plastic disease', *Annals of the New York Academy of Science*, New York.

Levenson, B. (1961) 'Bureaucratic succession' in A. Etzioni (ed.) *Complex Organisations*, New York: Holt, Rinehart & Winston.

Levinger, G. & Snoek, J. D. (1972) *Attraction in Relationships: A New Look at Interpersonal Attraction*, Morristown, N.J.: General Learning Press.

Levinson, D. J. (1972) 'A psychological study of the male mid-life decade', unpublished, Yale University.

Levinson, D. J. et al. (1974) 'The psychosocial development of men in early adulthood and the mid-life transition' in Ricks, Thomas & Roff (eds.) *Life History Research in Psychotherapy*, Vol. 3, Minneapolis: University of Minnesota Press.

Lewin, K. (1935) *A Dynamic Theory of Personality*, New York: McGraw.

Lewin, K. (1947a) 'Frontiers in group dynamics', *Human Relations*, 1, pp. 5—41.

Lewin, K. (1947b) 'Group decisions and social change' in T. M. Newcomb & E. L. Hartley (eds.) *Readings in Social Psychology*, New York: Holt, Rinehart & Winston.

Lifton, R. J. (1954) ' "Home by ship" reaction patterns of American prisoners of war repatriated from North Korea', *American Journal of Psychiatry*, 110, pp. 732—9.

Lopata, H. (1971) *Occupation Housewife*, New York: Oxford University Press.

Lowenthal, M. F., Thurnher, M., Chiriboga, D. & Assoc. (1975) *Four Stages of Life*, Washington, D.C.: Jossey-Bass, Behavioral Science Series.

Luft, J. (1970) *Group Processes*, Palo Alto: National Press Books.

Lundstedt, S. (1963) 'An introduction to some evolving problems in crosscultural research', *Journal of Social Issues*, 19, pp. 1—9.

McQuade, W. & Aikman, A. (1974) *Stress*, New York: E. P. Dutton & Co.

Maddison, D. & Viola, A. (1968) 'The health of widows in the year following bereavement', *Journal of Psychosomatic Research*, 12, 297.

Maizels, J. (1970) *Adolescent Needs and the Transition from School to Work*, London: Athlone Press.

May, R. (1969) *Love and Will*, New York: W. W. Norton.

Mead, M. (1943) *Coming of Age in Samoa*, Harmondsworth, Middx: Penguin; 1st edn. 1928.

Mead, M. (ed.) (1955) *Cultural Patterns and Technical Change*, New York: UNESCO.

Mencke, R. A. & Cochran, D. J. (1974) 'Impact of a counselling outreach workshop on vocational development', *Journal of Counseling Psychology*, 21, pp. 185–90.

Merton, R. K. (1957) *Social Theory and Social Structure*, London: The Free Press of Glencoe.

Miller, G. A., Galanter, E. & Pribram, K. H. (1960) *Plans and the Structure of Behavior*, New York: Holt, Rinehart & Winston.

Morris, R. T. (1960) *The Two-Way Mirror: National Status in Foreign Students' Adjustment*, Minneapolis: University of Minnesota Press.

Morse, N. C. & Weiss, R. S. (1955) 'The function and meaning of work and the job', *American Sociological Review*, 20, pp. 191–8.

Neff, W. S. (1968) *Work and Human Behavior*, New York: Atherton Press.

Oberg, K. (1960) 'Culture shock: adjustment to new cultural environments', *Practical Anthropology*, 7, pp. 177–82.

O'Neill, N. & O'Neill, G. (1971) *Open Marriage*, New York: M. Evans & Co.

O'Neill, N. & O'Neill, G. (1974) *Shifting Gears*, New York: M. Evans & Co.

Otto, H. A. (1970) *Group Methods to Actualize Human Potential: A Handbook*, 2nd edn., Beverley Hills: Holistic Press.

Packard, V. (1972) *A Nation of Strangers*, New York: McKay.

Pagés, M. (1971) 'Bethel culture 1969: impressions of an immigrant', *Journal of Applied Behavioural Science*, 7, pp. 267–84.

Parkes, C. M. (1970) 'The first year of bereavement', *Psychiatry*, 33, pp. 444–67.

Parkes, C. M. (1971) 'Psycho-social transitions: a field for study', *Social Science and Medicine*, 5, pp. 101–15.

Parkes, C. M. (1972) *Bereavement: Studies of Grief in Adult Life*, London: Tavistock Publications/New York: International Universities Press.

Parkes, C. M. & Brown, R. (1972) 'Health after bereavement — a controlled study of young Boston widows and widowers', *Psychosomatic Medicine*, 34, 449.

Peck, E. (1971) *The Baby Trap*, New York: Bernard Geis Associates.

Pfeiffer, I. W. & Jones, J. E. (1970) *A Handbook of Structured Experiences for Human Relations Training*, Vol. II, Iowa: University Associated Press.

Piaget, J. & Inhelder, B. (1958) *The Growth of Logical Thinking from Childhood to Adolescence*, New York: Basic Books.

Porat, F. (1974) *Changing your Life Style*, Secaucus, N.J.: Lyle Stuart, Inc.

Porter, E. H. (1973) *Strength Deployment Inventory*, Personal Strengths Assessment Agency, P.O. Drawer 397, Pacific Palisades, California 90272.

Prather, H. (1970) *Notes to Myself*, Moab, Utah: Real People Press.

Rahe, R. H. & Lind, E. (1971) 'Psychosocial factors and sudden cardiac death: a pilot study', *Journal of Psychosomatic Research*, 15, pp. 19–24.

Rahe, R. H. & Paasikivi, J. (1971) 'Psychosocial factors and myocardial infarction. II. An outpatient study in Sweden', *Journal of Psychosomatic Research*, 15, pp. 33–9.

Rahe, R. H., Meyer, M., Smith, M., Kajor, G. & Holmes, T. H. (1964) 'Social stress and illness onset', *Journal of Psychosomatic Research*, 8, pp. 35–44.

Rahe, R. H. *et al.* (1968) 'Life change — Patterns surrounding illness experience', *Journal of Psychosomatic Research*, 12, pp. 341–5.

Rapoport, R. & Rapoport, R. N. (1964) 'New light on the honeymoon', *Human Relations*, 17, 1, pp. 33–56.

Rogers, C. (1971) *Encounter Groups*, London: Allen Lane.

Rokeach, M. (1973) *The Nature of Human Values*, New York: Free Press.

Rollins, B. C. & Feldman, H. (1970) 'Marital satisfaction over the family life-cycle', *Journal of Marriage and the Family*, 32, pp. 20—8.

Rosoff, N. (1970) 'A study of the development of T-group trainers', unpublished paper, Case Western Reserve University, Cleveland, Ohio.

Rossi, A. (1968) 'Transition to parenthood', *Journal of Marriage and the Family*, 30, pp. 26—39.

Roth, J. A. (1963) *Timetables*, Indianapolis: Bobbs Merrill.

Rotter, J. B. (1966) 'Generalised expectations for internal versus external control of reinforcement', *Psychological Monographs*, 80, 1, Whole No. 609.

Rubin, A. (1973) *Liking and Loving*, New York: Holt, Rinehart & Winston.

Rubin, R. T., Gunderson, E. K. & Arthur, R. J. (1969) 'Life stress and illness patterns in the U.S. Navy', *Archives of Environmental Health*, 19, pp. 753—7.

Ryder, R. G. (1970) 'Dimensions of early marriage', *Family Process*, 9, pp. 51—68.

Saleh, S. O. & Otis, J. L. (1963) 'Sources of job satisfaction and their effects on attitudes toward retirement', *Journal of Industrial Psychology*, 1, pp. 101—6.

Schein, E. H. (1971) 'The individual, the organisation and the career: a conceptual scheme', *Journal of Applied Behavioural Science*, 7, 4.

Schoenberg, B. & Senescu, R. A. (1970) 'The patient's reaction to fatal illness' in B. Schoenberg *et al.* (eds.) *Loss and Grief: Psychological Management in Medical Practice*, New York: Columbia University Press.

Schutz, W. C. (1958) *FIRO: A Three-Dimensional Theory of Interpersonal Behavior*, New York: Holt, Rinehart & Winston.

Seashore, C. (1974) Public lecture, Washington, D.C., January 31.

Seeman, M. (1959) 'On the meaning of alienation', *American Sociological Review*, 24, pp. 783—91.

Seeman, M. (1971) 'Alienation: a map of its principal boundaries', *Psychology Today*, August, pp. 83—95.

Seligman, M. E. P. (1975) *Helplessness*, Reading: W. H. Freeman/San Francisco: W. H. Freeman.

Selye, H. (1956) *The Stress of Life*, New York: McGraw-Hill.

Selye, H. (1974) *Stress without Distress*, New York: Lippincott.

Sewell, W. H. & Davidson, O. M. (1961) *Scandinavian Students on an American Campus*, Minneapolis: University of Minnesota Press.

Shedlin, A. (1974) Personal communication.

Sheppard, H. L. & Belitsky, A. H. (1966) *The Job Hunt: Job-Seeking Behavior of Unemployed Workers in a Local Economy*, Baltimore: Johns Hopkins.

Sheresky, N. & Mannes, M. (1972) *Uncoupling: The Art of Coming Apart*, New York: Viking Press.

Silverman, S. (1968) *Psychological Aspects of Physical Symptoms*, New York: Appleton-Century-Crofts.

Skinner, B. F. (1938) *The Behavior of Organisms*, New York: Appleton-Century-Crofts.

Smalley, W. A. (1963) 'Culture shock, language shock, and the shock of self discovery', *Practical Anthropology*, 10, pp. 49—56.

Smith, M. B. (1955) 'Some features of foreign student adjustments', *Journal of Higher Education*, 26, pp. 231—41.

Smith, P. B. (1964) 'Attitude changes associated with training in human relations', *British Journal of Social and Clinical Psychology*, 2, pp. 104—12.

Sofer, C. (1970) *Men in Mid-Career*, Cambridge: Cambridge University Press.

Sokolov, E. N. (1963) 'Higher nervous functions: the orienting reflex', *Annual Review of Physiology*, **3**, pp. 545—8.

Stein, Z. & Susser, M. W. (1969) 'Widowhood and mental illness', *British Journal of Preventive and Social Medicine*, **23**, 106.

Strawson, P. F. (1959) *Individuals*, London: Methuen.

Super, D. E. (1953) 'A theory of vocational development', *American Psychologist*, **8**, pp. 185—90.

Super, D. E. (1957) *The Psychology of Careers*, New York: Harper.

Swank, R. L. & Marchand, E. (1946) 'Combat neurosis, development of combat exhaustion', *Archives of Neurology and Psychiatry*, LV, 236.

Terkel, S. (1974) *Working*, New York: Random House.

Theorell, T. & Rahe, R. H. (1971) 'Psychosocial factors and myocardial infarction: an inpatient study in Sweden', *Journal of Psychosomatic Research*, **15**, 1, pp. 25—31.

Tiedemann, D. V. & O'Hara, R. P. (1963) *Career Development: Choice and Adjustment*, Princeton, N.J.: College Entrance Examination Board.

Tiffany, D. W. & Tiffany, P. E. (1973) 'Social unrest: powerlessness and/or self direction?' *American Psychologist*, **28**, February, pp. 151—4.

Tiffany, D. W., Salkin, G. & Cowan, J. R. (1970) 'Generalised expectancies for control of reinforcement compared to experienced control', *Journal of Clinical Psychology*, **26**, pp. 519—20.

Toffler, A. (1970) *Future Shock*, New York: Random House.

Toffler, A. (1974) *Learning for Tomorrow*, New York: Vintage.

Tyler, L. (1961) *The Work of the Counsellor*, New York: Appleton-Century-Crofts.

Van Gennep, A. (1960) *The Rites of Passage*, London: Routledge & Kegan Paul.

Vernon, J. (1965) *Inside the Black Room*, London: Souvenir Press.

Veroff, J. & Feld, S. (1970) *Marriage and Work in America*, New York: Van Nostrand, Reinhold.

Webb, E. J., Campbell, D. T., Schwartz, R. D. & Sechrest, L. (1966) *Unobtrusive Measures: Nonreactive Research in the Social Sciences*, Chicago: Rand McNally.

Wedderburn, D. (1964) *White-collar Redundancy: A Case Study*, University of Cambridge, Dept. of Applied Economics, Occasional Paper No. 1.

Wedderburn, D. (1965) *Redundancy and the Railwaymen*, University of Cambridge, Dept. of Applied Economics Monographs.

Weiss, Jay M. (1972) 'Psychosocial factors in stress and disease', *Scientific American*, June, pp. 104—13.

White, R. W. (1959) 'Motivation reconsidered: the concept of competence', *Psychological Review*, **66**, pp. 297—333.

Wilder, R. M., Hubble, J. & Kennedy, C. E. (1971) 'Life changes and infectious monoculeosis', *Journal of the American College Health Association*, **20**, 2, December, pp. 115—19.

Williamson, R. C. (1972) *Marriage and Family Relations*, 2nd edn., New York: Wiley.

Wilson, D. (1975) 'Personal re-evaluation workshops: a critical examination', unpublished M.A. thesis, Dept. of Management Studies, University of Leeds.

Winch, R. F. (1971) *The Modern Family*, 3rd edn., New York: Holt, Rinehart & Winston.

Wolf, S. (1965) *The Stomach*, New York: Oxford University Press.

Wolpe, J. & Lazarus, A. A. (1969) *The Practice of Behavior Therapy*, New York: Pergamon.

Work in America (1972) Report on a special task force to the Secretary of Health, Education and Welfare, M.I.T. Press.

Young, M., Benjamin, B. & Wallis, C. (1963) 'Mortality of widowers', *Lancet*, 2, 454.

Zawadski, B. & Lazarsfeld, P. F. (1935) 'The psychological consequences of unemployment', *Journal of Social Psychology*, 6, pp. 224—51.

Name Index

Subject Index